THE

WELSH CASTLES

OF EDWARD I

ARNOLD TAYLOR

THE HAMBLEDON PRESS
LONDON AND RONCEVERTE

Published by The Hambledon Press 1986

35 Gloucester Avenue, London NW1 7AX (UK)
309 Greenbrier Avenue, Ronceverte, West Virginia 24970 (USA)

ISBN 0 907628 71 0

Originally published as part of *The History of the King's Works*,
Vols. I and II (1963), pp 293 – 408, 1027 – 39.
Editor: H.M. Colvin

British Library Cataloguing in Publication Data

Taylor, A.J. (Arnold Joseph)
    The Welsh castles of Edward I.
    1. Castles——Wales——History
    2. Architecture, Medieval——Wales
    I. Title
    728.8'1'09429   NA497.G7

Printed in Great Britain by
WBC Print Ltd, Bristol

Contents

List of Illustrations

PLATES

FIGURES

Foreword

In 1982 Her Majesty's Stationery Office completed publication, on behalf of the Ministry of Public Building and Works and its successor the Department of the Environment, of the great six-volume *History of the King's Works* edited by H.M. Colvin. The *History* traces the story of the erection and care of the official buildings of the Crown from Saxon times through to 1851. When the first two volumes appeared in 1963, they contained a section entitled 'The King's Works in Wales 1277–1330'. This section was re-issued by the Stationery Office as a separate publication in 1974, but for some time it has not been obtainable. The present re-issue by The Hambledon Press, under the title of *The Welsh Castles of Edward I*, makes it available once more, revised and re-edited as an independent work. It is hoped that in this way it will provide, in handy form, for the growing numbers who visit them from all over the world, the story of the castles' original construction. As a closely related contemporaneous group of medieval fortresses, several of them buildings of surpassing architectural and scenic beauty, the North Wales castles are unique in Britain. The aim of this historical study is to assist in their under-standing. At the time of its first publication in 1963, the spelling of the names of the castles was still that which had been customary for generations. Though in the case of Hope ('Caergwrle'), Criccieth ('Cricieth'), Conway ('Conwy') and Caernarvon ('Caernarfon') alternatives have since been generally (but by no means universally) applied, the forms used in the original edition and 2nd impression (1973) of vols. I and II of the *History of the King's Works* are here retained.

24th June 1985   Arnold Taylor

Fig. 1. The impressment of workmen for the King's Works in North Wales,
1282–3.

THE WELSH CASTLES
OF EDWARD I

THE king's decision, announced on 17 November 1276, to go against Llywelyn as a rebel and a disturber of his peace,[1] had, as not the least notable of its consequences, the inauguration in Wales of a programme of castle-building of the first magnitude. During the next twenty years no fewer than ten new castles,[2] the majority of them major works and some of them with substantial town fortifications attached, were begun and carried far towards completion; contemporaneously with these royal foundations, work proceeded on four new 'lordship' castles,[3] no less the creation of royal policy and not improbably owing at least their plan and general conception to the advice of officers of the royal works. During the same period, royal building of some consequence was also undertaken at three of the native Welsh castles which fell into the hands of the Crown as prizes of war,[4] as well as at several of the existing border castles from which the English operations were launched.[5]

It is with the creation of the first of these groups, the royal castles of the North Wales sea-board, that we are here primarily concerned. Their building was undertaken in three main stages, corresponding to the military campaigns of 1277, 1282–3 and 1294–5, and it will be convenient to examine their construction, together with works at the 'lordship' and native castles, in the order in which they were commenced.

Castles of the War of 1277

1. BUILTH

The first of the new works to be begun was the castle of Builth, on the Upper Wye, not one stone of which is now to be seen above ground. It took the form of a complete refortification of the motte-and-bailey castle established by Philip de Braose at the

---

[1] *Cal. Close Rolls 1272–9*, p. 359; *Foedera* (Rec. Comm.), I i, p. 535.
[2] Builth, Aberystwyth, Flint, Rhuddlan, Ruthin, Hope, Conway, Caernarvon, Harlech and Beaumaris.
[3] Hawarden, Denbigh, Holt and Chirk.   [4] Dolwyddelan, Bere and Criccieth.
[5] E.g. Chester, Oswestry, Shrewsbury, Montgomery, St. Briavel's.

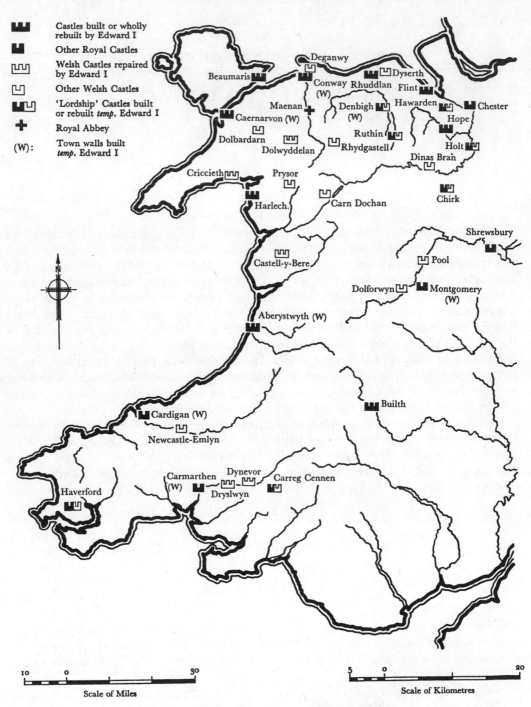

Castles built or wholly
rebuilt by Edward I

Other Royal Castles

Welsh Castles repaired
by Edward I

Other Welsh Castles

'Lordship' Castles built
or rebuilt *temp*. Edward I

Royal Abbey

(W): Town walls built
temp. Edward I

Fig. 2. The Edwardian Castles in Wales.

end of the eleventh century[1] and refortified under John, the defences of which had been razed to their foundations by Llywelyn in 1260.[2] The initial accounts[3] run from 3 May 1277, when John fitz Adam of Radnor began to receive a wage of 12d. a day as *custos operacionum*.[4] The first task was the construction and roofing, at a cost of £5, of timber buildings to serve as chapel, hall, chamber, kitchen and smithy for the use of the garrison quartered there during the war against Llywelyn. The hall and chamber are described as being *donio loco*,[5] and were presumably placed on the motte. These were all temporary buildings, and by mid-November had already been demolished (*avulse*) and replaced by a new great hall, kitchen, brewhouse and stable.[6] Work also appears to have been begun forthwith on the erection of the keep or great tower. Before 29 May 19 carpenters were sent to Builth from Abergavenny *ad quandam Turrim ibidem construendam*, together with 28 men with picks and shovels *ad operaciones Turris predicte*,[7] and by November the building was sufficiently advanced to require covering in with straw against the winter, as were also a brattice (*bretasche*) and two *camere*.[8] By the close of the first accounting period on 13 January 1278, when the works had been in progress for less than nine months, over £218 had been spent on wages of masons and quarrymen, more than double the amount paid under this head throughout any one of the three succeeding years,[9] while the carpenters' wages similarly amounted to £85, as compared with £20, £11 and £12 in the 1278, 1279 and 1280 seasons respectively.[10] The progress of the work by the end of the 1277 season is reflected in gratuities of 40s. paid at Chester in November to the 'engineer' in charge (*Magistro Henrico Machinatori del Buet de dono Regis xl.s.*)[11] and of 2s. paid at Builth to the masons when the king visited the castle at the end of the same month.[12]

On 4 March 1278, shortly before the onset of the second building season, William fitz Warin, a household knight, was sent from the court (then at Quenington, Glos.) to inspect the king's castles in Wales and the March,[13] amongst them the works at Rhuddlan and Builth:[14] and when, on 8 April, Master James of St. George, later to emerge as master of the king's works in Wales, went back from a visit to the court[15] to direct the works of the Welsh castles,[16] Builth was presumably one of the works under his control. The accounts[17] show that at this date operations were still at a winter level—a dozen men clearing earth from the quarry and two carts bringing stone and sand to the site—with weekly expenditure restricted to a total of 12s. 1¼d. In the week beginning 18 April (Easter Monday) there is a rise to £3 14s. 7½d., increasing in the following week to £6 12s. 0d. and in the first week in May to £7 3s. 10d., at about which figure it stood until mid-September: thereafter there is a downward trend until, in the first weeks of January 1279, only 3s. 10d. is paid out for cartage of

[1] Lloyd, *History of Wales* ii, p. 402.   [2] *H.K.W.*, I, p. 583.   [3] E 101/485/20; E 372/124, rot. 24.
[4] Liberate Roll 56.   [5] E 101/485/21.   [6] E 372/124, rot. 24.   [7] Liberate Roll 53.
[8] E 101/485/21; E 372/124, rot. 24.   [9] E 101/485/20.   [10] *Ibid.*   [11] E 101/3/19.
[12] C 47/4/1, m. 4; cf. B.L., Add. MS. 36762.   [13] C 47/4/1, m. 6d.   [14] Add. MS. 36762.
[15] His arrival at Down Ampney on 27 March is noted in C 47/3/49.
[16] C 47 4/1, m.11d. 'eunti in partibus Wallie ad ordinandum opera castrorum ibidem'.
[17] E 101/486/22 (which now includes three hitherto unidentified fragments formerly in E 101/501/25, mm. 4, 5 and 33) comprises the Builth particulars for the year 17 January 1278 to 16 January 1279, wanting only the 22nd–24th and part of the 26th and 27th weeks.

materials. The full seasonal resumption of work is marked by the presence, from 25 April 1278 onwards, of two named master masons, viz. Master Henry of Leominster[1] as *magister* at a weekly wage of 4s. 4½d. and Master William of Winchcombe[2] as *submagister* at 3s. od. From 9 May 'Master R.' and Master 'W' of Bromborough (*Wrombreg*'), at 3s. od. and 2s. 6d. per week respectively, are named as master carpenters.[3]

In the course of the year lead brought from Shelve in Shropshire was being cast and laid by a master plumber, an indication of the completion of permanent buildings, while £16 6s. 8d. was paid for a great palisade, 49 perches in length, made round the outer bailey.[4] This was intended to give place later to a stone curtain, and in the following April orders were given to the constable, 'so soon as the castle shall be closed with a wall, whereby it will be necessary to remove the brattishing, . . . to let Roger Mortimer have the best brattishing of the king's gift'.[5] In October 1280, however, this wall had still only been begun (*operaciones . . . unius muri lapidei incepti . . . ad includendum ballium forinsecum*).[6] In a summary of the works undertaken up to that date reference is made to (*a*) the great tower, (*b*) a stone wall with six lesser towers (*turriculis*) surrounding the castle, (*c*) a 'turning' bridge with two great towers (*magnis turrellis*) presumably flanking it on either side, (*d*) a stone wall near to this bridge and enclosing the inner bailey, (*e*) a ditch outside this stone wall, and (*f*) a stone wall begun across this ditch (*super idem fossatum*) to enclose the outer bailey.[7] That the great tower may have followed the pattern of a shell keep is suggested by a later reference (1343) to 'houses' within it; like Conway, Harlech, Caernarvon and Holt, and probably other castles for which evidence is now lacking, it appears to have had surmounting watch-turrets.[8]

The works continued, apparently without a break but at a diminishing tempo, until 14 August 1282, when they were brought to a halt for want of money (*et tunc cessavit opus pro defectu pecunie*).[9] There was a resumption for a few weeks only, and although the accounting period was continued until 1 November,[10] the last recorded payments are for the week ending 19 September 1282[11]: Stephen of Knill, John of Radnor's successor as clerk of works,[12] was paid his wage of 12d. a day *ad sustentacionem suam circa custodiam operacionum predictarum* until 6 December.[13] Thereafter he remained at Builth on the king's business until 15 August 1283, but the

[1] Presumably to be identified with the *Magister Henricus machinator del Buet* mentioned above as having been rewarded at Chester in November 1277.
[2] A William of Winchcombe is also named among the masons at Vale Royal abbey in 1278 (*Ledger-Book of Vale Royal Abbey*, Lancs. and Cheshire Record Soc. 1914, pp. 196 ff.)
[3] E 101/486/22.   [4] E 101/485/21, m. 2.   [5] *Cal. Close Rolls 1272–9*, p. 527.
[6] E 372/124, rot. 24.   [7] *Ibid.*
[8] . . . *omnes domus in magna turre et garrette minute eiusdem turris*—E 163/4/42 (Emeldon's Survey). That the *garrette minute* were turrets is inferred from the description of the four Harlech turrets as *garrite* in 1289–90 (E 101/501/25, no. 63) and as the *quatuor garrettours in dicto castro* in 1343.
[9] E 101/486/21, m. 3. In this last year Master Henry no longer appears as master mason, Master William being present alone for the twenty-four weeks from 4 April to 19 September (*ibid.* m. 1*d.*) at a weekly wage of 3s. He had drawn the same pay as *submagister* in 1278, but in 1280, when Master Henry was still receiving 4s. 4½d., Master William received only 2s. (E 101/485/23).
[10] E 372/127, rot. 2*d.*   [11] E 101/486/21, mm. 1*d*, 4.
[12] At first, from 28 October 1280, he accounts as John of Radnor's clerk and attorney (E 372/126, rot. 6): he is paid as clerk of works from 2 February 1282 (Liberate Roll 58). From 1292 to 1297 he was clerk of the works at Westminster and the Tower of London.   [13] Liberate Roll 58.

terms in which his wages for this final period were authorised show that the works were now officially regarded as closed down (*dum ibidem stetit, peractis operacionibus predictis, circa diversa negocia nostra que ei iniunximus expedienda*).[1] That they remained incomplete is clear from a report of 1343, which says that the twin gate towers had never been finished.[2]

In the 1278 season masons' wages for the 12 months ending 13 January 1279 amounted to £88 9s. 5d.,[3] the major proportion being laid out between May and October. During these six months the number of masons varied from 14 to 20.[4] It follows that during the preceding season, when £203 7s. 6½d. was spent on masons' wages between 3 May 1277 and 13 January 1278, their number must have averaged about 40 and may have reached a peak appreciably in excess of this figure. In the absence of writs calling specifically for the enlistment of masons for the Builth works in the adjacent counties of Hereford and Shropshire, it is to be inferred that the majority of them were drawn in the initial season from the general body of masons assembled at Chester on 18 July, 150 of whom appear to have been dispersed from Flint a fortnight later to go to various unspecified works.[5] It is, however, worth noting that it was from Leominster that the Builth master mason took his surname, and that some of the workmen came from Leominster also.[6]

The Builth 'particulars' record much other detailed information about labour and wages, materials and carriage. In an average week in 1278 there were, besides the master mason at 7½d. a day and the deputy master at 3s. a week, 4 masons at 2s., 5 at 1s. 8d. and 3 at 1s. 6d.: 10 workmen clearing away earth and breaking stone at two quarries included 2 masters at 1s. a week each, the remainder being paid 9d.: 4 mortar makers and 10 faulkners or mortar carriers (*portitores mortarii qui dicuntur fauconarii*)[7] were also each paid 9d. a week, as likewise were 4 sand throwers: 4 water carriers and 34 hodmen (*hottarii*) were paid 7d., 30 diggers (*fossatores*) and 20 barrowmen (*portatores ciuerum*) 8d.: a carpenter was employed on making things needed for the works (including 'falcons' (*falcon*') for the *fauconarii*) at 1s. 8d. a week, while 2 others who were making the stairs to the brattice over the gate (*gradus ad Brustag' ultra portam*) were each paid 3d. a day: there were 2 smiths sharpening the tools and making whatever iron work was required, one of them paid 2s. and the other 1s. 2d. a week, while 2 watchmen employed to control the workmen (*virgarii existentes ultra operarios*) were also each paid 1s. 2d.; 3 cart drivers belonging to the works were each paid 10d. Altogether there were 140 on the pay-roll.[8] In the corresponding week in 1282 the total was 126[9]: there were then 34 men working at the quarries, while a body of 80 diggers at the castle was made up of 1 master *fossator* at 8d. a week, 43 men at 7d. and 36 women at 6d. The names of many of the employees at this time, including those of 23 women, have been preserved: most of them are surnamed from

[1] Liberate Roll 60.   [2] E 163/4/42.
[3] E 101/485/20.   [4] E 101/486/22.
[5] The recruitment and assignment of masons and others in the summer of 1277 is further discussed in *Studies in Building History*, ed. E. M. Jope (1961), pp. 104 ff.
[6] E 101/485/23, m. 1: 'in expensis cuiusdam nuncii missi apud Leomister' post operarios .ij. den'.
[7] A different interpretation is given in Salzman, *Building in England*, p. 70, note 3, and p. 324: cf. also J. G. Edwards, *Cal. Anc. Correspondence concerning Wales*, p. 251, note 1.
[8] E 101/486/22.   [9] E 101/486/21. In each case the week chosen is that beginning 25 April.

places in Radnor, Herefordshire and Brecon.[1] As a rule a seven-day week was worked, but the 1278 accounts indicate a three-day break at Whitsun and two days at All Saints', one John le Hert being paid 1s. for looking after the keep during the holidays; work also stopped throughout Christmas week and on the three preceding days.[2]

Stone for the works came from at least three sources. Probably the bulk of the rough-hewn stone was from a quarry near at hand referred to in the 1282 accounts as the black quarry (*nigra quarrera*).[3] Freestone, on the other hand, was brought from Cusop (19 miles) and Clifford on the Wye (20 miles).[4] Stone to be burnt for lime was quarried at Talgarth (15 miles) and brought in hired ox-drawn wagons to Llyswen on the Wye (12 miles), a lime kiln being built in the castle bailey.[5] Lime was also bought at Hay (18 miles) and Radnor (15 miles).[6] For lead it was necessary to go farther afield. In 1278, 3 waggon-loads were brought 40 miles from Shelve in Shropshire, while two years later 24½ loads were bought at Mold, involving a haul of about 90 miles. This may imply that a mine opened the previous year at Morugge, a place as yet unidentified and perhaps nearer at hand, had failed to yield the required quantity.[7] The accounts include regular weekly payments for fodder for carthorses used in hauling materials, especially stone and sand, to the site. Three such horses were bought for 45s. at the beginning of the 1278 season, and 2 carts, much worn and held together with iron (*ferro ligatis et multum usitatis*), were obtained for 13s. 11d.[8]

Financial provision for the Builth works came principally from the revenues of the lordship of Abergavenny (£792 6s. 8d. in the period 1278–82), from the Wardrobe (£466 13s. 4d. in the period 1278–80), from the farm and other revenues of the lordship of Builth (£375) and from a fine of £200 levied on the men of Builth in 1277 on their readmission to the king's peace, giving a total allotment of £1834; recorded expenditure amounted in all to £1666 9s. 5¼d.[9]

In 1301 the newly-built castle was among those conferred on Edward of Caernarvon by his father.[10] Repairs were carried out from time to time during the next twenty-five years, as much as £93 being spent in 1316–17, chiefly on the ditches and peel.[11] In 1327 Builth was one of the castles appropriated by Queen Isabella, who handed it over to Roger Mortimer, Earl of March.[12] On Mortimer's fall in 1330 it was granted to Ebles le Strange and his wife Alice for their lives,[13] but in 1343 Edward III reasserted the rights of the Crown in favour of his son Edward, Prince of Wales.[14] In a survey made in that year the cost of necessary repairs was estimated at £180 13s. 4d., besides £200 to complete the unfinished gatehouse.[15] There is no evidence that any major repairs were put in hand, however, and in 1359 the castle

[1] They are printed in Edwards, *op. cit.* pp. 250–1.
[2] Most wages show a reduction in the week beginning 22 July 1280, *quia fuerunt duo dies festiuales in septimana* (E 101/485/23).
[3] E 101/486/21.   [4] E 101/485/21.   [5] E 101/486/21.   [6] E 101/485/23.
[7] E 101/485/21.   [8] E 101/486/22.
[9] E 372/124, rot. 24; 126, rot. 6: 127, rot. 2d; for classified summaries of works expenditure at Builth and elsewhere, see J. G. Edwards, 'Edward I's Castle-building in Wales', *Proceedings of the British Academy* xxxii (1946), pp. 66–73.
[10] *Cal. Charter Rolls* iii, p. 6.
[11] Pipe Roll 10 Edward II, rot. 35d (. . . *fossatis eiusdem castri faciendis et emendandis et pelo castri per loca de novo faciendo* . . .). See also *Cal. Close Rolls 1307–13*, p. 3; *1313–18*, pp. 153, 248, 394; *1323–7*, p. 81.
[12] *Cal. Pat. Rolls 1327–30*, p. 68; *1358–61*, pp. 262–3.   [13] *Cal. Pat. Rolls 1330–4*, p. 74; *1334–8*, p. 34.
[14] *Cal. Charter Rolls* v, p. 15; *Cal. Pat. Rolls 1338–40*, p. 448; *1348–50*, p. 461.   [15] E 163/4/42.

was restored to the house of Mortimer in the person of Roger, Earl of March, who was allowed to hold it of the prince in fee-farm.[1] Early in the fifteenth century the castle suffered serious damage at the hands of the Welsh rebels.[2] As the then Earl of March was a minor, the castle was temporarily in the king's hand, and in 1409 the royal constable, John Smert, was stated to have spent over £400 on repairs at his own expense.[3] With the accession of Edward IV Builth became once more a royal castle, and in the reign of Henry VIII it was still 'a fair castel of the Kinges'.[4] According to the historian of Breconshire it was probably destroyed in the reign of Elizabeth in order to provide materials for new mansions then being built in the neighbourhood.[5]

2. ABERYSTWYTH

According to the *Red Book of Hergest* version of the *Brut y Tywysogion*, or 'Chronicle of the Princes', the Latin original of which was compiled at the neighbouring abbey of Strata Florida, the king's brother Edmund of Lancaster came with a host to Llanbadarn on 25 July 1277, and began to build the castle of Aberystwyth.[6] Though in effect the successor of a castle established beside the estuary of the Ystwyth by Gilbert Fitz Richard of Clare in the time of Henry I,[7] Edmund's castle was erected on a new coastal site near the mouth of the Rheidol and in the territory of Llanbadarn Fawr.[8] Accordingly in contemporary records it is generally named the castle of Lampader or Lampadarn, but lasting tradition and a northward shift in the outfall of the Ystwyth together tended to attach the name of the old location to the new and eventually it prevailed.

The draft of a directive for the enlistment in the counties of Somerset, Dorset and Wiltshire and the town of Bristol of 120 masons and 120 carpenters *pro operibus in SuWall'*, and for their assembly at Bristol by 8 July 1277, may be taken as an indication that plans for building the new castle were already being worked out some weeks before that date.[9] The task of recruiting the men was entrusted to Master William of March. He obtained the numbers required and arranged for their pay as far as Carmarthen,[10] where they may be assumed to have arrived by water from Bristol on or about 10 July. On that day Edmund of Lancaster, who was himself

---

[1] *Cal. Pat. Rolls 1358–61*, p. 262. [2] *Cal. Pat. Rolls 1405–8*, pp. 94, 114.
[3] *Cal. Pat. Rolls 1408–13*, p. 75. [4] *Leland's Itinerary in Wales*, ed. Toulmin Smith, p. 109.
[5] Theophilus Jones, *History of Brecknockshire*, ed. Lord Glanusk, iii, p. 7.
[6] *Brut y Tywysogion, Red Book of Hergest version*, ed. T. Jones (Cardiff, 1955), p. 267.
[7] J. E. Lloyd, *The Story of Ceredigion* (Cardiff, 1937), p. 44.
[8] *Aedificatum est castellum apud Llan Padarn super mare* (*Annales Cambriae*, R.S., p. 105); for evidence that the position had not been previously fortified, see Sir John Lloyd's paper 'Aberystwyth' in *Archaeologia Cambrensis* (1931), p. 207.
[9] C 47/2/2, no. 14. The draft had first provided for 100 carpenters instead of 120, and for a quota from Gloucestershire and not from Bristol.
[10] E 101/485/19, last paragraph: 'Pro vadiis Cxx. cementariis et Cxx. carpentariis xx. dierum quos magister Willelmus de Marchia conduxit in Comitatibus Wiltes', Som' et Dors' ad destinand' apud Kaermerdin in tempore estiuali, Lx.li. Eidem magistro Willelmo percipienti per diem xij.d. pro vadiis suis eorundem xxx. dierum, xxx.s.'

still at Carmarthen, minuted the constable of Bristol to send to him either there or at Cardigan 2 good smiths and 4 other smiths, together with 40 measures of iron and 4 great *chars* of lead,[1] presumably to make tools for the large labour force that had just joined him. The men and materials asked for were despatched by boat from Bristol, the lead going to Carmarthen, the iron and the smiths with their gear to Aberystwyth, the whole journey to the west coast taking eight days.[2] On 18 July Henry of Hereford, who appears to have been the mason chosen, at least initially, to be in local charge of the work, was sent off to Carmarthen from Chester, where he had presumably been given his final instructions by the king and the officers of the Wardrobe.[3]

Work on the new site appears to have begun on 1 August,[4] and ten days later a further mandate from Edmund to the constable of Bristol called for the despatch to Aberystwyth of 3 more smiths, 9 quarrymen and 24 workmen.[5] They in turn were likewise shipped via Carmarthen, taking with them a barrel of 6000 nails,[6] to be used perhaps in the erection of the first *bretagium* or boundary fence round the works area, following the practice already recorded at Builth[7] and later to be encountered at Flint, Conway, Caernarvon and Beaumaris. During the first five months' operations (1 August–25 December) disbursements amounted to £595 13s. 4d.,[8] representing an average monthly expenditure considerably in excess of that applied to the initial effort at Builth but little more than a quarter of the £100 a week authorised during the following summer for works at the Tower of London.[9] Some £440 of this figure was absorbed by wages, the bulk of the remainder being accounted for by the cost of shipping stone, lime and other necessaries, including four consignments of money for the works. Before the end of the year, on 28 December 1277, the new town was made a free borough, with a ditch and a wall (the latter being still to be built), a gild merchant and hanse, the liberties and customs of Montgomery, a weekly market, and fairs at Whitsun and Michaelmas.[10]

Early in 1278, on 8 March, Roger de Molis, lately one of the 'barons of the lord king's garrison in West Wales',[11] who had been left in charge at Aberystwyth on Edmund's return to England on 20 September,[12] was appointed to keep 'the castle and honor of Lampadervaur together with all the king's lands in the county of Cardigan . . . provided that Ralph of Broughton, whom the king has appointed keeper and viewer of his works at Lampadervaur, shall receive the issues of the said castle, honor and lands and shall answer for them at the Exchequer by the view and

---

[1] Edwards, *Cal. Anc. Corr. Wales*, p. 158.

[2] E 372/ 122, rot. 28; Liberate Roll 53. The lead comprised 38 whole pieces and 29 *pecias scissas et separatas per medium*, the iron 800 pieces at 22s. od. a hundred, 7 *summae* at 8s. 6d. each and 1 *summa* at 8s. od.

[3] E 101/3/15: 'Henrico de Hereford, Cementario, eunti apud Kaermerdyn pro castro de Lampader firmando, ad suas expensas x.s.' He is presumably to be identified with the Master Henry of Hereford named as a burgage tenant at Caernarvon in a rental of 1298, where his position fourth from the head of the list and next but one to Master Walter of Hereford, at that time master of the Caernarvon works, may possibly point to kinship with his more famous namesake (*Bull. Bd. Celtic Stud.*, ix, pp. 238–9).

[4] SC 6/1218/10, m.1, printed in M. Rhys, *Ministers' Accounts for West Wales, 1277–1306*, p. 9; this is the date from which the first wages payments are reckoned.

[5] Edwards, *op. cit.* pp. 54 and 158.   [6] Liberate Roll 53.   [7] Above, p. 3.

[8] Rhys, *loc. cit.*   [9] *Cal. Pat. Rolls 1272–81*, p. 273.   [10] *Cal. Charter Rolls*, ii, p. 206.

[11] *Littere Wallie*, ed. J. G. Edwards, pp. 36–7.

[12] J. E. Morris, *Welsh Wars of King Edward the First*, p. 138. Closer reading of the Pipe Roll of 7 (not 6) Edward I (no. 123, rot. 23*d*) shows no evidence for Morris's assertion (*ibid.* p. 146 and note) that the work was under the superintendence of the Earl of Lincoln.

testimony of Roger'.[1] The works were apparently not fully resumed until 29 June, running thereafter for nineteen weeks until 11 November.[2] On 28 August the king sent William de Valence to South Wales, and in particular to Llanbadarn, to 'ordain and complete certain of the king's affairs there, and to do all things there that the king himself would do if he were there.'[3] Shortly afterwards William wrote to Henry of Bray, the king's steward of Abergavenny, saying that he had been to Llanbadarn and seen the work, and that owing to the great number of workmen there the king's money had already run out (*pur la graund multitude des ouerours ke il a les deners le Roy ke la sunt ja tot fayliz*). He therefore ordered Bray to send £50 or £60 to Carmarthen at once, and the rest[4] as soon as possible to reach Carmarthen by mid-October, if he wanted to save the king's work from failing for lack of funds (*si cum vous voler sauver le ouerayne le Roy e ke ele ne se fayle par le enchesiem de ceus deners*). While at Aberystwyth de Valence also arranged to compensate the abbot and convent of Strata Florida for a parcel of the abbey's land taken by the king 'for his castle of Lampadervaur';[5] it was presumably this transaction which involved the surrender of the piece of land called Ranbran which prior to 1278 had yielded a rent of 10s. 8d., but which an account of that year notes as having been given in exchange for the site of the new town and castle.[6] Doubt as to the precise length of the period of account in 1278 precludes calculation of the average weekly payments, but in the season as a whole some £265 were spent on the wages of masons, quarrymen, etc., *ad operamen castri*, and £413 on shipping stone and timber for the castle and town and on making and repairing the town ditch and mill pool.[7]

In the following season, 1279, the works made a great stride forward, Aberystwyth and Rhuddlan constituting between them the two principal operations of the year.[8] In March writs were addressed to the sheriffs of Gloucestershire, Devon and Hampshire requiring them each to send to Aberystwyth, by the octave of Easter (9 April), 60 good masons who should be chosen by the master of the work (*quod eligantur per Magistrum operis*), and to the constable of Bristol to provide for their passage down the Severn to Carmarthen.[9] The sheriff of Somerset and Dorset was ordered to send 120 masons and 40 good carpenters to Bristol by the day which Ralf of Broughton would tell him 'so that he could take the said workmen back with him to Aberystwyth'; and the constable of Bristol was himself required to furnish 20 carpenters and 40 good masons, besides despatching 30 boatloads of

[1] *Cal. Welsh Rolls*, p. 166.
[2] Dates of Broughton's works payments as given in SC 6/1218/10 (printed in *Ministers' Accounts for West Wales*, p. 11); according to the prior of Cardigan's audit, however, they ran from Easter (17 April) to All Saints (1 November), a period of twenty-eight weeks (*Littere Wallie*, p. 131). Contact with the central authority during the earlier part of the period is indicated by the despatch of three letters from the king to officials at Aberystwyth between 2 May and mid-July (E 101/308/4).
[3] *Cal. Welsh Rolls*, p. 177.
[4] Bray's total payment to the Aberystwyth works from the issues of Abergavenny was £120 (E 101/3/20, m. 2). Valence's letter is printed in *E.H.R.* xiv, pp. 506–7; cf. also *Cal. Anc. Corr. Wales*, p. 169.
[5] *Cal. Welsh Rolls*, p. 177.
[6] SC 6/1158/1, m. 4d, printed in *Trans. Cymmrodorion Soc.*, 1895–6, p. 122.
[7] *West Wales Ministers' Accts.*, p. 10.
[8] A writ of *allocate* was issued on 1 May 1279 to allow 'to Thomas of Normanville, our seneschal, £900 which on 28 April he delivered to Master Thomas Bek, keeper of the Wardrobe, *ad constructionem castrorum nostrorum de Lampaderuaur et de Rothelan*' (Liberate Roll 55).
[9] C 81/1766, no. 1.

freestone for the works.[1] Expenditure between 19 March and 1 November fell little short of £2200,[2] an average of £68 a week. Of this figure £1944, or about £60 a week, is accountable to wages. On 18 July the constable of Bristol was allowed 8s. for the shipment of 400 iron picks and crowbars, and 20s. for the expenses of two sergeants conveying a consignment of money for the works.[3] For a consignment of £333 6s. 8d., also in July, John the usher of the Wardrobe, with 10 men and 6 horses, received £4 12s. 10d. for the journey from Bristol and back; and in October, Michael Weston, sergeant-at-arms, had 28s. 1½d. for carrying a similar sum.[4] The labour quotas from the shires were only partly met. Somerset and Dorset sent 80 of their 120 masons, but no carpenters, Gloucestershire 46 masons out of 60; apparently none of the 60 Hampshire masons were forthcoming, but 27 are recorded from Wiltshire instead; Bristol mustered only 48 'carpenters, masons and other workmen' of the 40 masons and 20 carpenters demanded; Devon alone did more than was asked, sending not 60 masons but 64.[5] Thus only 265 men were found as against 400 called for. When the season was drawing to its close in October, 176 of the masons were still on the books.[6] With them were 14 carpenters, 5 smiths, 2 plumbers and 1120 other workmen, 'all the which workmen aforesaid did in fact get none of their pay during the said month, nor is there mention of it in the discharge of the account of the aforesaid Ralf' (i.e. Ralf of Broughton, the receiver and clerk of the works).[7] Of the actual constructional progress of the castle we know little, but it is doubtful if it could yet have begun to wear the aspect of nobility implied in the description *castrum insigne* given to it by the chronicler Trevet.[8] That some internal buildings were going up by this time is apparent from a claim by Roger de Molis for £17 9s. 2d. spent *pro domibus in castro constructis*, while the acquisition from the five neighbouring commotes of ten oxen 'to draw timber' suggests that the material to build them was being brought in from the country round.[9]

In January 1280, Bogo de Knovill, keeper of the castles of Oswestry and Montgomery and formerly sheriff of Salop and Stafford, was appointed justiciar of West Wales and keeper of the castles of Llanbadarn, Cardigan, Carmarthen, Dynevor and Carreg Cennen.[10] He soon visited Aberystwyth, and we are fortunate in having the report he made to the king and Council. In it he says that when he came to take over from Roger de Molis, he found a castle without arms, garrison or provisions, and had either to send to Montgomery for supplies or leave all to the mercy of

[1] C 81/1766, no. 2.
[2] £2192 4s. 5½d., including £120 still owing for the men's final month's wages at the conclusion of the account (*West Wales Min. Accts.*, pp. 15, 17).
[3] Liberate Roll 55. Probably this was the sum of 400 marks (£266 13s. 4d.) which the constable said in 1290 he had received from the chattels of the condemned Jews of Bristol (cf. Powicke, *The Thirteenth Century*, p. 633 and nn.) and had had taken to Aberystwyth by the king's order to be delivered to Ralf of Broughton for doing the king's works there ('monstravit Regi quod cum ipse anno vij⁰ ... CCCC. marcas de catallis Iudeorum de Bristoll dampnatorum recepisset, et eas usque Lampader per preceptum Regis cariari et Radulfo de Broughton tunc custodi operacionum Regis ibidem liberari fecisset ad easdem operaciones inde faciendum, quod quidem cariagium Rex eidem Petro [sc. de la Mare] postmodum fecit allocari ...'), E 159/64, m.12.
[4] Liberate Roll 55; E 101/3/20; *Cal. Anc. Corr. Wales*, p. 114.
[5] Liberate Rolls 55 and 56.
[6] *West Wales Ministers' Accts.*, p. 15.   [7] *Ibid.*
[8] *Annales*, ed. Eng. Hist. Soc. (1845), p. 298.
[9] *Cymmr. Trans.*, 1895-6, p. 107.   [10] *Cal. Welsh Rolls*, p. 182.

Providence.[1] The gates of the town had neither locks nor bars and were left open day and night.[2] At the place where the king had ordered stone to be prepared and mortar made for the building of the town walls, neither mason nor quarrier was to be found, and if the king wanted the works to be done Bogo advised him to enlist immediate help from Ireland; if he wished them to start on time, then he must order the constable of Bristol to send a shipload of corn without delay.[3] If there was to be enough lime to make the mortar, there would have to be regular shipments of stone from Tenby, 'for no other stone in the country would serve to make lime except this.'[4] Some of the work already begun was said to be unsatisfactory and the king must send the master of the works at Rhuddlan (i.e. Master James of St. George) or some other skilled master to Llanbadarn to look at it; no new work could begin, because the gate tower, which was already started, was itself proving a big enough task through its foundation having been placed too near to the castle ditch, where it was shaken day in and day out by the great crash of the waves.[5] With the Rhuddlan works at their height[6] Master James could perhaps not be spared; at all events de Knovill was told to send instead to Bristol for a Master Thomas. This was done, and arrangements discussed with him for the sending of masons and workmen.[7] The new justiciar also pointed out that it would be possible to make a good harbour, adding that the town would never thrive without one; both from what people had told him and what he had seen himself, it could be done at no great cost.[8] Finally, he says, with regard to the king's orders to collect moneys from sources made known to him by Ralf of Broughton for the purpose of preparing stone and making mortar, it has

[1] '. . . E sachet sire ke ieo resu le chastel tut nu, sauns vitayle e garneysun e sauns alblastes e baudricks . . . E kaunt ieo sir ceoce chose vi, ieo envea a Mungomeri a quire armures alblastes quarreus e vitayle par quei, si deus plest, nus ne auerum garde du chastel ne de la vile al eide deus.' (C 49 [Chancery, Parliamentary Proceedings], 1/19).
[2] '. . . kaunt ieo vint ilekes, il ni ont loc ne clostur a nule porte de la vile, mez esturent totes ouertes de iour e de nuit, de quei ieo ai fet mettre locs e gardeyns de portes ke respunderunt de portes de iour e de nuit si deus plest' (*ibid.*).
[3] Much of the passage is illegible, but this seems to be the general sense: '. . . a mustrer a nostre seynur le Rey ke la ou il me comaunda de pesser pere e fere mortier (*sc.* pur le mur) de sa vile de Lampader, ke ieo ne troue nul maun ne quarr . . . en le pays e ke ieo ne . . . nul ouerour . . . . sire si vus plest vos ouerayne fere ieo . . . et ke vus comaundet a vostre Iustice de Irlaunde . . . . vener hors de Irlaunde ilekes pur metr mut en hast, e ke vus comaunde a vostre conestable de Bristowe ke il face vener ilekes une nave de ble par mer mut en hast si vus volet ke le ouerayne comes par tens' (*ibid.*).
[4] 'E ke une nave de pere venge par tens ilekes de Dynbyec a fere chaus, pur ceo ke nul autre pere du pays ren ne vant a fere la chaus fors cele pere' (*ibid.*). That the reference is to Tenby is made clear by a record of payments for lime bought 'apud Tynebeyam' for the town wall of Aberystwyth in 1282 (C 47/2/4, m. 1d).
[5] This passage also is only partly legible, but the sense seems to be as given: '. . . ke il maunde a Lampadarvaur le meistre del ouerayne de Rothelan ou aukun autre meistre ke sotil oume seit de ouerayne . . . . ke nul ouerayne seit comese du chastel pur ceo ke icouent ke la tour de la porte ke est comese seit tut de fet ke mut ad tasce au Rey, pur ceo ke le fundement de la tour est assis trop pres le fosse du chastel, dunt le fundement crachet de iour en iour pur le graunt carck del mayre . . .' (*ibid.*).
[6] P. 29, below.
[7] The evidence for this is two notes added at the end of the last quoted section: (i) *mittatur usque Bristowe pro Magistro Thome cementario*, and (ii) *et postmodum mittetur ibi et cum ipso tractetur de cementariis et operatoribus mittendis ibi*' (*ibid.*).
[8] 'Et a mustrer a nostre seynur le Rey ke il purra fere bone hauene a sa vile de Lampaderuaur e ke james bone vile ne auera ilekes si hauene ne seit. E sachet, sir, a ceo ke lom me fet entendre e a ceo ke ieo vei memes vus, purriet fere la hauene ilekes saunt trop de custage. Mettre de quei, sir, vost pleisir me maundet' (C 47/2/2, no. 3, but apparently originally part of C 49/1/19). According to the endorsement on the latter, Bogo was ordered to examine with three other knights the possibilities of making a good and commodious harbour ('. . . videat si unus melius et commodus portus fieri possit tam ad opus Regis quam ad securitatem ville eiusdem et aliorum ibidem applicancium').

been quite impossible for him to levy and obtain them so quickly. Consequently he has no money at all, neither for those purposes nor for beginning nor doing any other part of the work. 'Therefore, Sir', he ends, 'please let me know clearly what is your pleasure for your work at Llanbadarn, and what you wish me to do in regard to all the things that I have told you of.'[1]

The sequel to these shortcomings and uncertainties was a recorded expenditure of only £12 12s. 10d. on the works of the castle in 1280 and 1281.[2] On the other hand the year 1280 saw the expenditure of £199 1s. 7½d. on the building of the town wall,[3] half of this sum being found 'from the new money' by the constable of Bristol castle in his capacity as keeper of the king's exchange there,[4] and the other half by way of loan from Orlandino di Podio, the king's banker.[5] In 1281 came the construction, near to the castle, of a weir in the River Rheidol, at a cost of £11 12s. 0d.,[6] and indeed it appears that works of one kind or another were being actively pursued right up to the outbreak of the revolt which marked the beginning of Edward I's second Welsh war in March 1282. Thus in November 1281 there is a note of the delivery of 200 marks of the issues of the Jewry to Ralf of Broughton for the works of Lampader,[7] while in January 1282 the Bishop of St. David's was ordered to pay 250 marks to William de Canvill 'for the works of the castle of Lampaderware'.[8]

On 24 March, two days after the revolt had broken out in North Wales, the Welsh gained access to Aberystwyth Castle by treachery. According to first reports they did not immediately demolish anything,[9] but within a day or two 'they burned the town and the castle and destroyed the rampart that was around the castle and the town'.[10] About the middle of May Master James of St. George himself was sent to Aberystwyth; the nominal purpose of his visit was to 'construct' the king's castle (*ad castrum Regis ibidem construendum*),[11] a phrase which seems to point to something more than the mere repair of damage, and may indeed rather indicate some radical attempt to overcome major weaknesses of the kind pointed out two years earlier by Bogo de Knovill. On 25 May, no doubt as a result of Master James's report, writs were issued to the sheriffs of Gloucester and Somerset instructing each of them 'to choose 15 good masons immediately and have them conducted to Bristol, to be there with their tools on 25 June ready to set out in the king's service for Lampader,

---

[1] 'Et a mustrer a nostre seynur le Rey ke la ou il me comaunda de leuer deners ke dues li furunt, la ou Rauf le Clerc del ouerayne me freit a sauer, a depesser pere e morter fere, sachet sir ke ieo ne pus nul de ces deners si en hast leuer ne auer. E sachet, sire, ke ieo uai nul dener de quei ieo pus pere depesser ne morter ne autre chose del ouerayne comser ne fere. Dunc, sire, si vus plest vostre pleisir de vostre ouerayne de Lamp' ceo ke vus volet ke ieo face, e do totes choses ke ieo vus ai mustre certeinement par vostre lettre me maundet si vus plest' (C 47/2/2, no. 3).
[2] *West Wales Ministers' Accts.*, p. 35.
[3] E 372/125, rot. 2; Liberate Roll 56.
[4] *Cal. Close Rolls 1279–88*, p. 24; G. C. Brooke, *English Coins* (3rd edn., 1950), pp. 116–17.
[5] Liberate Roll 56. For Orlandino, see Tout, *Chapters* ii, p. 29.
[6] '. . . in factura cuiusdam gurgitis in aqua de Reddor iuxta castrum nostrum de Lampadervaur' (Liberate Roll 57).
[7] *Cal. Close Rolls 1279–88*, p. 137.
[8] *Ibid.* p. 145.
[9] *Cal. Anc. Corr. Wales*, pp. 44–5.
[10] *Brut y Tywysogion, Red Bk. Version*, ed. T. Jones, p. 271; *Annales Cambriae*, p. 106.
[11] E 101/3/29. The entry of his 20s. expenses allowance is undated but follows closely on an entry covering the period 17–22 May.

to do there what the king shall enjoin upon them.[1] At the same time provision was made for the resettlement of the borough by empowering the Earl of Gloucester to admit and enfeoff burgesses.[2]

It was presumably by Master James's arrangement[3] that the ensuing works were placed in the charge of a master who must have been one of his close associates. This was a Master Giles of St. George,[4] whose wages were paid as from 7 June 1282 by Walter of Nottingham, named both as paymaster of the king's Wardrobe (*pacator de garderoba domini Regis*)[5] and clerk of works for the castle.[6] No record of cost has survived; but it seems fair to suppose that a substantial part of a sum of £1260 issued from the Wardrobe at Hartlebury at the time of Master James's visit, and conveyed to Walter of Nottingham at Lampader by two clerks of the Bishop of St. David's, may have been for works payments.[7] We know equally little of the nature of what was done; the only fact that remains on record is that by mid-September Master Giles had agreed with five purveyors of lime at Tenby for the production, when the king should need it, of 75 lasts (1800 quarters) of lime at 3s. the last for work on the town wall (*versus murum de Lampaderuaur*), Henry the vicar of Tenby both witnessing the account and taking charge of the tools provided for breaking the limestone.[8]

The main repair is assigned by the *Annales Cambriae* to the following year, 1283,[9] when expenditure on wages, at any rate in September and October, was running at the rate of rather more than £27 a week. The labour force, already apparently running down from its summer peak, included over 80 masons, 9 smiths, 28 carpenters and 257 quarriers, hodmen, etc. The master mason, at 7s. a week, was Master John de Ocleye, the master carpenter Master John of Maghull (*Moghale*).[10] A writ of 11 September 1283 to the constable of Bristol to send two cartloads of lead without delay for the works at Lampadervaur[11] may be an indication that some of the re-erected 'houses' in the castle were ready to receive their roofs.

[1] *Cal. Welsh Rolls*, p. 250. The Gloucester men were allowed 3d. each, the Somerset and Dorset men 2d., for their day's journeying to Bristol; the latter had another 2d. for a further day spent waiting for orders to come from Robert Tybetot (Liberate Roll 59). Their return journey appears to have been by way of the Hospice of Slebech, 20s. being paid for the expenses of the 30 of them *in redeundo versus hospicium* (C 47/2/4, m.1d); for the far-famed hospitality of Slebech, *see* William Rees, *A History of the Order of St. John of Jerusalem in Wales* (Cardiff, 1947), p. 33.

[2] *Cal. Pat. Rolls 1281–92*, p. 24; *Cal. Welsh Rolls*, p. 222.

[3] Cf. his appointment a few weeks later of the resident master mason at Hope, below, p. 39.

[4] C 47/2/4, m. 3. No other instance of the use of his full name is known to have survived in English records; he is probably identical with the 'Giletus' named at Harlech in 1286 (Appendix C, III, 9) and with the Giles of St. George, mason, who in 1279–81 was joint contractor with his brother Tassin of St. George for building the keep of Philip of Savoy's castle at Saxon (Valais), Switzerland (Turin, Archivio di Stato, Inv. Sav. 69, Fo.69, Mazzo 1, no. 1.).

[5] C 47/2/4, m. 2.   [6] *Cal. Welsh Rolls*, p. 324.

[7] E 101/3/29. The purpose of the £1260 is unstated, but it was separate from a sum of £200 issued from Worcester about the same time to Walter of Nottingham for paying soldiers' wages at Lampader.

[8] Details on C 47/2/2, no. 7, a schedule formerly attached to C 47/2/4 ('Visus compoti Magistri Egidii cementarii de expensis per ipsum Egidium factis per visum et testimonium domini Henrici vicarii de Thinbek').

[9] *Annales Cambriae*, p. 108 and note; 'Eodem anno reaedificavit rex Edwardus castrum de Lanpadarnvawr'.

[10] C 47/2/2, no. 13. J. G. Edwards, 'Edward I's Castle-building in Wales', p. 31, note 3, rightly supposed this fragmentary undated account to belong to 1283 and not 1277; attribution to the later year is made almost certain by the presence of John of Maghull, who is named in the previous April (C 47/2/4) as one of 74 carpenters engaged at the siege of Castell y Bere and in erecting a palisade round the town of Towyn, the base for the operation (*ad villam de Towin cum pilis claudendam*).

[11] *Cal. Anc. Corr. Wales*, p. 63.

There was still work to be done, however, and preparations for the resumption of building in the 1284 season included the delivery in February of £300 of the proceeds of the thirtieth, held in the keeping of the sheriff of Nottingham, to the clerk of the works.[1] Progress during the ensuing months may be inferred from the shipment of a further 28 carrats of lead from Bristol, for which payment of £64 13s. 6d., plus £1 3s. 6d. freight, was made by the keeper of the Wardrobe on 21 September.[2] The king himself visited Aberystwyth from 10 to 16 November 1284.[3] In 1286 another £100 was delivered from the issues of the county of York to the justiciar of West Wales, 'wherewith to carry out our works in Wales'.[4] When Walter of Nottingham died, his accounts could not be found. Accordingly in January 1290 the Bishop of St. David's, the Abbot of Whitland and Peter Lof, viewer of the king's works in West Wales, were appointed to go to Aberystwyth and examine the works there 'and the costs and expenses of Walter on them during the king's absence abroad by those engaged upon them in Walter's time' and report how much he had spent on them over and above the £100 furnished by the sheriff of York.[5] Their enquiry resulted in an account which gives us our earliest information about different parts of the castle.[6] Its first section records an expenditure of £247 10s. 0d., i.e. £147 10s. 0d. more than had been received from the sheriff of York, and must be in respect of the 1286 season. It includes the following items:

> Making the outer wall of the castle on the N. side over the sea, containing 50 perches, with wages of masons and other workmen   £37 10s. 0d.
> Doubling the chamber over the gate on the side towards the sea[7] and renewing its lead roof   £50.
> Remaking the well in the middle of the castle   £20.
> Making a stable and bakehouse under one roof below the wall on the W. side of the castle: making a chamber and a wall adjacent to it under the King's Chamber; making a lead-roofed porch over the door of the Great Chamber; with carpentry, etc.
>   £60.
> Making an outer barbican towards the town, together with its foundation, besides the expenses previously incurred on it by Geoffrey Clement   £50.
> Heightening a tower over the middle of the gate towards the town, and raising the wall on either side of the same gate   £30.

In the second part, covering £73 18s. 4d. spent on works executed between 27 April 1287, and 1 August 1289, the following particulars are given:

> For a new wall raised on either side of the bridge in the time when Geoffrey Clement was constable of the castle   £4 13s. 4d.
> Wages of divers workmen about the said wall   £6 6s. 0d.
> Making two new posterns in the outer bailey and stopping one up (*claudend'*) there, and repairing the wall of the kitchen *ad tascham*   £2 4s. 0d.
> To diggers for repairing and mending the ditches round the castle *ad tascham*
>   £5 16s. 8d.

[1] *Littere Wallie*, p. 190.   [2] E 101/351/9.   [3] *Cal. Pat. Rolls 1281–92*, pp. 138–45.
[4] C 47/35/18, no. 37.   [5] *Cal. Welsh Rolls*, p. 324.   [6] Pipe Roll 134, rot. 2d.
[7] 'Et in camera ultra portam versus mare gimellata et plumbata de novo facienda.'

To Robert and Nicholas, carpenters, staying in the castle during the war of Rhys ap Maredudd from 8 June to 21 September 1287, to put the castle on a war footing (*ad batillandum castrum predictum*),[1] and for other works done in it   £3 10s. 0d.

For 10 measures of iron for the works   £3 0s. 0d.

To John the smith and his assistant, working in the castle from 8 June to 26 October 1287   £2 10s. 0d.

Burning charcoal, making lime and carrying stone   £7 18s. 4d.

To Robert the mason for making a new wall on the sea front, with a new tower, outside the outer bailey, *ad tascham*   £6 13s. 4d.

To carpenters for making the woodwork of the said tower and repairing certain other 'houses' in the castle *ad tascham*   £2 10s. 0d.

For 2½ loads of lead for roofing the said tower and other 'houses' in the castle   £4.

To William the plumber for roofing the said tower and another tower *ad tascham*   15s. 0d.

To David the carpenter for making a new granary in the castle *ad tascham* £8 10s. 0d.

To Thomas of Buildwas (*Thome Beldwas*) for paving two towers and a wall-walk *ad tascham*   £5 10s. 0d.

To the same for deepening a well *ad tascham*   £1.

For covering the well and for a rope for it   10s.

Mending a window and gutter in the king's wardrobe *ad tascham*   12s. 0d.

To David the mason for whitewashing (*dealbacione*) the top of a tower and the battlements in the outer bailey   £3.

Wages of William the plumber's assistant, in roofing the 'houses' of the castle, for 1 year at 2d. a day   £3 0s. 8d.

The works covered by the above payments appear to be the last to have been carried out. To some extent they comprised the repair and replacement of the parts of the castle damaged in the incursion of 1282, while such an evident innovation as the new eastern barbican may represent an addition to the original plan designed to help prevent a repetition of the Welsh success. Certainly when the castle was besieged in 1294–5 the Welsh with all their numbers were unable to reduce it and, though completely cut off from relief by land, sea-borne supplies, sent as usual from Bristol, saved it from surrender by starvation.[2] The works had gone on more or less continuously for twelve years and had cost at least £4300, but it is to be remembered that some £3470 of this was spent in the first three seasons of building. These figures compare with a total expenditure at Builth of little more than £1650 in five-and-a-half years.

The new castle became in 1301 one of the possessions of Edward, Prince of Wales, and thereafter its maintenance was the responsibility of the ministers of the principality of Wales. The sums spent on repairs under Edward II were generally small, and a survey made in 1321 disclosed that the roofs of the towers and other buildings were nearly all defective, and that the bridge of the outer bailey needed immediate

[1] Literally 'battlementing', but probably in the sense of equipping the battlements with timber *hourds* and galleries to assist in repelling close siege engines.
[2] Morris, *Welsh Wars of Edward the First*, pp. 249 and 260.

attention as its condition endangered the security of the castle.[1] Orders were then given for the bridge to be mended, and £15 19s. 0¼d. were spent on this and other repairs.[2] Further repairs were carried out early in the reign of Edward III,[3] but when the Black Prince took possession of the castle in 1343 it was found to be in a poor state. The Long Chamber had collapsed for want of prompt repair. The windows of the King's Hall needed renewing, as did the lead on the tower near the Old Hall—itself in need of roof repairs. The kitchen, bakehouse, stable and two granaries were all in need of repair. The great gate, the two draw-bridges and the timberwork of three towers in the inner bailey were all more or less rotten. The walls and towers in the 'third bailey' had been largely destroyed by the sea, and only the building of a sea-wall at a cost of £200 could save it. As the other dilapidations were estimated at £106, the total estimate for repairs was £306.[4] All that in fact was done was to buy four fothers of lead to mend the roofs at a cost of £6, to repair the 'new granary' at a cost of 7s. 7d., and later (in 1349–50) virtually to rebuild (*quasi de novo facere*) two bridges in the outer ward.[5] By now the prince had got into the habit of granting the custody of the castle to favoured retainers for life, and this practice was continued by his widow Princess Joan, who held it in dower after his death.[6] In these circumstances little or nothing was spent on the castle by the chamberlain of South Wales until after Princess Joan's death in 1385.

From 1403 to 1408 Aberystwyth Castle was in the hands of Owain Glyndŵr.[7] When it was recovered some repairs were carried out, but the expenditure at Aberystwyth was much smaller than upon other castles recovered from the Welsh, amounting to less than £10 between 1409 and 1415.[8] Possibly this indicates that here there was less damage to make good, but no survey is available to indicate whether this was in fact the case. £18 7s. 0d. were spent on repairs early in the reign of Henry VI,[9] and in 1450–1 the lead roofs of the Knights' Hall, the 'Somerhall' and the chapel were repaired at a cost of £20.[10] In 1456–7 a further £27 17s. 2d. were spent on unspecified repairs.[11] Under Edward IV recorded expenditure on the castle amounted to £7 14s. 0d. (chiefly on a new bridge) in 1465–6, 7s. 8d. in 1466–7, £32 6s. 2d. in 1467–8, £10 17s. 6d. in 1478–9, and £5 2s. 0d. in 1480–1.[12]

3. FLINT[13]

Simultaneously with the building of Builth and Aberystwyth, two new royal castles, Flint and Rhuddlan, were established along the north coast between Chester and the

[1] B.L., Add. Roll 7198.   [2] *Cal. Close Rolls 1318–23*, p. 296; E 101/13/32; E 372/171, rot. 35.
[3] E 372/178, rot. 43; *Cal. Close Rolls 1333–7*, p. 616.   [4] E 163/4/42.   [5] SC 6/1221/5; SC 6/1306/1.
[6] *Cal. Pat. Rolls 1348–50*, p. 11; *Black Prince's Register* i, p. 131; *Cal. Pat. Rolls 1381–5*, pp. 405, 453.
[7] J. E. Lloyd, *Owen Glendower* (1931), pp. 81, 136.   [8] SC 6/1222/10–14.   [9] E 101/487/18.
[10] SC 6/1224/4.   [11] SC 6/1224/2.   [12] SC 6/1224/5–9, 1225/1–8.
[13] The documentary evidence for the building of Flint is studied by Sir Goronwy Edwards in *Flints. Hist. Soc. Pubns.* xii (1952). Since that date five further fragments of Flint 'particulars' have come to light in the Public Record Office, viz: (i) Costs of necessaries and carriage (part) 1281–4 (cf. A. J. Taylor, 'The Building of Flint a Postscript', in *Flints. Hist Soc. Pubns.*, 1957, pp. 34–41); (ii) Wages of masons, April–August 1281 (E101/674/23); (iii) Wages of *minuti operarii* April 1279–August 1281 (E 101/674/23); (iv) Wages of carpenters, smiths and *minuti operarii*, 1286; (v) Wages of *minuti operarii*, 1286 (C 47/3/52, no. 31.).

Conway estuary. Their purpose was to bring under permanent control the disputed territory of Englefield, which had changed hands many times since its initial English conquest in the seventh and eighth centuries and had only recently been ceded to Llywelyn by the Treaty of Montgomery (1267). Both were associated with dependent boroughs for English settlers and both were planned to be directly accessible to sea-going shipping. They superseded the castles of Dyserth and Deganwy which henceforward disappear from the records. At the same time the building of a new castle was initiated at Ruthin in the Vale of Clwyd.[1]

Measures to provide the necessary labour force for these works were being put in hand at least as early as June 1277. On 11 June the king's clerk, Master William of Perton, was given his expenses to set out from High Wycombe, where the court then was, to recruit masons in the counties of Leicester, Lincoln and Nottingham, while about the same time his colleague Master Robert of Belvoir was sent to 'divers parts of the realm' to enlist carpenters.[2] A third clerk, presumably the *M. clericus* through whom their wages were subsequently paid,[3] must have been similarly sent on tour to recruit diggers in the counties of Warwick and Leicester, Salop and Stafford, Lancaster and Chester. A fourth, John of Spofforth, was responsible for obtaining woodmen (*cissores bosci*) in Cheshire and elsewhere. From 16 July onwards the bodies of men thus enlisted were converging on Chester, where the king and the army had arrived the previous day from Worcester and where the Cinque Ports fleet joined them a day or two later.[4] On or about 21 July the whole array moved forward to field headquarters on the Dee estuary at a site which the records name variously as 'the camp near Hawarden', 'the camp near Basingwerk' and the camp *apud le Flynt prope Basingwerk*.[5]

For the first few weeks each labour category was treated as a military unit and placed under a knight who shared with the clerk who had directed its recruitment responsibility for the issue of its wages. Thus the masons and carpenters were respectively under Sir Peter de Campania and Sir Walter de Jaye, the diggers and woodmen under Sir Peter of Brampton and Sir Gilbert of Birdsall. By the end of July there were already assembled, at the place ever since known as Flint,[6] approximately 1850 workmen, made up as follows:

Ingeniatores	Diggers	Carpenters	Woodmen	Masons	Smiths	Charcoal Burners
1 Master(a)	970 plus 3 Masters(b)	330	320	200 plus 1 Master(c)	12	10

(a) Master Richard of Chester (b) Master William and two others unnamed (c) Master Thomas of Grantham

[1] See below, p. 35.   [2] E 101/350/26; *Cal. Pat. Rolls 1272–81*, pp. 213–14.   [3] E 101/485/19.
[4] J. E. Morris, *Welsh Wars of Edward the First*, pp. 127–8.   [5] E 101/350/25; E 101/3/19; *Foedera* i, p. 544.
[6] There was previously no such place. The site lay territorially within the bounds of the lost vill of Redington and its hamlet of Ondeston, ecclesiastically in the parish of Northop (see J. E. Lloyd, 'Edward I and the County of Flint', in *Flints. Hist. Soc. Jnl.*, 1916–17, pp. 21–22; for a suggestion as to the origin of the name 'Flint', see *Studies in Building History*, ed. E. M. Jope (1961), p. 129, note 3).

During the next two weeks the numbers continued to increase; the arrival on
9 August of a contingent of 300 *fossatores* led by Master William of March on a seven-
days' journey from Boston and the parts of Holland in South Lincolnshire, with
three mounted sergeants to keep them from deserting en route (*ne fugerent per viam*),
no doubt brought to the conquest of the Dee and Clwyd marshes something of the
dyking experience of the fens, and meant that by that date the diggers alone numbered not less than 1800; by the end of the month they had increased to nearly 2300.
Such manpower figures as we have[1] are, however, perplexing by reason of the fluctuations to which they bear witness. Thus the 200 masons disappear from the record
after 31 July, there are no masons at all from 1 to 14 August, and when they reappear
on the following day they number only 50. It seems probable that the camp at Flint
at first served partly as a dispersal centre from which men were sent as needed to
other embryo works—to Ruthin, to Builth, perhaps to Vale Royal to prepare for the
laying of the foundation-stone on 13 August, and, after 19 August, to Rhuddlan.

For the chief activity of these early weeks we have the Welsh annalist's statement
that the king 'fortified a court in Flint with huge ditches around it'.[2] This would
suggest that the first main task was the digging of the double bank and ditch of the
future town, which to begin with may have served to protect the camp of the army
and the labour force.[3] Something of the sort seems to be implied in the wording of the
enrolment of the wages account quoted above,[4] where it is described as being in
respect of workmen *operantium fossata et alia in castris Regis de Flint et Rothelan ad securitatem Regis et comitive sue dum Rex erat in partibus illis*.[5] A sense of the urgency with which
the work was pressed forward is reflected in the award of bonuses 'by the king's gift' to
diggers who worked specially well between 2 and 7 August and to men who bestirred
themselves carrying the hand-barrows.[6] Conversely, during the first four months no
less than £9 7s. 8d. was deducted from the men's wages because of bad work or
absenteeism (... *denariis subtractis de diversis operariis propter defectum laboris*).[7] Stocks of
wood-cutting, clearing and digging tools were being accumulated at Chester before
the king's arrival and after it lime was bought and sent 'to the castle of Flint for the
works of the said castle by the king's command'.[8] Before the end of July timber was
being felled in the forests of Toxteth and Cheshire specifically for the construction
of the new castle.[9] At least some of it was ferried to the site on rafts, 250 boards being
purchased 'to make rafts to carry the timber by water'.[10] A special payment made on
10 August on the high recommendation of Otto de Grandson to men raising timber

[1] Given in E 101/485/19, which is the keeper of the Wardrobe's account of wages paid to the carpenters,
masons, smiths, diggers and other workmen 'who were in the king's army at Flint and Rhuddlan'.
[2] *Brut y Tywysogion*, Red Book Version, ed. T. Jones, p. 267.
[3] Expenditure of nearly £200 on wages of diggers *operancium circa clausturam ville* between March 1281
and November 1286 (Pipe Roll 131, rot. 26) suggests, however, that the town defences were not completed
tout à coup in the earliest phase of the work, even accepting that part of this figure may be accountable to war
damage repairs after March 1282.
[4] Cf. note 1 above.   [5] E 372/123, rot. 23.
[6] '... quibusdam fossatoribus bene laborantibus per eosdem dies de dono Regis, iij.s; ... duobus garc'
festinantibus portit' ciueriarum pro vadiis suis duorum dierum, vj.d.'
[7] Cf. note 1 above.   [8] Liberate Roll 55.
[9] 'C. carpentariis ... euntibus in foresta domini Edmundi germani Regis de Toxtar, ad cindendum
arbores pro constructione castri de flind' (E 101/485/19); 'Gilberto fil' Roberti militi eunti in foresta Cestr' ad
faciendum prostracionem arbores ad constructionem castri de flind' E 101/3/15).   [10] E 101/3/15.

at Flint may perhaps have been to do with erecting these first consignments to form the palisade.[1] An obscure item in the earliest account, possibly connected with the setting out of the positions of the castle walls and towers, is the purchase of more than 150 'tables' (*tabule*) *ad constructionem castri de Flynd*. They were mostly bought from archers, which suggests 'targets' rather than 'tables': thus 37 'tables' were bought for 1s. 6½d. 'from divers archers', while 19 'tables' bought 'from the Macclesfield archers' cost 3s. 4d.[2] Meanwhile in the Wirral 10,000 stones were being obtained for the works from a quarry near Shotwick.[3]

From 25 July, the date of the first payments recorded as being made at Flint, until 23 August, when the king established his headquarters at Rhuddlan,[4] a sum of £722 13s. 5d. was expended by the keeper of the Wardrobe on workmen's wages,[5] and it is probably fair to assign the greater part of this amount to the works of Flint itself. From the latter date William of Perton, the clerk who had been sent out in June to recruit masons from the east midlands, reckoned his appointment as keeper of the works of the castles of Flint and Rhuddlan.[6] His first Flint account, from 23 August to 21 November 1277, shows a further expenditure of £470. The bulk of the payments are in respect of wages, up to 88 masons, 102 carpenters and 684 diggers being on the roll prior to 10 October; wages paid to knights include 2s. a day to Gilbert Fitz Walter as *custos operariorum* from 10 August to 19 October.[7] By mid-November the maxima of the three main categories of workmen had dropped to 35, 61 and 176 respectively,[8] but continuance of work during the winter is evidenced by payments between 21 November 1277 and 28 February 1278 of £76 13s. 5d. from the issues of Chester.[9] That progress had been made in laying out the town is suggested by the authorisation, in February 1278, for the granting of burgages at fixed rents in Flint as well as in Rhuddlan.[10]

The next account[11] covers the fifteen months from 30 November 1277 to 5 March 1279, and is thus broadly in respect of the 1278 building season. The accountant was the king's clerk Nicholas Bonel, who before the king's departure from the district had been appointed by word of mouth to be receiver of the cantreds of Rhos and Englefield and surveyor of the works of Flint and Rhuddlan.[12]

The figures show that at this time the major effort was being concentrated on Rhuddlan, the expenditure of £830 on Flint being little more than a quarter of that absorbed by the sister castle (£3160) during the same period. The biggest items are £485 for diggers' and £176 for carpenters' wages. Masons' work amounted to only £53 (compared with £1267 at Rhuddlan) and was limited to preparing stone in the quarry across the Dee at Nesshead for revetting the castle ditch.[13] Some of the towers were far enough advanced to be roofed in lead, and may thus possibly have already

---

[1] 'Vincencio clerico pro duobus solidis quos dedit diversis hominibus precepto O. de Grandisono pro maremio leuando apud Flind, ij.s.' (E 101/3/15)   [2] *Ibid.*   [3] E 372/124, rot. 29.
[4] E 101/350/25.   [5] E 101/485/19.   [6] E 372/124, rot. 29.   [7] *Ibid.*
[8] For the interpretation of these figures, see J. G. Edwards, 'The Building of Flint' (*Flints. Hist. Soc. Pubns.*, 12), p. 15, no. 27.
[9] *Cheshire in the Pipe Rolls*, p. 124.   [10] *Cal. Welsh Rolls*, p. 165.
[11] E 372/122, rot. 28d.   [12] *Cal. Welsh Rolls*, p. 160.
[13] The account notes that the stone was not used in Bonel's time, the ditch being temporarily dressed (*paratum*) with a revetment of turves.

stood completed;[1] as will be seen shortly, however, it is clear from a later account[2] that the Great Tower and a tower towards the river were still under construction in 1282, while the former was not finally roofed until 1286.[3]

The fortunate survival of the detailed rolls of wages paid to masons at Flint from April 1279 to August 1281,[4] to labourers (*minuti operarii*) from April 1279 to December 1280,[5] and to carpenters, smiths and others for part of the year 1286,[6] together with some details of purchases and carriage charges for the period 1281–4,[7] enables us to trace the progress of the work in its later stages rather more closely. In the seven months of the 1279 building season, from 9 April to 29 October, only £61 was accounted to masons' wages, practically half this amount (£29 3s. 0d.) being paid on 9 July for the construction of about 200 feet of the revetment wall of the castle ditch,[8] presumably with the stones quarried at Nesshead during the previous year. During approximately the same period £126 was paid to *minuti operarii*, whose numbers reached maxima of 428 at the end of April and, after a drop to 20 in June, 380 in mid-July; their task was to serve both the masons and the quarrymen, details of whose operations have not survived, though it looks as if they rather than the masons may have made the heavier call on their services. The last operation of the year was to clear out a lime kiln, and for the next ten months (November 1279–August 1280) work at Flint appears to have been entirely suspended.

The quarrying of stone was resumed about 15 August 1280 and shortly afterwards two buildings were constructed in which to store lime. About 6 October an existing limekiln was repaired and work begun on the construction of a new and larger one. From 1 November the wages of Master James of St. George begin to be entered on the Flint masons' account,[9] where from 3 November he is joined by John Pycard and five others unnamed, from 20 January 1281 by William of Southwell, from 2 March by Walter of Lincoln and from 16 March by Master Richard of Chester.[10] Another indication of increased activity to come is the preparation, in November 1280, of accommodation for the masons.[11] Between mid-October and mid-March (1281) the number of masons receiving pay in addition to Master James averaged only 4. In the last two weeks of March the corresponding figure leapt up to 132 and by the end of April stood at 196. Between then and 17 August, after which date detailed figures are

---

[1] Besides the four towers of which substantial remains still stand, it should not be forgotten that there was a fifth—the outer gate tower shown in the plan of Flint inset in Speed's map of Flintshire (1610). When the Pipe Roll records the purchase of lead *ad turres cooperiend' in eodem castro* and the wages of a plumber executing the work, the reference might be to this tower and only one of the others. Early completion of the gate tower is suggested by the fact that the grant of 'the custody of the gate of the king's castle of Flint' to Ralf of Broughton in June 1281 was evidently not the first such grant to have been made (*Cal. Welsh Rolls*, p. 189).

[2] E 101/674/23.   [3] C 47/3/52, no. 31.   [4] E 101/674/23.   [5] *Ibid.*

[6] C 47/3/52, no. 31.   [7] E 101/674/23.

[8] 'Et Ricardo de Franckevill' et Waltero de Bridelton cementariis pro factura viij perticatar' et viij pedum muri fosse Castri ad tascham xxix.li.iij.s., viz. pro qualibet perticata lxx.s. et pro viij pedibus xxiij.s.'

[9] The last of the major Rhuddlan accounts terminated only two days later (3 November 1280, E 372/124, rot. 29). The entering of the pay of the master of the works on the Flint account reflects the transfer of the main building effort to the latter castle from the former.

[10] Their daily wages are: Master James, 2s. 0d.; Master Richard, 10d.; William of Southwell, 6d.; Walter of Lincoln, 5½d.; John Pycard, 5d. Only Master James is paid continuously, i.e. 7 days a week; normally a 6-day week is worked at Flint, and the others are paid only for days so worked.

[11] '. . . xij Baardariis portantibus lapides ad Godefridum carpentarium et coadiuvantibus eundem ad suppodiendum postes Astelarii cementariorum per xj dies, xvj.s.vj.d.' (E 101/674/23).

lost, an average of 190 masons were constantly employed. The contrast in terms of money is no less striking. Whereas in the seven months April–October 1279 masons' wages amounted to only £61, in the ten months October 1280–August 1281 they totalled £650; and on the assumption that the average weekly expenditure on masons' wages from 6 October onwards was continued through to the end of the season, i.e. to the second week of November 1281, the full year's figure would have come to about £835, making with the 1279 expenditure a total of £896. As the total bill for masons' wages from April 1279 to November 1284 amounted to £1672, this means that approximately £60 more was spent under this head in the 1281 season than in the three following seasons put together. There can thus be little doubt that the year 1281 saw the biggest single advance of any in the progress of the Flint works. It is perhaps no coincidence that the Welsh attack on the new castles in March 1282 was timed for the very week in which, a year earlier, the expansion of work at the less finished of them had been inaugurated.

The weekly wage accounts tell us little or nothing about what parts of the building were under construction at any given time. The gap can, however, at least partly be filled from details given in the accounts of payments for work executed *ad tascham*.[1] Thus in May 1281 £15 8s. 1½d. was paid to 5 masons and their assistants[2] for dressing 2545 stones at 1½d. a stone for the sides of the moat (*talliatis ad costeras fosse castri*), and £5 11s. 8d. for making and dressing during the winter 67 steps at 1s. 8d. each for stair-cases in the towers; John White (*le Blund*) of London was paid 19s. for dressing 152 stones for the well in the Great Tower, and Peter Morel 12s. for dressing stones to make the heads for three windows in the 'little' (? S.W.) tower (*pro lapidibus talliatis pertinentibus ad tres voyzur' faciend' ad tres fenestras minoris turris*). Other masons, many of them named,[3] were paid for task work in dressing 30,515 stones at 1d. or 1¼d. each during the preceding winter. Items paid for in July 1281 include 140 stones dressed 'for the work of the Great Tower' by Peter Morel, Flauner and their fellows; stones dressed by Thomas de Hardingesham 'for the doorways of the Great Tower'; a further 150 steps; 88 stones called *eschonchons*; and 1871 stones called *serches*.[4] A further 929 *serches*, dressed by Flauner and his fellow masons, were paid for in August, 121 of them at 1¼d. apiece for the north-west tower (*ad paruam Turrim versus Mare*) and the remainder at 1½d. apiece for tower staircases generally (*ad gradus turrium*). The same group also provided 147 buttress stones (*lapidibus scilt. Botriz*) for the Great Tower. Another contractor, Ingeram by name, provided stones called *roydes* for 13½ feet of the 'little' tower (*pro lapidibus scilt. roydes talliatis pertinentibus ad xiij pedes et dim' Minoris turris in altitudine*). That at least one of the curtain walls was under

---

[1] E 101/674/23.

[2] Those named are Robert de Hardingesham, 'Baron', 'Yngeram', Peter Morel and 'Flauner'. For Morel, see below, p. 29, note 2; for 'Flauner', p. 50, note 9.

[3] Those named are 'Brentford' (*Breynford*), Master John of Chester, Walter of Lincoln, William of South-well, William of Craven, Henry of Kirby, Elias of Moston, Michael le Normand', Robert of London, Robert of Ocle, John of St. Faith's, William Seysil, Geoffrey Francis, Richard of Carlington, William of Burton (*Bortun*'), and Matthew Jardine (*de Gardino*); *et sociis suis cementariis multis et diversis*.

[4] 'Serches' were apparently stones cut with a concave face, for use in forming the sides of wells, newel staircases, etc.; thus at Westminster in 1365–6 John Mordon provided 240 'petras de Raygate operatas vocatas Sherches, emptas *pro quadam vice* in Turri iuxta gardinum Regis' (E 101/472/14); cf. Salzman, *Building in England*, p. 109.

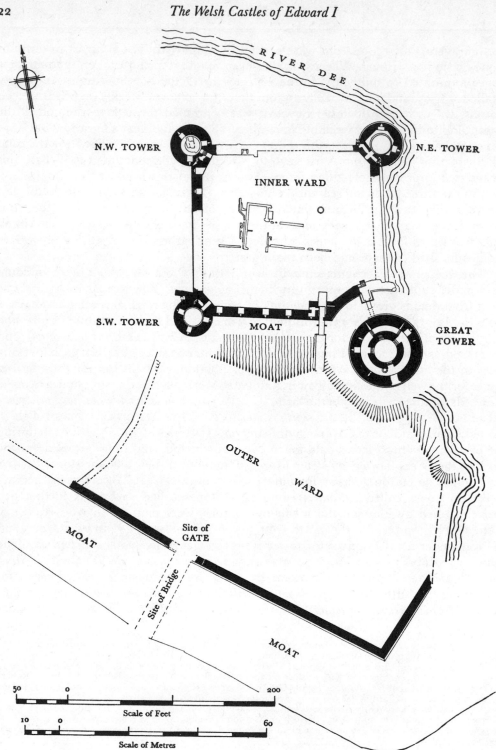

Fig. 3. Flint Castle.

construction at courtyard level at this time is shown by the payment of 51s. to John of Clifford, Richard of Wellingborough (*Wenglingberg'*) and John Page, masons, for making eight embrasures in it (seven at 6s. 3d.—*pro factura vij archeriarum muri castri ad tascham*—and one at 7s. 3d.).

The surviving particulars in regard to materials and necessaries supplied[1] are concerned with lime for making mortar, items required in connection with the horses and carts used to bring supplies of every kind to the site, parchment for the writing of the accounts, joists for the tower floors, thatch for temporary roofs on the towers and brushwood required for use by the plumber.

The cost of lime supplied within the period of the account was £112 9s. 9d.; at 4d. a 'ring' or bag, this represents something like 87,000 bags—a reminder of the scale of the supply organisation behind the works. It is notable that the 17,000 'rings' recorded on the section of the account still extant are stated to have been supplied 'in the 10th year, before the war' (*anno regni Regis Edwardi x° ante guerram*), i.e. between 20 November 1281 and 22 March 1282. The great bulk of this amount probably belongs to the weeks immediately preceding the Welsh rising and the quantity points to preparations having been in train at that time for the commencement of another full-strength building season. Some of the lime was brought from Basingwerk, some from 'Holston' (Whelston in Bagillt).

A number of items of interest concerned with cartage and the purchase of necessaries emerge from the account. Master Henry of Oxford, one of the chief master carpenters employed at Conway in 1285-6, here makes an earlier appearance at Flint, where he accounts for carting timber from the woods for making brattices. There is also mention of a hitherto unknown master mason, Master Robert of Boulogne, and of a master plumber, Master William of Lichfield. Grease is bought for lubricating a crane (*pro quadam machina*) used to lift joists on to one of the towers facing the river (*pro gistis trahendis super Turrim versus Mare*), and the date the joists were supplied, presumably for one of the tower floors, is specifically stated to have been during the Welsh war and in the king's tenth year, i.e. between 22 March and 19 November 1282 (*pro una turri de Flynt versus Mare gistanda in guerra Wallensi anno regni Regis Edwardi x°*).[2]

Further light is thrown on the building of the towers by entries recording the purchase of 44 bundles of straw thatch for covering the walls of the towers against the winter in the tenth year (the winter of 1281-2), the purchase by Master Henry of Alcester[3] of straw thatch for protecting the Great Tower against the winter in the eleventh year (1282-3), the purchase of spars for holding down this temporary roofing over the Great Tower, and the supply in July 1284 of 12 cart-loads of brushwood for the use of the plumbers. These entries seem to show that part of the major operations of the 1281 season consisted of building work on at least two towers which thereafter required temporary covering to protect them during the succeeding winter period;

---

[1] The substance of the following paragraphs, based on E 101/674/23, has appeared in *Flints. Hist. Soc. Pubns.* (1957), pp. 37-8.

[2] Early in April 1282 five master carpenters from London travelled to Devizes, where the court then was, before going on to Flint *pro constructione eiusdem castri* (E 101/3/29, para. 1). James of St. George was with the court at this time (*ibid.* para. 2) and would perhaps require to give directions for the work they were to do.

[3] If from Alchester, co. Oxon., possibly identical with Master Henry *de Oxon'*.

that one of these towers, namely one of those facing towards the Dee, was having its floor joists built into it during the following season, the war summer of 1282; that the Great Tower was still unfinished and itself required a temporary roof during the next winter, that of 1282–3; and that plumbers were operating on a fair scale, which could mean the permanent roofing of at any rate one tower, in the summer of 1284. Timber to construct the king's chamber in the castle was paid for by the keeper of the Wardrobe in July 1283.[1]

The termination of the masons' wages account at Martinmas 1284 probably reflects the termination of constructional work, and during 1285 there was no expenditure on the castle at all. This year may, however, have accounted for a major share of the £171 7s. 5d. assigned between May 1284 and November 1286 in payment to diggers working on the town defences (*fossariorum operancium circa clausturam ville*). A sum of £22 9s. 6½d. had been similarly spent between March 1281 and September 1283,[2] but the later work is noted as being *post guerram* and may have been at least partly in the nature of war damage repairs.[3] A final year's work on the castle in 1286 saw the smiths busy forging and fitting hinges and locks for doors and windows, the carpenters making the bridge between the castle and the town and preparing the framing for the roof of the Great Tower,[4] and finally, between 8 September and 30 November, the plumbers rounding off the whole achievement by giving the Great Tower its covering of lead. Master Henry of Oxford now being engaged at Conway, the carpenters were under the direction of Philip the carpenter, here named as Philip Sente (2s. 6d. per week),[5] who had with him Robert Ireland (2s. 3d.), Robert of Barrow and Roger of Bakewell (2s. 2d. each). For the sum of 1s. Richard of Lancaster made 400 laths for the roof of the Great Tower. At All Saints' tide 1284 and again at Martinmas 1285 it had been necessary to repair the thatch of its temporary covering. Now, on 9 August 1286, 8d. was paid to 8 men for a day's work striking the temporary roof and pulling the thatch away from the woodwork (*circa cooperturam magne Turris frangendam et literam cooperture dicte Turris dividendam de meremio*); by mid-September the lead to replace the thatch was being cast and weighed and guarded day and night at a foundry in the woods.[6] Whether the roof thus constructed marked the completion of the Great Tower to its full intended height, or whether, as was afterwards the case with the Eagle Tower at Caernarvon, it only marked what it was by then clear would have to be a prolonged postponement of the building of a final storey or storeys, may never now be known. The additional works carried out in timber in 1301–3, which are referred to below, and the relative evenness with which the outward-facing stonework is broken off at

[1] E 101/351/9.
[2] Also, between these dates, authority was given on 14 November 1282 to William of Perton and James of St. George to grant burgage tenements in Flint free of rent for 10 years and at a rent of 6d. a year thereafter (*Cal. Close Rolls 1279–88*, p. 172). This may reflect a reorganisation following disturbances in the Welsh rising, authority for letting burgages having already been given in February 1278 (*Cal. Welsh Rolls*, p. 165).
[3] E 372/131, rot. 26.   [4] Details in C 47/3/52, no. 31.
[5] For Philip the carpenter, see Appendix III, p. 126.
[6] 'Et quibusdam minatoribus pro diverso plumbo ponderando per vices iuxta hotam plumbi in silvis, quod quidem plumbum prouisum fuit pro dicta magna turri cooperienda, pro stipendiis suis x.d. Et cuidam vigilatori custodienti plumbum predictum in siluis iuxta hottam per iiij dies et per iiij noctes, pro stipendio suo ix.d.' (C 47/3/52, no. 31).

the top of the tower's surviving first-floor level, might together suggest that little more than the height represented by the existing ruin was ever achieved as designed.[1] On the other hand the impression of Speed's drawing of 1610 is that of a building standing to a sufficient height to dominate the adjacent towers and curtains.[2] The likelihood that by 1284 at least one more stage of the Great Tower than now survives had been built in stone is, moreover, much increased when it is recalled that in 1652, only six years after the slighting ordered by the Parliament, an eye-witness described the castle as being 'now almost buried in its own ruins',[3] and that for many years afterwards those ruins supplied materials for the building of houses in the town and neighbourhood.[4]

The recorded cost of the Flint works, both of the castle and the town defences, from 23 August 1277 to 25 December 1286, is £6068 7s. 5¾d.[5] To this there have to be added sums of £722 13s. 5d. expended by the keeper of the Wardrobe on workmen's wages at Flint between 25 July and 23 August 1277; £55 paid by him to the justiciar of Chester for felling and carrying timber to Flint and making rafts (*pontes*); £26 13s. 4d. paid by him to Robert of Belvoir for hiring and bringing carpenters to Flint; £20 3s. 0d. for materials and necessaries supplied for the works by the justiciar of Chester during the same period; and £76 13s. 5d. noted earlier as having been expended by the chamberlain of Chester during the winter of 1277–8. The total may be given in round figures as £7000.

The town and castle of Flint were in 1301 conferred on Edward of Caernarvon as part of his earldom of Chester, and were thereafter administered by the justiciar

[1] Cf. A. J. Taylor, 'The Building of Flint: a Postscript' in *Flints. Hist. Soc. Pubns.* xvii, pp. 38–40, and D. J. C. King, 'The Donjon of Flint' in *Chester Arch. Soc. Jnl.*, xlv (1958), pp. 67–8.
[2] John Speed, *Theatre of the Empire of Great Britaine* (London, 1611), inset to map of Flintshire.
[3] John Taylor, 'A Short Relation of a Long Journey, etc.' (printed in C. Hindley, *Old Book Collector's Miscellany* iii, 1873).
[4] The unique plan of the Flint Great Tower gives rise to some reflections as to the purpose or purposes for which it was commissioned. The basement, with its open central space communicating through wide archways with a broad circular vaulted gallery, can only have been intended for storage, here at Flint most probably for the kind of stores which in time of war would be more usefully held in advance of Chester, in other words the arms and armour, ammunition and clothing, which in the Tower of London came within the sphere of the Great Wardrobe; the fact that Adam the Tailor, one of the 'buyers' of the Great Wardrobe at the Tower (Tout, *Chapters* iv, pp. 369–73), held a burgage in Flint (E 179/242/52) lends credence to such a suggestion. The first floor was planned as a self-contained apartment, with four small intercommunicating segment-shaped rooms and a chapel, all built round an open light well after the fashion of the rooms at Castel del Monte. The provision of ample accommodation for the king and queen at Chester and Rhuddlan seems to make it unlikely that this small isolated suite at Flint would have been intended for their use, even granted its duplication on a now lost upper storey. We are left with two possible alternative explanations, viz. (i) that it was planned as the residence of the first constable, Sir Gerard de St. Laurent (? 1277–November 1281, *Cal. Pat. Rolls 1272–81*, p. 464), or (ii) that it was designed to provide, in view of the constitutional dependence of Englefield and its successor Flintshire on Chester (for which see Tout, 'Flintshire: its History and its Records', *Flints. Hist. Soc.*, 1911, pp. 20–21), a 'judge's lodging' for the use of the justiciar of Chester when coming to hold the pleas of the Crown at Flint. Gerard of St. Laurent was with Edward I at Acre in 1271–2 (arrears of wages *de tempore quo stetit in servicio nostro in Acon*, Liberate Roll no. 49) and if he accompanied the king on the first part of the land journey back through Apulia could have known Castel del Monte at first hand; his high standing in the king's inner circle is indicated by his having preceded Edward to England from Gascony and by his having been ordered to stay at Dover apparently to make arrangements for the king's passage and arrival there on 2 August 1274 (Liberate Roll no. 51, m. 12). He is probably the 'Géraud de Laur' who was Edward's envoy to Gaston de Béarn in Sept. 1273 and was maltreated and imprisoned by Gaston's men, probably at Orthez (J.P. Trabut-Cussac, *Administration Anglaise en Gascogne* (Paris-Genève, 1972), 42). His origins are unknown, but the fact that Savoyard or Burgundian knights were chosen as the first constables of Rhuddlan and Conway (in each case Sir William de Cicon), Harlech (Sir John de Bonvillars) and Caernarvon (Sir Otto de Grandson) makes it not unlikely that St. Laurent was a Savoyard also, possibly from St. Laurent-Grandvaux in the Jura; he appears to have died before 8 May 1282 (*Cal. Anc. Corr. Wales*, p. 201).　　[5] E 372/124, rot. 29; 122, rot. 28; 131, rot. 26.

and chamberlain of Chester. The castle appears to have been maintained in good order throughout the fourteenth and fifteenth centuries, expenditure on its repair figuring regularly in the chamberlains' accounts except during the years 1422–37 when it was held in dower by Queen Katherine of Valois.[1]

In 1301–3, some fifteen years after the castle's completion, substantial works were undertaken at a cost of £146. The principal item was the addition of a large work of timber to the top of the great tower, together with what seems to have been a particularly handsome circular timber gallery (*unam magnam operacionem ligneam super magnam Turrim Castri de Flynt, unacum una carola lignea nobili et pulchra*).[2] Its construction apparently involved the tower's complete reroofing, for which 15½ cartloads and 3 fothers of lead were provided at a cost of £25. The cost of the whole addition was £76 6s. 9¾d. The contracts were assigned by Master Richard of Chester, whose design the *carola lignea nobilis et pulchra* is therefore likely to have been. Its execution was entrusted to the Chester carpenter Master Henry de Rihull.[3]

When the castle was surveyed for the Black Prince in 1337 the necessary repairs were estimated to cost only £25, the biggest item being the completion of the *alura* or parapet-walk on the peel round the outer bailey, which required an expenditure of £8.[4]

In 1382–3 the chamberlain of Chester paid £26 13s. 4d. to masons, carpenters and quarrymen working on the construction of a new hall 'within the castle of Flint in which pleas may be heard by the king's justices'.[5] This hall probably stood in the outer bailey, and its repair figures from time to time in subsequent accounts.

In 1452 a hall and chamber were built in the castle at a cost of £51 1s. 8d.[6]

4. RHUDDLAN

Llywelyn ap Gruffydd's destruction of Henry III's new castle of Dyserth in 1263 had left the northernmost reach of the traditional frontier line of the Dyke without a military focus. To restore such a focus must have been a main objective of the war of 1277. It could be achieved either by rebuilding Dyserth or by a return to the much older Anglo-Norman centre of Rhuddlan.[7] Dyserth, essentially a castle of the hills, had been cut off once by the Welsh and might be cut off again. Rhuddlan, on the other hand, occupying lowland ground on tidal water, offered infinitely greater advantages, especially to a power whose strategy for the conquest of Gwynedd relied in no small measure on the use of maritime resources. For its successful exploit-

[1] *Rot. Parl.* iv, pp. 202–6.   [2] SC 6/771/1.
[3] For further details see *Flints. Hist. Soc. Pubns.* iii, pp. 15–16, 32–5, 45.
[4] SC 12/22/96. Repairs to the *jarellum* (palisade) of the outer bailey are recorded in 1328 (E 101/487/6).
[5] SC 6/1302/11.   [6] SC 6/779/1.
[7] For the earlier history of the castle see Lloyd, *History of Wales* ii (1911), pp. 500, 519–20, 640, and James Tait in *Flints. Hist. Soc. Pubns.* xi (1925). Founded by Robert of Rhuddlan in the eleventh century, it had been fortified by Henry II in 1157, captured by Owain Gwynedd in 1167, but refortified by John in 1211, only to be taken from him by Llywelyn in 1213. Henry III recovered it in 1241, and fortified the site while his new castle was building nearby at Dyserth, but like Dyserth, it fell to Llywelyn ap Gruffydd in 1263.

ation, however, it was necessary that the River Clwyd should be rendered navigable to sea-going shipping. This required the construction of a new 'cut', between two and three miles long, to take the place of the river's serpentine meanderings through the *morfa* to the sea. How early this project was planned is unknown, but the visit to Woodstock, in June 1277, of Master William, the master *fossator* whose name is soon afterwards regularly appearing in the earliest Flint and Rhuddlan accounts, may not have been unconnected with it.[1] Probably he was the William of Boston who, on 20 July, at Chester, was paid his expenses for going to the parts of Lindsey and Holland to enlist diggers, and, as we have already seen, 300 of them were brought across under mounted guard from the fens.[2] Some at least of their number are likely to have been included among the 968 *fossatores* who were receiving pay on the keeper of the Wardrobe's account at Rhuddlan in mid-September, and one may suppose that a proportion of this veritable army of diggers will have been employed on the work of the canal from the beginning. After 30 November, the date of the commencement of the first enrolled Rhuddlan works account, conjecture is replaced by certainty, and between that date and November 1280 no less a sum than £755 5s. 3d. is explicitly recorded as being spent on the wages of diggers engaged in constructing the *fossa maris* or *magnum fossatum . . . a mari usque castrum*.[3] With 3d. as the daily wage of a *fossator*, this represents the continuous employment of an average of 66 diggers six days a week throughout the three years on this work alone, though seasonal fluctuations will no doubt have involved peak figures that were substantially higher. That the undertaking was successful is implied in a reference in October 1282, within two years of its completion, to land lying between the old channel of the river and the new,[4] and it seems probable that the course of the Clwyd from Rhuddlan to the sea to-day is still broadly that to which it was diverted by Edward I.

This feat of civil engineering is here given priority, for its achievement was fundamental to Rhuddlan's resurgence as a castellated borough. Plans for the new castle and town, both sited a little downstream of their Norman predecessors,[5] were no doubt worked out and approved during the king's three-month sojourn at Rhuddlan in the autumn of 1277,[6] and a beginning may have been made on the site

[1] E 101/350/24: 'Willelmo Fossatori ad suas expensas de veniendo ad Regem quando erit apud Cestriam, de dono Regis, vj.s. viij.d.' (Woodstock, 23 June).

[2] From 9 August, when the 300 Lincolnshire diggers first appear on the payroll, wages are paid also to a Master William *fossator* (E 101/485/19); it seems reasonable to suppose that he was their master, and to identify him with the William *fossator* who in June was engaged to come to the king at Chester, the William of Boston who in July went from Chester to Lincolnshire to recruit such diggers, and the William *magister fossator* who at the end of September had his travelling expenses for going home again (E 101/3/19: *Willelmo Magistro fossatori eunti in patriam suam ad suas expensas de dono Regis*, xxx.s.).

[3] E 372/122, rot. 28d.   [4] *Cal. Welsh Rolls*, p. 241.

[5] For positions of the old and new towns, see plan in *Rhuddlan Castle, Official Handbook* (H.M.S.O., 1982).

[6] Edward was at Rhuddlan intermittently from 19 August and continuously from 27 September to 18 or 19 November, when he left for the south on a progress which included visits to the works at Flint, to Montgomery and to Builth (p. 295 above). For part if not all of his stay he was accommodated by the Rhuddlan Dominicans, who were paid for their hospitality and given a donation towards the glazing of their new church (E 101/350/23: *Fratribus Predicatoribus per elemosinarium Regis ad suam sustinacionem, pro elemosina sua, x.li.; . . . Fratribus Predicatoribus de Rodelano ad fenestras vitreas faciendas in ecclesia sua iuxta altare beate Virginis de dono Regis, L.s.* The king also subscribed 13s. 4d. to the building of an almshouse (*pro constructione unius domus ad ponend' intus infirmos et pauperes apud Rodelanum*), which the queen founded and endowed with 70 acres of land (P.R.O. Chester 30/2, m. 22). Later (October 1284) the queen contributed to the cost of materials bought *ad constructionem ecclesie sancti Johannis in villa Rodolani* (E 101/315/15).

works. Of the £252 shown by the Wardrobe account as having been spent on work-men's wages between the king's arrival from Deganwy on 14 September and the middle of November, about £165, or over 65 per cent, went to *fossatores*, £55 or 22 per cent to carpenters, and £11 or 4 per cent to masons. The only specified item of the work at this time was the building and plastering of a *camera* for the queen,[1] probably a timber-framed apartment or suite of apartments of temporary character like those erected for the royal households in the earliest stages of the Caernarvon works in 1283.[2]

The next year, 1278, witnessed a full and intensive building campaign, operations on the castle alone amounting to £2746 in the fifteen months from December 1277[3] and thereby exceeding by practically £1000 the combined current expenditure at Flint (£830), Aberystwyth (£679) and Builth (£262).[4] In addition 54 per cent of the Clwyd canal expenditure was also incurred in this period, bringing the total outlay between December 1277 and March 1279 to over £3160. There can thus be no ques-tion that the Rhuddlan works were regarded at this time as the principal single undertaking in Wales. Their relative significance becomes apparent when it is recalled that in approximately the same period works expenditure at the Tower of London amounted to only £2970.[5] They were directed, jointly with those of Flint, by Master James of St. George, who left the court in April to go to Wales 'to ordain the works of the castles there' and whose pay during the succeeding months remained at the 'away' rate of 2s. a day because of his absence 'to visit the castles of Flint and Rhuddlan'.[6] Local control, at least in the period between the court's departure from Rhuddlan in November 1277 and Master James's arrival in the spring, appears to have been in the hands of Master Bertram,[7] who on 1 March 1278 was paid for acquiring buildings presumably intended for use as site huts and a site office.[8] Though booked in February 1278, a bonus payment of 6d. 'by the king's gift' to car-penters working on Rhuddlan bridge, in order perhaps to enable it to bear the weight of building materials coming to the castle from the Vaynol direction, no doubt belongs to the period when the king was still present. Similarly the payment of 16s. to Richard, canon of St. Asaph, for stone bought of him for the castle works, though entered on the *rotulus necessariorum* among payments made between 13 and 18 January 1278,[9] was actually in respect of a transaction dated elsewhere to

---

[1] E 101/485/19.   [2] P. 80, below.   [3] E 372/122, rot. 26d.

[4] The comparative figures are in respect of accounting periods which correspond approximately only; for details see J. G. Edwards, 'Edward I's Castle-building in Wales', pp. 66–9.

[5] E 372/123, rot. 21. Both figures embrace one summer season, namely 1278, that for the Tower covering the 12½ months from April of that year. The main components are: wages of masons and carpenters £1428 (Rhuddlan), £1163 (Tower); wages of diggers, £965 (Rhuddlan—including the *fossa maris*), £608 (Tower).

[6] For further details of Master James's employment and movements at this time, see *E.H.R.* (1950), pp. 434–7.   [7] For Master Bertram see Appendix III, p. 126, below.

[8] B.L., Add. MS. 36762: 'Pro duabus domibus emptis apud Rothelan ad ponendum in castro Rothel' per manus Magistri Bertrami Ingeniatoris, xxvj.s.viij.d. Pro una alia domo ad idem castrum, xij.s.' Cf. references between 19 October and 11 November 1277 to the servant of Master Bertram *machinator* assisting the carpenters at Rhuddlan (E 101/485/19).

[9] *Ibid.* E. Neaverson, *Mediaeval Castles in North Wales, A Study of Sites, Water Supply and Building Stones* (Liverpool, 1947), p. 42, points out that the only visible source for the large squared blocks of distinctive purple sandstone, used as a facing for the lower courses of the towers and curtains of the inner ward of the castle, is an old quarry on the river Elwy, 2 miles S.S.W. of St. Asaph. The same stone was found in excavated buildings at the Prestatyn Roman station and is used in thirteenth-century work at St. Asaph Cathedral.

20 November 1277.[1] With Master James and Master Bertram we should probably also reckon among the Rhuddlan building masters a Master Peter, whose wages from the Wardrobe begin on 2 March and are booked, like theirs, until the termination of the account at the end of the regnal year.[2] In the Wardrobe account all three are named as *ingeniatores*, Master James alone being also referred to as *le Mazun*. By far the largest item of the enrolled expenditure in the 1278 season is in respect of masons' wages, which amounted to £1267; diggers' wages absorbed a further £965, nearly half of this being for work on the canal; carriage and transport costs accounted for £710, the purchase of materials and necessaries for only £30.[3]

The next enrolled account,[4] rendered by William of Perton by view and testimony of Master James of St. George, runs from 5 March 1279 to 3 November 1280 and records expenditure amounting to £5611 in the course of a further two building seasons. On the castle, the largest item, at £2083, is again the wages of masons; diggers' wages are £204 and carpenters' £124; transport charges amount to £1531 and purchase of materials, tools, etc., to £182. There is also a separate entry for the works of the town, with carpenters' wages at £487, diggers' at £418, and cartage costs at £120. In addition, between June 1279 and September 1280, £341 was paid in wages to diggers working in the *fossa maris*. While Bonel's account for 1277–9 makes no differentiation on the receipt side to show which moneys were assigned to Rhuddlan and which to Flint, Perton's for 1279–80 gives the figures separately. They show that on the Rhuddlan account he received in all £7133. £3206, or nearly half, came from the Wardrobe, £1842 from the revenues of the vacant dioceses of York and Winchester, and £1000 from the treasury at the Tower of London. Welsh sources were limited to the £666 13s. 4d. provided by one of the annual renders of 1000 marks owed by Prince Llywelyn for the island of Anglesey under the terms of the treaty of 1277, and £375 derived from a wide variety of local receipts, including 18s. from the sale of buildings at the old castle.[5] Thus less than 15 per cent of the building costs was found from Welsh or local sources, the whole of the remainder being provided out of the ordinary revenues of the Crown.[6]

By the autumn of 1280 Rhuddlan Castle was substantially a finished structure and preparations were being made, as we have seen above, to transfer the weight of the building effort to Flint. In the following season (the period of account is from 3 November 1280 to 15 March 1282) specifically castle expenditure dropped sharply to £157,[7] compared with an average of over £2450 in each of the preceding three

---

[1] E 101/3/15. Earlier still, on 11 November, the prior of Rhuddlan was paid £3 6s. od. *pro petra et calce emptis a Fratribus Predicatoribus de Rodolano ad constructionem castri de Rodolano (ibid.).*

[2] C 47/4/1, ff. 14, 19ᵛ, 29ᵛ, 34, 42ᵛ. It was probably this same Master Peter *Ingeniator* who in January 1277 had been given his expenses at Dover, presumably on arrival from across the Channel, to travel on to join the king (subsequent allowance to constable of Dover Castle of 13s. 4d. *quos per preceptum nostrum soluit Magistro Petro ingeniatori nostro ad expensas suas in veniendo ad nos apud Wigorn' in hieme proxima preterita ad mandatum nostrum*—Liberate Roll 53), and who on reaching the court at Oddington (Glos.) on 15 January was given money to purchase a saddle. He is probably to be identified with Peter Morel, paid for shipping seven boatloads of stone from Boulogne for the Tower of London works in 1278 (E 101/467/7 (b)), who as Master Peter Morel is named at Flint (1281), Hope (1282) and Harlech (1286).

[3] E 372/122, rot. 28*d*.   [4] E 372/124, rot. 29.   [5] 'de duabus domibus venditis apud la Mote.'

[6] Bonel's receipts for the combined Flint and Rhuddlan works show a similar division, with approximately 83 per cent from national and 17 per cent from local revenues. (E 372/122, rot. 28*d*.).

[7] E 372/131, rot. 26.

years, a preponderance of carpenters' over masons' wages (£50 and £38 respectively) suggesting that attention was now being directed mainly to internal buildings, roofs and fitting out. On the works of the town, however, a good deal must have remained to be done. New burgages were being granted as early as February 1278,[1] and in March 1279 we hear of the 'king's men' erecting burgages near the castle.[2] In the following July the bailiffs and tenants were notified that 'the king is sending to his town of Rhuddlan Master William of Louth, his clerk, to view the void sites (*placeas*) and other sites in that town, and to assess and rent burgages in the same plots and to demise the burgages at the king's will, and to [*blank in original*] the king's ditches about the town and the king's port there as shall seem expedient.' William of Perton and Master James of St. George, 'keepers of the king's works at Rhuddlan', were instructed to assist him.[3] A month later the 'men of Rhuddlan' were granted the fee-farm of the town at £80 a year for seven years.[4] In March 1280 the justiciar of Chester was associated with Louth in a new commission to assign lands and places in Rhuddlan to all desiring to receive and hold the same from the king; they omitted to carry out their task, and in May 1280 Perton and St. George were ordered to execute it in their stead.[5] By the time the 1279–80 accounting period closed in the following November no less than £1025 had been spent on the works of the town,[6] and on it being reported to the king that the burgesses 'are now building the town and are expending and will expend great costs about making the town, building and improving it, as they promised to him', commencement of payment of their annual fee-farm was deferred until 1286.[7] At about this time or a little later proposals were also being made, and papal approval sought, for transferring to the new borough the nearby cathedral of St. Asaph, the king offering an ample site and a contribution of 1000 marks towards the building of the church.[8] In the ensuing accounting period (November 1280 to March 1282) a further £251 was applied to the town works, £120 of it on wages of diggers *operantium circa claus(t)uram ville* and £61 on wages of carpenters similarly engaged.[9] The enclosure, as at Flint, was to be a palisade (*palicium*) and not a town wall of stone.

It is probable that when the Welsh rebels entered Rhuddlan on 22 March 1282 these defences were still unfinished. The documents tell a tale of looting and plunder, and, while there is no explicit reference to the destruction of either burgages or palisades, the church of St. Mary and the convent of the Friars Preachers received 50 marks and £17 10s. od. respectively as compensation for damages sustained in the war.[10] The castle was besieged, and some of the lead prepared at Northop and awaiting transfer for use on the king's works at Flint was seized by the rebels and sent to Rhuddlan for Llywelyn's siege engines there.[11] After about a month the siege was

---

[1] *Cal. Pat. Rolls 1272–81*, p. 259; *Cal. Welsh. Rolls*, p. 165. In November 1278 the burgesses were granted a new charter (*Cal. Charter Rolls* ii, p. 209).
[2] *Cal. Welsh Rolls*, p. 180.   [3] *Op. cit.* p. 178.   [4] *Op. cit.* p. 188.
[5] *Cal. Pat. Rolls, 1272–81*, pp. 366 and 370.   [6] E 372/124, rot. 29.   [7] *Cal. Welsh Rolls*, p. 188.
[8] For documentation, see A. J. Taylor, 'Rhuddlan Cathedral: A "might-have-been" of Flintshire History' *Flints. Hist. Soc. Pubns.* xv, pp. 43–51.
[9] E 372/131, rot. 26.   [10] *Littere Wallie*, ed. J. G. Edwards, pp. 63, 70.
[11] Flint Pleas, 1283–1285', ed. J. G. Edwards, *Flints. Hist. Soc. Pubns.* viii, p. 3; also *op. cit.* xiii, pp. 51–2. The Chester annals, usually a reliable source, say David laid siege to Rhuddlan castle on the first day of the rebellion, i.e. 22 March (*Annales Cestrienses*, Lancs. and Cheshire Rec. Soc. xiv (1887), p. 108).

raised by forces from Chester led by the king's cousin Amadeus of Savoy.[1] That the castle actually fell to the Welsh has been denied,[2] but the extent of the reparations carried out over the next two years would appear to contradict this. Money was being applied to them, as also to the repair of Flint, as early as July 1282.[3] Even before this, at the end of June, arrangements were being made to accelerate the haulage of timber from Delamere Forest to Rhuddlan 'to enclose the town and make dwellings there',[4] though so far as the *claustura* is concerned this seems to point to the carrying out of work still wanting at the time of the Welsh attack rather than the remaking of defences the insurgents had destroyed. In July a Chester wardrobe clerk, Stephen of Howden, was sent to Lancashire to supervise the cartage of the timber earmarked 'for the palisade at Rhuddlan',[5] and on its arrival by water on 6 and 7 August 20 carts were employed to move it up into the town from the riverside.[6] Thereafter, from 6 September until Christmas Eve, a watchman was paid $2\frac{1}{2}$d. a day for guarding it.[7] Early in December another clerk, Godfrey le Meryloun, went to Chester to see to the carting of further wood from Delamere and the shipment of a further consignment of palisading.[8] On the 26th, boats were sent to load it and bring it to Rhuddlan.[9] It was not, however, destined to be used there. On 20 June 1283, in a writ which is itself the earliest known reference to the beginning of the new works at Caernarvon, the king issued orders from Rhuddlan (whither he had come with the queen from Conway to spend his birthday)[10] that all the material prepared for the town's enclosure should be sent forward to where it was now much more urgently needed,[11] and on 5 July payment was duly made for nine shiploads of timber sent from Rhuddlan to Caernarvon 'for the construction of the castle and town there'.[12] Its surrender to the needs of the future capital was symptomatic of an early decline in Rhuddlan's foreshadowed pre-eminence, inevitable perhaps as new and greater fortifications began to rise beyond the Conway. In the event, Rhuddlan's promised cathedral was never built,[13] the shire-town status at one time proposed for her was conferred on Flint,[14] and the endowment of the almshouse (*domus infirmorum*) founded by Queen Eleanor was before long being appropriated to other uses, for want of inmates.[15] Even the rebuilding of the town church seems to have hung fire,

[1] A relief expedition is known to have left Chester on or about 21 April and to have returned about four days later (C 47/35/18, no. 20). Amadeus's command of it appears from a letter of 9 May in which he testified to one John Wnall having served with him at the raising of the siege (. . . *fu ozd nos a lever le sieche de Rodelan*, SC 1/24/94). For Amadeus's part in the Welsh wars see A. J. Taylor, 'A Letter from Lewis of Savoy to Edward I', *E.H.R.* lxviii (1953), pp. 56 ff.
[2] J. E. Morris, *The Welsh Wars of Edward the First*, pp. 153 and 162; but Edward's letter to Queen Margaret, *Cal. Anc. Corr. Wales*, p. 56, explicitly states that one of the royal castles was already occupied by 8 April. For damage at Flint Castle, cf. the king's letter of 25 March to Roger Mortimer in *Cal. Welsh Rolls*, p. 212.
[3] *Cal. Pat. Rolls 1281–92*, p. 30.   [4] *Cal. Welsh Rolls*, p. 228.   [5] E 101/3/29.
[6] . . . *car' palicium de aqua Rothel' usque superius in villa* (ibid.).   [7] E 101/351/9.
[8] Ibid.; see also SC 1/29/116.   [9] *Cal. Anc. Corr. Wales*, p. 262.   [10] *Annales Cestrienses*, p. 112.
[11] Writ of privy seal to William of Perton to provide Thomas le Charrur, sergeant-at-arms, with whatever might be necessary *pro cariagio Pele et maeremii, que prouisa fuerunt ad claudendum villam Rothelane, ut ea cariare possit usque Carnaruan prout ei iniunximus*' (C 47/35/11, no. 122, printed in *Studies in Building History*, ed. E. M. Jope (1961), p. 125).   [12] E 101/351/9.
[13] An indication that the proposal to vacate St. Asaph was already abandoned by 1290 is afforded by a writ of that year ordering Reginald de Grey to make good the lack of a highway between St. Asaph and Rhuddlan, that it might be used for ever (*Cal. Close Rolls 1288–96*, p. 104).
[14] Cf. J. G. Edwards, 'The Building of Flint' (*Flints. Hist. Soc. Pubns.* xii, 1951–2), p. 5, note 1.
[15] '. . . quia nulli infirmi morabantur ibidem', P.R.O., Chester 30/2, m. 22.

for in 1303 the sheriff was ordered to bring the trustees to court to explain what had happened to the moneys given them for that purpose.[1]

When war broke out in March 1282 all the castle works hitherto considered had been in progress for rather more than four-and-a-half years. Those of Rhuddlan had entailed expenditure totalling little short of £9500, or nearly twice the combined cost of Builth and Aberystwyth and some £2500 more than the sum spent on Flint. From July 1282 until the advance to Conway in March 1283 the king made Rhuddlan his headquarters, and during this period and for about a year afterwards further works were carried out. They included the rebuilding, no doubt as a result of war damage, of the king's water-mills between Rhuddlan and Dyserth and of the town bridge over the Clwyd, and also the construction of bridges across three of the water-courses of Rhuddlan marsh. In addition, expenditure amounting to some £244 was incurred on works in the castle, details of some of which are specified in the accounts. First there was the 'queen's work', including the construction of a timber-framed *camera* roofed with lead brought from Flint, a building for the queen's goldsmith, and, encircling the head of the castle well (which had a boarded roof), a little fish-pond lined with four cartloads of clay brought from the marsh and set around with seats; the adjacent courtyard was laid with 6000 turves and the lawn fenced with the staves of discarded casks.[2] Some of the wood used in the queen's work was shipped specially from Gascony.[3] The principal item in the 'king's work' was the erection of a new hall, chamber, kitchen and wardrobe. As was customary the chamber was a painted one[4] and was no doubt ready for occupation when the king kept Christmas at Rhuddlan in 1283.[5] Phrases such as *pro operacione noue aule Regis a principio construc-tionis eiusdem aule* point to entirely new construction; on the other hand the almost simultaneous mention of materials bought *pro reparacione aule Regis* suggests a pre-existing building, and it may thus be supposed that the damage inflicted by the rebels had been such as to require repairs amounting to total replacement. The castle granary was similarly pulled down and rebuilt, an almonry erected, the stable repaired and provided with a new porch, timber galleries (*alure*) constructed near the king's chamber, and a postern put up outside one of the gates (*posterna facienda ante portam*). Most of the cost of these works was borne by the keeper of the Wardrobe, from whose accounts the foregoing particulars are taken.[6] Besides many items discharged in the names of individual accountants, £132 13s. 1½d. was allowed between February 1282 and May 1284 to the constable, Sir William de Cicon, 'for making and repairing the hall and other buildings in the castle', while a further £38 16s. 3d. was subsequently allowed to the justiciar of Chester, Reginald de Grey.[7] A final

---

[1] . . . ad ostendendum qualiter administrauerunt L. marcas et L. solidos eisdem liberatis pro ecclesia de Rothelan construenda et reparanda' (P.R.O., Chester 30/2, m. 22.); cf. also *Littere Wallie*, p. 70.

[2] '. . . quemdam parvum fossum prope puteum in castro Rothel' pro pisce vivo imponendo'; wages of Master William of Flint and 4 *fossatores* working *circa vivarium Regine iuxta puteum;* turves bought *ad ponendum circiter vivarium Regine in castro;* Willelmo le Plomer *facienti bancos circiter dictum vivarium.*

[3] '. . . pro portagio bord' de serruz que fuerunt misse Regine de Vasconia usque in castrum de Rothel' de aqua, ij.d.'

[4] '*Stephano pictori depingenti cameram Regis et pro coloribus emptis per ipsum et pro stipendiis suis xiiij s.*' For Stephen see Appendix III.   [5] *Cal. Pat. Rolls 1281–92*, pp. 108–9, 139.

[6] E 101/3/29 and 351/9, as also the account of Richard de Bures of miscellaneous expenses laid out in 1282–3 (wrongly dated to 1281–2) printed in *Archaeologia* xvi (1806), pp. 32 ff.   [7] E 372/143, rot. 33*d.*

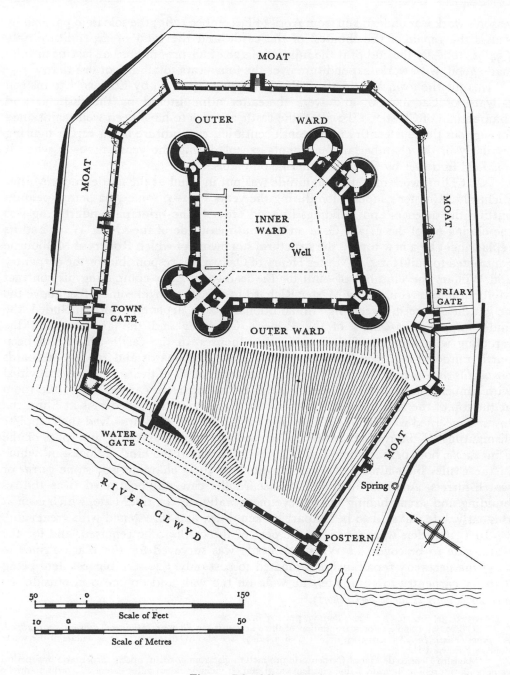

MOAT

OUTER WARD

MOAT

MOAT

INNER WARD

○ Well

FRIARY GATE

TOWN GATE

OUTER WARD

WATER GATE

MOAT

Spring ○

RIVER CLWYD

POSTERN

50 . 0 150
Scale of Feet

10 0 50
Scale of Metres

Fig. 4. Rhuddlan Castle.

season's work was undertaken from April to December 1285; the sole item particular-ised is the repair of the 'houses' of the castle and the total of expenditure only £54 9s. 10d.[1] By the end of it the injuries of 1282 had presumably at last been fully made good, with works expenditure over the four years totalling not less than £365.

In 1301 the town and castle of Rhuddlan were granted by Edward I to his son Edward of Caernarvon, and were thereafter administered by the justiciar and chamberlain of Chester. Like Flint, the castle appears to have been well maintained throughout the fourteenth and fifteenth centuries, expenditure on its repair figuring regularly in the chamberlains' accounts except during the years 1422–37 when it was held in dower by Queen Katherine of Valois.[2]

As at Flint, work of some magnitude was put in hand at the castle under Master Richard of Chester's supervision during the years 1301–4, some £82 being spent on putting the defences and buildings in good order.[3] The principal undertaking was the closing up of the Friary Gate on the south-east side of the Outer Ward and its replacement by a new turret, the structural stonework of which Robert of Melbourne contracted to build for £4: Master Henry of Oxford was responsible for the carpentry and William the Plumber of Flint for the leadwork. After completing his contract Melbourne was required by Master Richard to raise the turret some 7 feet above the height first agreed, receiving an additional 30s. Carpentry work included the underpropping (*apodiend*') of the Prince's Chamber and the granary, and the reroofing with shingles of these and other 'houses' in the castle which had been partly unroofed in a gale. The purchase of 400 7-foot boards and 100 4-foot boards *pro turellis eiusdem castri batilland*' suggests that some or all of the towers were provided with timber hourds. Major alterations, all in timber, were carried out to the room at the top of the north tower, on which an 'oriel' was also added.[4] As at Flint, the tower concerned was the one nearest the town, and the work involved the complete dismantling of the roof. Possibly the Rhuddlan 'oriel' was the counterpart of the Flint *carola*, both perhaps being added in order to afford the kind of 'look-out' which in the castles built after 1283 was provided by their characteristic stone *garrite* or watch-turrets. Another operation, whose results can still be traced, was the re-building and strengthening of the revetment wall near the river gate, which even at this early date was said to be 'in part broken down and threatened with great ruin'.

In 1326 orders were given for the peel of the castle to be repaired, and for the water-gate to be covered.[5] When the castle was surveyed for the Black Prince in 1337 the necessary repairs were estimated to cost only £22, the biggest item being £10 for carpentry to complete 'the walk on the wall and on the peel outside' (*le aler sur le muyr et sur le peel dehors*).[6]

[1] E 373/131, rot. 26.   [2] *Rot. Parl.* iv, pp. 203–6.
[3] SC 6/771/1, 2 and 4. For a translation of these accounts see *Flintshire Ministers' Accounts 1301–28*, ed. A. Jones (*Flints. Hist. Soc.* 1913), pp. 16–17, 36–7, 46–7. See also SC 6/1287/2(9), particulars of the works done in 2 Edward II.
[4] 'Magistro Henrico de Oxon' Carpentario pro factura gistarum et tocius operis carpentarie in superiori camera illius turelli in interiori ballio eiusdem castri que est vicinior eidem ville; eidem . . . pro uno oriello faciendo super predictum turellum' (SC 6/1287/2(9)). To distinguish it from the new outer tower the north tower is also referred to as the tower 'in le Dongoun': cf. the similar usage at Deganwy, Montgomery and Builth.
[5] *Cal. Close Rolls 1323–7*, p. 450.   [6] SC 12/22/96.

Though the maintenance of Rhuddlan Bridge was legally the townspeople's responsibility, their resources were insufficient to keep it in repair, and in 1358 and again in 1372–3 it was repaired at the prince's expense.[1] In 1331–2 it had been rebuilt by the king,[2] and it was again extensively repaired, if not wholly rebuilt, in 1395–7 at a cost to the Crown of £100.[3] The present bridge is dated 1595.

5. RUTHIN

In 1247 Dyffryn Clwyd, with its centre at Ruthin, passed with the three other cantreds of Perfeddwlad into English rule under the terms of the Treaty of Woodstock.[4] Included in the endowment of the lord Edward in 1254, this whole 'middle territory' had then been declared inseparable from the Crown of England.[5] It was, however, overrun by Llywelyn ap Gruffydd in 1256 and subsequently assigned to him by the Treaty of Montgomery (1267).[6] Meanwhile, in July 1263, Prince Edward had granted the cantreds of Dyffryn Clwyd and Rhufoniog (the latter centred on Denbigh) to Dafydd, Llywelyn's brother and antagonist, 'to hold until he shall have obtained all his inheritance as well beyond the Conway as elsewhere in North Wales'.[7] In the summer of 1277 the Four Cantreds were recovered by English arms, and as the tide of war flowed against Llywelyn concrete proposals were promulgated by the king on 23 August for restoring to Dafydd his patrimony in Gwynedd.[8] Had they materialised, Dafydd would no doubt have been required to surrender in return his claim to hold Dyffryn Clwyd and Rhufoniog under the grant of 1263, thus leaving the lordships either to be retained by the Crown or granted to an English feudatory.

That the former alternative was contemplated is suggested by the beginning, contemporaneously with the works at Flint and Rhuddlan, of a new castle at Ruthin. For reasons which will be apparent its documentation is slender. But its undoubted inception as one of the royal works is attested by the payment in July or August 1277 of £20 to the king's clerk William of Blyborough *eunti apud Ruffyn super constructione castri de Ruffin.*[9] That these operations were, at least initially, integrated with those of the other new castles, is indicated by a note that 120 diggers who arrived at Rhuddlan on 7 November had just come from Ruthin (*qui tunc venerunt de Ruffyn*), in the same way as other groups were noted as having come from Flint.[10] The disappearance by 16 August, from the keeper of the Wardrobe's day-to-day account of payments to workmen, of all but 50 of the 200 Lincolnshire masons who had arrived at Chester with their master, Thomas of Grantham, on 17 July,[11] may be explicable at least in part in terms of the demands of the works at Ruthin, as may be the king's gift on 10 August of a half-mark's expenses to presumably this same Master Thomas on his

[1] *Black Prince's Register* iii, pp. 162, 262–3; SC 6/771/22; SC 6/772/8.   [2] SC 6/771/13.
[3] SC 6/774/4–6.   [4] Lloyd, *History of Wales* ii, p. 708.
[5] Sir Maurice Powicke, *Henry III and the Lord Edward* ii, p. 649.   [6] Lloyd, *op. cit.* pp. 717 and 740.
[7] *Inspeximus* in *Cal. Pat. Rolls 1272–81*, pp. 231–2, and *Cal. Welsh Rolls*, p. 160.
[8] *Littere Wallie*, p. 103.   [9] E 101/3/16; cf. E 372/123, rot. 23.   [10] E 101/485/19.
[11] Above, p. 17.

leaving Flint for an unspecified destination.[1] If so, it may be no coincidence that eighteen years later the earliest surviving Ruthin court rolls include amongst the burgesses the name of a Master Thomas the Mason.[2]

In the event, the Treaty of Conway (November 1277) postponed Dafydd's recovery of his inheritance in Snowdonia for the period of Llywelyn's lifetime, the king undertaking to recompense him with suitable lands elsewhere which would revert to the Crown on the death of either brother.[3] The recompense had in fact already been provided by the confirmation, on 10 October, of Dafydd's former grant of Dyffryn Clwyd and Rhufoniog.[4] The effect of this arrangement on the castle works is unknown. But if, as seems likely, they were continued, they would henceforward be the concern of the lordship and of David as its tenant-in-chief and no reference to them during the ensuing five years has survived.

Dafydd's rebellion in March 1282, however, created a new situation, and by the end of August Ruthin had been regained for the king by English forces under the justiciar of Chester, Reginald de Grey. Edward himself was at Ruthin from 31 August to 8 September, addressing an urgent demand to the Chester Wardrobe on 2 September for £500 to be sent by return 'to expedite certain special business of the king in those parts'.[5] There are two pieces of evidence which suggest that the special business in question may have included a resumption of work on the castle, an operation with which both the personal presence of the king and the size of the sum called for would be fully consistent. One is a reference connecting Master James of St. George with Ruthin at about this time;[6] the other is a letter of 21 October 1282 from Grey to Robert Burnell, in which Grey tells the Chancellor that on that day the king had come over from Denbigh to Ruthin to inspect the work there and see what Grey was doing.[7] The wording of the original letter implies that what was being done was the king's work, executed by Grey as the king's agent.[8] Two days later the king's charter was issued from Denbigh, granting Grey 'the castle of Ruthin and the cantred of Defferencloyt . . . to hold as freely and wholly as other neighbouring cantreds are held'.[9] Thereafter further works will have been a charge on the lordship and the subject of local, not central, record. Reference has already been made to the presence at Ruthin in 1295 of a Master Thomas the Mason and to his possible identity with the Master Thomas of Grantham who brought masons from

---

[1] 'Thome cementario recedenti, ad suas expensas de dono Regis, vj.s.viij.d.' (E 101/3/19).

[2] 'The Court Rolls of the Lordship of Ruthin or Dyffryn-Clwyd', ed. R. A. Roberts (*Cymmrodorion Record Series*, No. 2, London, 1893), pp. 21–2.

[3] *Littere Wallie*, p. 120.

[4] *Cal. Pat. Rolls 1272–81*, pp. 231–2.

[5] *Cal. Anc. Corr. Wales*, p. 202; SC 1/45/6: '. . . ad quedam negocia nostra specialia inde expedienda in partibus ubi ad presens commoratur'.

[6] 23–26 October: 'Et Magistro Jacobo Machinatori pro Clays' empt' apud Ruffyn, v.d.' (E 101/3/29 para. 14). These 'clays' (wicker screens used in the scaffolding of building works) were being obtained from a number of sources for the works then being begun at Denbigh.

[7] *Cal. Anc. Corr. Wales*, p. 121.

[8] SC 1/23/118: '. . . vint notre seignur le Rey de Dinbeygh au Ruthin a sun ouereygne voir e ce ke nus y feymes sue mercy.'

[9] *Cal. Welsh Rolls*, p. 243. The specific reference to the castle, as to something already in being, is noteworthy as confirming Ruthin as a foundation of 1277–82; the absence of any corresponding mention of Denbigh Castle in de Lacy's charter of 16 October 1282 (*op. cit.* p. 241) reflects the fact that the Denbigh works were then only just being begun. See further below, p. 41.

Lincolnshire to Chester and Flint in 1277; it may be noted that John of Helpston, who contracted to build the Water-tower at Chester in 1322[1] and who was working at Flint in 1324,[2] also appears as a burgess of Ruthin in 1296.[3]

6. HAWARDEN

According to the Waverley annalist the castle of Hawarden was completely destroyed by Llywelyn ap Gruffydd in September 1265.[4] In 1267 the lordship was restored to Robert de Mohaut under the Treaty of Montgomery, but only on condition that no castle should be built there for thirty years.[5] By March 1282, however, the castle had been re-established, for we read that at that time Dafydd's men 'went by night to the castle of Hawardyn . . . and burned the houses of the castle' while others did the same at the king's castle of Flint.[6] What had happened in the meanwhile?

In the settlement of 1277 custody of the land of Hawarden was granted to a Welsh 'friendly', Kenwrick Seys,[7] a grant unlikely to have been made had buildings on the scale of the present castle been erected by that date. Nor indeed is it conceivable that such a castle could already have existed so near to the scenes and activities of that summer, or, like Ruthin, have been commenced under royal aegis at that time, and have passed altogether unmentioned in the records of the period. Afterwards, between 1277 and 1280, the lordships of Mold and Hawarden reverted to the Crown. Their custody was then granted, in the continued minority of the heir, Roger de Mohaut, to Maurice de Craon, who in June of the latter year sold it back to the king for £300.[8] After a short interval it was granted, in January 1281, to Roger de Clifford.[9] Then, after a lapse of only fifteen months, we have the record, already quoted, of the castle of Hawarden taking its place with the castles of Flint and Rhuddlan, Aberystwyth, Carreg Cennen and Llandovery as a primary objective in the opening attack of the Welsh rebellion. In at least three of these cases the aim of that attack was a new royal castle under construction, and it is not improbable that works were in progress at the southern lordship castles also.[10] There is therefore a strong likelihood that similar circumstances underlay the attack on Hawarden, and that here too the Welsh purpose was as much to destroy a castle that was rising again as to capture Roger de Clifford. Roger, like Maurice de Craon before him, was of the king's closest circle, and a start on the rebuilding of the castle would be a natural sequel—if indeed it may not have been an orally agreed condition[11]

[1] J. H. Harvey, *Mediaeval Architects*, p. 125.   [2] *Flintshire Ministers' Accounts 1301–1328*, p. 83.
[3] *Ruthin Court Rolls*, p. 34. There may be a concealed reference to the works at Ruthin in a record of wages paid to Master William, the king's master plumber, and his two mates (*garciones*), who were noted as being on the Rhuddlan strength from 3 September 1283 to 21 January 1284 'except for 3 weeks when they were attached to (*steterunt cum*) the justiciar of Chester' (E 101/351/9, para. 47); such an attachment could well have been in connection with the roofing of Grey's buildings at Ruthin.
[4] Lloyd, *History of Wales* ii, p. 738.   [5] *Op. cit.* p. 740.   [6] *Cal. Welsh Rolls*, p. 212.
[7] *Cal. Pat. Rolls 1272–81*, p. 232.   [8] *Op. cit.* p. 380.   [9] *Op. cit.* p. 422.
[10] Cf. Morris, *Welsh Wars of Edward the First*, p. 125.
[11] For Roger de Clifford and Maurice de Craon, see Powicke, *Henry III and the Lord Edward* ii, pp. 698 and 722, n. 3.

—of the grant of the lordship to either of them. If so, Hawarden finds its proper place among the works begun as a result of the war of 1277.

If it was the beginning of new construction that impelled the Welsh attack, its achievement, now principally represented by the circular keep surmounting the earlier motte, is most likely to have post-dated their defeat. This building in particular shows affinities with the royal castles that are close enough to suggest at least the guiding hand of the master of the king's works, whose responsibilities were not limited to the more fully documented Crown buildings, but who was also certainly involved, as we have seen in the case of Ruthin and shall see again at Hope and Denbigh, in the works of castles begun in one sense or another as royal enterprises but destined to be held by tenants-in-chief. In plan the keep's main floor, with its octagonal apartment, mural chambers, and wall-passage on the sides towards the field, is allied in conception to Caernarvon, designed and begun in 1283. And though it is true that at Caernarvon the quarter-round corbelling of the Hawarden wall-passage is in the main a characteristic of the later (i.e. post-1304) work, nevertheless the wave moulding of the Hawarden chapel doorway, seen also on a surviving jamb at the south end of the hall block, is found in some of the earliest Caernarvon work of all.[1] Hawarden's octagonal upper interior carried on a circular basement interior is an arrangement paralleled in the Great Tower at Flint, which was under construction at the time of the 1282 rising, and is likewise found before 1282 at Rhuddlan as well as after 1282 at Harlech and Beaumaris. Thus, though Clark was inclined to attribute it to the time of the last Robert de Mohaut (i.e. after 1296), the building's architecture in no way precludes its having been built during Roger de Clifford's tenure of the lordship in the 1280s.[2] Such a date, besides being likely on general grounds, would accord with Roger's standing and dignity. And if we are right in seeing indications which link the design with others that are reasonably associated with James of St. George, it is perhaps worth noting that Roger de Clifford's own second marriage had taken place at St. Georges-d'Espéranche in the course of his sojourn with the king there in June 1273.[3]

Castles of the War of 1282–3

1. HOPE

English reaction to the Welsh outbreak of March 1282 was immediate and far-reaching. Within a month writs were on their way to every part of England, and to

---

[1] Hist. Mon. Comm., *Caernarvonshire* ii, fig. 103 and pp. 127–8.
[2] G. T. Clark, *Mediaeval Military Architecture* ii, p. 99. In August 1282 the king restored possession of Mold and Hawarden to the heir Roger de Mohaut, while still under age: but it was on the condition that he should answer for the issues to Roger de Clifford (*Cal. Close Rolls 1279–88*, p. 165).
[3] E 36/274 ('Liber A'), f. 193*b*.

Ireland, Ponthieu and Gascony, calling for the provision and early concentration at Chester of supplies and services of every kind on a scale clearly intended to ensure massive and final retaliation.[1] Amongst them were orders to the sheriffs of twenty-eight shires from the Channel coast to Northumberland to muster local levies of diggers and carpenters, needed by the king 'for his works in Wales', to a total strength of 1010 and 345 men respectively, and to have them at Chester by 31 May.[2] The spearhead of the English advance was directed against the castle of Hope, the centre of the lordship of that name which the king had granted to Dafydd ap Gruffydd in 1277[3] and from which the recent raid on Hawarden had in all probability been mounted. When Reginald de Grey's forces arrived on 16 June they found the castle slighted (*prostratum*) by Dafydd,[4] but in less than a week the full company of 340 carpenters, reorganised into seventeen groups of twenty men each, commenced the work of repair.[5] Initially this was directed by Master Richard of Chester, with Masters Henry of Oxford, William of Eleston, Henry Marshal and Laurence of Canterbury as chief carpenters.[6] By the beginning of July there were also over 600 diggers and 30 to 35 masons. Final responsibility for the works lay with James of St. George. It was he who gave the order for Henry of Turvey to pull down the old keep,[7] and he who authorised the payment of Master Ralf of Nottingham's first four weeks' wages as resident master mason.[8] On two occasions masons who were employed for short periods only, possibly on work of a special nature, are similarly noted as being paid *per preceptum Magistri Jacobi* or *Magistro Jacobo denunciante*—four unnamed masons on two days in July and Roger of Corve for a week in October. The four may well have been the same four who make a previous appearance on the pay-roll during the five days immediately preceding the arrival of Ralf of Nottingham, namely John Pykard, Peter Morell, 'Bonetus' and 'Flauonarius'. Pykard, Morell and Flauner we have met already at Flint; Morell we shall meet again at Harlech and Flauner at Conway. Pykard and Morell were both paid at the high weekly rate of 3s. 6d., i.e. 6d. more than Ralf himself received as resident master. In the Hope account they are reckoned separately from the main body of masons who are there on long-term assignment, and it looks as if they may be men whom Master James looked upon as lieutenants whom he could depute to undertake or oversee special tasks.[9]

[1] *Cal. Welsh Rolls*, pp. 212–250, *passim*.
[2] *Op. cit.* pp. 247–8; related drafts in B.M. Cott. MS. Vitellius CX, f. 162b, and P.R.O. C 47/2/21, 18. For details of labour recruitment, assembly, pay, journeys to Chester, etc., see A. J. Taylor, 'Castle Building in Wales: the prelude to construction,' in *Studies in Building History*, ed. Jope (1961), pp. 110 ff.
[3] *Cal. Pat. Rolls 1272–81*, p. 227.   [4] *Annales Cestrienses*, p. 108.
[5] C 47/2/3: account of John of Lincoln, clerk, of receipts and payments at Hope Castle, viz. in wages of knights and squires, stipends of masons and carpenters, purchase of necessaries, wages of constables, foot soldiers and archers and stipends of diggers, Tuesday 16 June to Sunday 1 November 1282. Unless otherwise noted details given are based on this roll.
[6] For the names of the 17 *vintenarii*, or carpenters' group leaders, and also of 29 leading masons, see *Studies in Building History*, pp. 117–19.
[7] 4 July, 'Heyn (als. Henr') de Thoruy [*sc.* cementario] prosternenti turrim de Hope ad tascham, xij.d., Magistro Jacobo precipiente'; presumably this was the 'high' tower from which a workman fell a few days later, receiving compensation on the recommendation of Sir John de Mohaut ('cuidam operario qui cecidit de alta Turri de Hop' et fuit lesus, ex dono Regis xij.d., domino J. de Monte Alto precipiente').
[8] 3s. per week from 4 July, *per preceptum Magistri Jacobi*; in 1278 he had served under Walter of Hereford at Vale Royal (*Ledger-Book*, pp. 209–12).
[9] For Peter Morell, see above, p. 29, note 2.

The account gives details of many items próvided for the works, such as 'clays' for scaffolds, lime for making mortar and two sieves for mixing it, a pair of scales, locks for the entrance gate and hinges for the little gate. The Welsh having destroyed and blocked the well, water had at first to be carried up to the castle in a tank bought for the purpose. An early payment is for a rope 'to draw stones from the well of Hope Castle' and the work of clearance, entrusted *ad tascham* to Master Manasser,[1] went on until the middle of August. To mark its successful conclusion a servant was sent with two barrels of the newly recovered supply as an offering to the king and queen at Rhuddlan.[2] The internal buildings constructed were evidently mainly of timber, and included a chapel (apparently with a louver, for cords were bought *ad Loueras capelle*), a chamber for the pay clerks (*camera ubi compoti scribebantur et pacaciones fiebant*), another chamber, and a chamber over the gate.

The record covers a period of nineteen weeks from mid-June to the end of October 1282. 'Necessaries' amounted to £15 and wages averaged £15 a week, making a total outlay of almost exactly £300. On 24 February 1283 the king granted the castle and land of Hope to his consort Queen Eleanor,[3] by whom the works may have been continued. On the 27th August following, however, the castle was damaged if not destroyed by an accidental fire; the king and queen were at Hope at the time and were in danger.[4] The castle was subsequently conferred on Edward of Caernarvon as Prince of Wales and Earl of Chester,[5] but there is no evidence that he repaired it, and after his accession he granted it to John of Cromwell for life on the understanding that Cromwell would restore it at his own expense.[6] Whether Cromwell did so may be doubted, for when he died in or about 1335 the castle passed to Edward the Black Prince, whose surveyors reported that they found there 'only a place called the castle of Hope, whose walls and towers are largely thrown down and there is no housing there.'[7] In 1351 the men of Hope tried to persuade the prince to build a tower in the castle to serve as a prison for local malefactors, but were told that 'as to building a tower or anything else in the castle the prince will consult his own wishes'.[8] After the prince's death Hope was granted by Richard II to the Holand Earls of Huntingdon, and later passed into the possession of the Stanleys. In Henry VIII's reign Leland saw 'greate walles' of the castle still standing on the hill above Hopedale,[9] and considerable portions of these still remain. But the ruins have not been cleared or explored in modern times, and it is uncertain how far the standing remains are the work of 1282 or how far they may embody parts of the earlier castle.[10]

---

[1] For Manasser, see Appendix III, p. 127 below.

[2] '. . . cuidam garcioni deferentï duos barillos impletos aque de fonte Castri de Hop domino Regi et Regine apud Roth', pro expensis suis eundo et redeundo, iij.d'.

[3] *Cal. Welsh Rolls*, p. 265. A payment at the end of Octobeï 1282 to 10 men *cooperiuntibus muros castri* suggests that the works had been covered in for the winter, implying the intention of continuing them in the next season.   [4] *Annales Cestrienses*, p. 112.   [5] Hilda Johnstone, *Edward of Carnarvon* (1946), pp. 55–57.

[6] *Cal. Pat. Rolls 1307–13*, p. 79.   [7] SC 12/22/96; *Cal. Charter Rolls 1327–41*, p. 300.

[8] *The Black Prince's Register* iii, pp. 30–1.   [9] *Leland's Itinerary in Wales*, ed. Toulmin Smith (1906), p. 73.

[10] Since the above account was written, evidence has come to light that on 12 November 1278 Edward I made a contribution of 100 marks to Dafydd ap Gruffydd towards the construction of his castle of Hope (*David filio Griffini, ad construendum castrum suum de Kaierguill, de dono Regis, Lxvj.li.xiij.s.iiij.d*). This entry is from a 'Dona' Roll of 6 Edw. I now in the possession of the Wellcome Historical Medical Library (Wellcome MS. No. 253). See A J Taylor, "The earliest reference to works at Hope Castle", *Journal of the Flintshire Historical Society*, 22 (1965–6), pp. 76–7.

2. DENBIGH

Prior to 1282 the tenurial history of the cantred of Rhufoniog, with Denbigh as its ancient centre, had followed the same pattern as Dyffryn-Clwyd.[1] Letters dated at Denbigh by Llywelyn in 1269 imply a residence, though not necessarily a castle, of the princes.[2] That it occupied the site of the present castle is, however, likely and would accord with both traditional and topographical probabilities.[3] The castle as we now know it was undoubtedly begun within a few days of the grant of the lordship, on 16 October 1282, to Henry de Lacy, Earl of Lincoln,[4] and throughout the last ten days of the month, while the king and de Lacy were both present at Denbigh in person, the royal resources were used to help with the initial operations. The details are recorded on the account of the keeper of the Wardrobe[5] and indicate a contribution to the value of £22. Of this amount, £19 18s. od. was expended on the purchase of more than 1200 'clays' 'for the construction of the castle' and most of the remainder on bringing 184 cartloads of timber from nearby woods to the site of the castle. A cartload of tools was also brought from Rhuddlan. All but two of the payments made are debited in the name of Henry of Greenford, one of the ushers of the king's chamber, for whose activity as a works officer of the household there is other evidence.[6] The exceptions are similarly in the names of officers of the royal works, one being a payment to Master James of St. George for procuring an unspecified quantity of 'clays' at Ruthin[7] and the other a payment to Master Henry of Oxford for obtaining charcoal for the smiths from Rhuddlan.

That is all that surviving records have to tell us directly about the building of Denbigh and it does not amount to very much. How far, for example, the labour employed, either during October 1282 or subsequently, may have been drawn from the general body recruited from the shires and first deployed at Hope, is altogether unknown. But it is likely, especially in the earliest stages, and the falling off in numbers which occurs at Hope just when the Denbigh works are beginning could be a pointer to it. Indirectly, however, the Denbigh entries are of great value. They serve to underline how close a connection there might be between the king's works, properly so called, and similar works carried out by feudatories from the resources of their

---

[1] Above, p. 35.   [2] *Cal. Anc. Corr. Wales*, p. 28.

[3] Cf. Lloyd, *History of Wales* i, p. 240. The proximity of the site to the hill-forts of the Clwydian range and its panoramic command of the surrounding country both point to its fortification in prehistoric times.

[4] *Cal. Welsh Rolls*, p. 241; cf. above, p. 36, note 9.   [5] E 101/3/29.

[6] When the court was in France and Gascony in 1286–7 it was Henry of Greenford who went ahead to make the advance arrangements for the king's accommodation in Paris (*preeuntis Paris ad providenciam faciendam ibidem contra adventum Regis*, C 47/4/3, m. 14ᵛ); bought partitions, doors, steps and stools and constructed private chambers for the king and queen in their apartments in the abbey of St. Germain-des-Prés (*ibid.*); paid carpenters and masons for building a *camera* for the king and queen in the bishop's palace at Agen (*ibid.* m. 23ᵛ); and constructed chambers for them in the archbishop's palace at Bordeaux (E 36/201, m. 4ᵛ– m. 8ᵛ). From 14 March 1283 he was the first English constable of Criccieth Castle (below, p. 73, note 8).

[7] Cf. above, p. 36, note 6. The 'clays' obtained through Master James cost only 5d. As other purchases were in the order of 101 for 23s. 3½d., 350 for 60s. 10d. and 655 for 90s. od., the average price of 'clays' worked out at something between 1½d. and 3d. according to quantity. It rather looks as if the 'clays' bought at Ruthin may have been a few that were surplus to the works there and for which only a nominal charge was made.

lordship in the furtherance of royal policy. Such a creation Denbigh undoubtedly was. If the king's master of the works was present at its inception, then the leading part in the planning and setting out of this lordship castle, and of its associated array of town walls, may fairly be supposed to have been his.[1] The characteristic symmetry of the castle plan as a whole and the striking originality of its triple-towered gate-house, which Leland thought if complete 'might have counted among the most memorable peaces of workys yn England',[2] are alike in favour of such an attribution.

3. HOLT

Holt Castle was built as a new foundation between 1282, when the king granted the lands of Bromfield and Yal to John de Warenne, Earl of Surrey,[3] and 1311, the date of the earliest recorded reference to it.[4] To-day little is to be seen beyond the artificially shaped sandstone rock around and against which the castle was constructed, and of its building history nothing is known. Sixteenth- and seventeenth-century surveys are, however, available, together with a plan and perspective drawing made by John Norden in 1620 and another plan and drawing of still earlier date.[5] These reveal a design of quite remarkable individuality, a single-ward castle planned as a regular pentagon, with a range of buildings against each of the five curtains and flanking towers with battered plinths at the corners. Though differing in other respects, both drawings show four of the towers as round and surmounted by watch turrets; in Norden's version these closely recall the four turrets of Conway and Harlech.

The award of Bromfield and Yal to the Earl of Surrey on 7 October 1282, as of Rhufoniog to the Earl of Lincoln on the 16th and Dyffryn-Clwyd to Grey on the 23rd, was a recompense for service rendered in war.[6] De Lacy's grant was followed, as we have seen, by the commencement of the new castle of Denbigh; Grey's was associated with a resumption of work at Ruthin. De Warenne's grant included, it is true, the native Welsh castle of Dinas Brân in Yâl, but its hilltop site was remote and difficult of access and for several years its buildings had stood ruined and neglected.[7] For Warenne and the Welshries assigned to him the counterpart of the works inaugurated or renewed by his fellow lords at Denbigh and Ruthin was accordingly the establishment of a new English castle and borough at Holt on the

[1] That the development of Denbigh was not delayed is made probable by the record of the stocking of de Lacy's park there with deer from Delamere Forest in 1284 (*Cal. Close Rolls 1279–88*, p. 278) and the grant of the first borough charter—to 39 named burgesses described as dwelling within the walls—at a date not later than 1290 (printed by J. Williams, *Ancient and Modern Denbigh*, Denbigh, 1856, pp. 302–9).
[2] *Itinerary*, ed. L. Toulmin Smith vi, p. 98.   [3] *Cal. Welsh Rolls*, p. 240.
[4] *Cal. Pat. Rolls 1307–13*, p. 405; cf. also the reference to the castle and its ditches in 1315 in T. P. Ellis, 'The First Extent of Bromfield and Yale' (*Cymmrodorion Rec. Ser.* No. xi, 1924), pp. 38–9.
[5] B.L., Harl. MSS., 2073 and 3696. The plans and drawings are figured, and the surveys printed *in extenso*, by A. N. Palmer in *Arch. Cambr.*, 6th Ser. vii, pp. 311 ff. and 389 ff.
[6] Morris, *Welsh Wars of Edward I*, p. 178.
[7] The Welsh had set fire to Dinas Bran in 1277. Henry de Lacy had recommended that it should be repaired and made serviceable again (*Cal. Anc. Corr. Wales*, p. 83), but the indications are that it was not rebuilt.

Dee.[1] We should expect, in the light of what happened in the other lordships, that its foundation would have followed closely on the royal grant and would have had the king's full cognisance. Whether, in these circumstances, the services of the master of the king's works would have been made available, as it has been suggested they were in those cases, for laying out the castle site and 'ordaining' the works, can only be conjectured. All that can be said is that the precedents make it likely and that the likelihood is strengthened by the evidently accomplished character of the resulting design.[2] The castle was demolished between 1675 and 1683 to provide building stone for Sir Thomas Grosvenor's Eaton Hall.

4. CHIRK

There is no basis of fact for the assertion that Edward I intended to construct a royal castle at Chirk in 1274.[3] The building of the earlier part of the present structure must fall between June 1282, when the king granted Chirkland to Roger Mortimer the younger, and 1329, when some of the castle buildings had been sufficiently long established to require substantial repairs to their stone-tiled roofs.[4] The grant to Mortimer, like the others made later in the same year, created a new marcher lordship held of the king by knight service, and may, as at Denbigh, have been closely followed by the setting out of the castle which would from the first have been envisaged as its *caput*. On the whole, however, both the plan and scale of the work, and particularly its general resemblance to the inner ward at Beaumaris, suggest that it may not have been undertaken before the last decade of the century, possibly not even until after Mortimer's appointment as justiciar of all Wales in 1308. Its building may well have proceeded but slowly, and the eventual failure to complete the southern half of the enclosure, with the great gatehouse presumably intended on that side, as perhaps also the failure to carry the towers above the tops of the curtains, may point to a cessation of work at the time of Roger Mortimer's downfall in 1322.

Alone of the North Wales castles Chirk has been continuously inhabited throughout its history. It has consequently undergone alterations which have obscured original affinities and limited the field of comparison. Whatever the precise date of its beginning, however, its creation reflected royal policy, and its inception, whether before or after 1300, may no less have owed something to the officers of the royal works.

[1] The ancient ford of the Dee between Farndon and Holt was a key point on the approaches to the highland zone. A letter of November 1282 from Roger Lestrange to the king shows that by the control of this route Warenne was expected to be able to hinder supplies from reaching Llywelyn as part of a concerted policy of blockade. Lestrange's advice to the king 'to tell Earl Warenne to keep watch at Brumpfeude, for much supplies enter the land without anyone's knowledge' (*Cal. Anc. Corr. Wales*, p. 84) goes far to account for the choice of this particular spot for the establishment of the new castle. For the Norman castles of Bromfield, see E. S. Armitage, *Early Norman Castles*, p. 268 f.

[2] The apparent kinship of Holt to the major North Wales castles was noted by the Welsh Ancient Monuments Commissioners when they visited the site in 1911 (*Denbighshire Inventory*, p. 75).

[3] *Op. cit.* p. 32. The suggestion arose from the erroneous ascription of a Chirk works account, E 101/485/18, dated 'Anno E.iij⁰', to 3 Edward I instead of 3 Edward III, which internal evidence shows to be its correct date. For the twelfth-century castle, which occupied a different site, see Armitage, *op. cit.* p. 269.

[4] E 101/485/18.

5. DOLWYDDELAN

In the opening weeks of 1283 King Edward's army moved from the Clwyd to the upper Conway, with the small but strongly sited native castle of Dolwyddelan as the first objective of the advance.[1] Symbolically important as the birthplace of Llywelyn the Great, Dolwyddelan's position on the edge of the central mass of Snowdonia and near the watershed of valleys leading down to Conway on the one hand and Harlech and Criccieth on the other, marked it out as a key point in the developing strategy of the war as well as for the future control of north–south movement behind the main mountain zone. The castle fell to the English on 18 January and building works were begun the same day.[2]

The works accounts as such are lost and Dolwyddelan must be assumed to be one of the 'divers other places' whose costs are included in the sum of £9414 4s. 11d. expended by the keeper of the Wardrobe between 22 March 1282 and 20 November 1284 on workmen's wages at castles named and unnamed.[3] Louth's account of miscellaneous Wardrobe expenditure for part of the same period[4] does, however, preserve the record of a number of auxiliary payments which throw light on what was done. The first operation was the building of a new *camera*, here used in the sense of a complete lodging and no doubt referring to the added two-story apartment whose ruins occupy the north-west angle of the courtyard;[5] from 18 January to 4 May 1283 one man, and from 4 to 16 May two men, received pay to help the masons carry mortar and stone used in its construction. Early in February Master James of St. George was being supplied from Chester with a quantity of steel for use at the castle, possibly in connection with its armament, possibly for hardening building tools.[6] In May there is a payment for making 'clays', supplementing others shipped earlier from Rhuddlan and brought 'to Snowdon' (i.e. up river as far as Trefriw or Llanrwst) in the *Holy Cross* of Hythe (John Hampton, master). In July work was in hand on a new bridge and a water mill. A year later, in August and September 1284, £7 11s. 5½d. was paid for repairs to the carpentry and leadwork of 'divers chambers' in the castle, which probably means the rehabilitation of the older tower or keep after damage inflicted by the retreating Welsh at the time of the siege; for 10 weeks Nicholas de 'Cufflet' (apparently identical with the Nicholas de Clyfford employed about the same time on the wardrobe works at Conway) was

---

[1] For the military details, see Morris, *Welsh Wars*, pp. 190–1.
[2] 'Et memorandum quod dicto die Lune [*sc.* in festo sancte Prisce Virginis] intrauerunt primo gentes Regis in dicto castro', E 101/351/9, para. 38. Two days earlier the keeper of the Wardrobe ordered 11 masons to be sent to the king, no doubt to be ready to start work at the castle (*Archaeologia* xvi (1806), pp. 38–9). Directly it was occupied steps were taken to equip the garrison with camouflage clothing suited to winter warfare in Snowdonia, Robert the king's tailor supplying for this purpose some 80 yards of a white Irish material (*pro lxiiij ulnis albi panni et dimid' de Hibernia:* ? Irish linen), 57 pairs of white stockings (*calige*), 100 pairs of shoes (*sotule*) and 100 pairs of gloves (*cirothece*), with 10 yards of canvas wrapping for transit from Chester to Dolwyddelan (E 101/351/9, para. 25).
[3] E 372/136, rot. 33.
[4] E 101/351/9, on which unless otherwise stated the rest of this paragraph is based.
[5] For plan and description see Hist. Mon. Comm., *Caernarvonshire* i, pp. 80–2.
[6] *Cal. Anc. Corr. Wales*, p. 204 (where *calabis* should be 'steel', not 'canvas'), supplementing E 101/351/9.

paid 4d. a day while he was *ultra operationes de Doluidaleyn*. Works appear to have been still in hand during the period when Robert of Belvoir was chamberlain of North Wales, i.e. after January 1286.[1]

6. CONWAY

The capture of Dolwyddelan having secured the rear of the English advance, Conway was reached from the south in the second week of March 1283. So far as is known there were at this time only two significant groups of buildings on the site of the future town. One, the Cistercian abbey of St. Mary, was the premier royal foundation of the northern princes, the burial-place of Llywelyn the Great and others of his line. The other, standing close by, was the princes' residence, or 'Hall of Llywelyn' as it is called in documents of little later date. The setting must have been familiar to the English leaders, especially to those who like Otto de Grandson and Anthony Bek had been here for the peace negotiations with Llywelyn's delegates at the end of the war of 1277 and who even then may have noted its advantages.

These were indeed considerable. On the east side of the abbey the land sloped gently to the margin of the Conway river, with its sheltered anchorage on tidal water; to the south a steeper fall gave on to the Conway's tributary the Gyffin, its power already harnessed to the abbey mill. Between the two and occupying the angle of their confluence, the abbey ground rose to end in a high, narrow, jutting spine of rock, its farthest footings water-washed on east, north and south. Such a site would anywhere have lent itself to the founding of a castle and attendant town.[2] Here it fitted a developing pattern of coastal castles, as naturally the successor to Deganwy as Rhuddlan had been to Dyserth. Moreover, besides the material assets of an abundant building stone[3] and direct water-borne access for other supplies, the presence of the abbey and the hall of the princes offered immediate facilities to the occupying power recalling those afforded by the Blackfriars at Rhuddlan and foreshadowing the similar role of the Llanfaes Greyfriars at Beaumaris. The expense involved in having in this case to uproot the convent and provide for its re-establishment elsewhere was offset politically by the demonstration thereby afforded of the eclipse of the native dynasty and its institutions.[4]

---

[1] *Cal. Anc. Corr. Wales*, p. 118.

[2] The natural strength of the position, now much disguised by the bridges, the railway, and the levelling of the Gyffin estuary, is brought out by Buck's engravings (1742) of Conway from the north-east and south-east.

[3] On this see E. Neaverson, *Mediaeval Castles in North Wales: a Study of Sites, Water Supply and Building Stones* (Liverpool, 1947), pp. 43–6.

[4] This was neither Edward's first nor last essay in activities of this sort: cf. in 1254 the demolition of the church of La Réole (Gironde) *que sita est prope castrum nostrum in eadem villa, eidem castro nocens est, et nuper quamplurimum nocuit*, J.–P. Trabut-Cussac, 'Un Rôle de Lettres Patentes emanées du Prince Édouard pendant son premier séjour en Gascogne', in *Receuil de Travaux offert à M. Clovis Brunel* (Paris, 1955), p. 608; and the order issued in 1300 to the mayor and community of Newcastle upon Tyne to make provision for the prior and brethren of the Carmelites, 'whose church and convent will be destroyed by the new fortifications there' (Bain, *Cal. Docs. Scotland* ii, p. 293).

The precinct and buildings of the abbey were at once pressed into use.[1] A temporary wardrobe, where treasure could be securely stored, was set up there; timber was unloaded from the river and stacked there; money shipped from Ireland was placed there; a cartload of iron, steel and arrows from Chester was ferried across 'to the abbey' from Deganwy and then carried into the wardrobe; anchors and ships' cables were stored 'in the abbey'. All this was in March and April. In June twenty men were paid for four days' work clearing a site to put up the king's tents and pavilions 'beside the abbey', and £22 15s. 3d. was paid to carpenters constructing the king's granary in the abbey and beginning work on the king's new mill. Timber and 'clays' were early provided for building a palisade to enclose the site of the new town (*ad Brittach' circa claustruram ville de Conewey*). Very early priority was given to the construction in timber, by Master Henry of Oxford, of permanent wardrobe buildings and a hall and chambers for the king and queen, now described as *apud Conewey*, now as *in castro de Conewey*. Later documents show the wardrobe and the king's hall to have stood somewhere to the south or south-west of the abbey close to the future Mill Gate,[2] and it is indeed inconceivable that room could have been found for any of these urgent wardrobe and household constructions on the restricted castle site, with all that must have been going on there to prepare for the immense building about to be erected on it. The 'houses' for whose construction 'in the castle' materials were being provided only a few days after the occupation may, it is true, have been works huts put up on the actual site;[3] on the other hand it appears that in this earliest account *castrum* is not limited to the castle proper but is also used loosely to describe the whole fortification.[4] At first the king must have lodged at Llywelyn's hall or the abbey, a payment on 23 March 1283 to four masons for 'repairing the chimney in the king's chamber' clearly implying an already existing building; 12 ells of canvas were provided for hangings for the queen's chamber. When, towards the end of June, her own newly built *camera* was nearly ready, a lawn was made beside it with turf shipped from up the Conway and fenced with the staves of an empty tun, and on a July evening Roger le Fykeys, one of her squires, saw to its first watering (*pro aspersione aque super herbarium Regine apud Conewey per j noctem, iij.d.*). While the king's wardrobe was being constructed, temporary quarters adjoining it were provided for the lodging of the Wardrobe clerks.

The removal and rehousing of the abbey must have been in the king's thought from the beginning, and the presence of the abbot of Vale Royal at Conway as early as 6 April 1283 may have been connected with it.[5] By September consent to the move had been asked of the General Chapter at Citeaux and given subject to the monks not being disturbed until, in the opinion of inspectors appointed by the Chap-

---

[1] Unless otherwise stated the details which follow are based on the keeper of the Wardrobe's miscellaneous expenses account, E 101/351/9, where many additional details are given.

[2] A different view is, however, taken by Edwards, 'Edward I's Castle-building in Wales', *Procs. of the British Academy* xxxii (1946), p. 39.

[3] Payment on 28 March 1283 of 15s. 10d. to Nicholas Smallwood of Newcastle for 7200 assorted nails *ad constructionem domuum et fenestrarum in castro de Conewey*.

[4] Cf. also *Cal. Welsh Rolls*, p. 285 (24 June 1284), where 'castle' clearly means 'castle and town'.

[5] *Littere Wallie*, ed. J. G. Edwards, p. 202.

ter, the alternative site was sufficiently built and made ready for them to observe the regular life of the order.[1] Arrangements having meanwhile been made with the Earl of Lincoln to release to the king the manor of Maenan in Rhos, 7 miles up the Conway on the right bank of the river, Master James of St. George was instructed on 11 September to go there in person, receive the estate from the earl's bailiff, and convey it in the king's name to the abbot and convent.[2] Two days later the keeper of the Wardrobe issued orders for William of Perton to pay the abbot £40 for the site of the Conway property.[3]

On 6 March 1284 the abbot of Aberconway, riding into England with fellow monk and servants to meet the king, fell in with the court at Haywood in Staffordshire; and on the 9th, as the royal cavalcade, returning to Wales from the direction of York and Lincoln, moved on towards Chester, it was joined at Tarporley by the abbot of Vale Royal. It was a momentous progress,[4] culminating as it did in the birth of the king's heir at Caernarvon in April and witnessing during a week's sojourn at Rhuddlan from 16 to 24 March the promulgation of the Statute on which the administration of the Principality is still essentially based. These were events which shaped the course of history. In the midst of them, on Passion Sunday (26 March), Edward found time to turn aside, as he had turned aside to Vale Royal in 1277,[5] for the inauguration of his new abbey on the Conway.[6]

Of the plan or design of the new abbey church nothing is known, though in the circumstances of the refoundation outlined above influence from Vale Royal may well have played a part.[7] By 15 October 1284 the abbot could say that not only had the site been moved to the abbey's advantage but also that the king had made a good start on the works there.[8] The extent of the royal contribution is unknown, but sufficient had now been done to allow the abbot, 'in recognition of the king's many benefits to the house' and in return for a final payment of 580 marks, to acquit the

---

[1] *Littere Wallie*, p. 203.
[2] *Cal. Welsh Rolls*, p. 275; for the tenancy exchanges involved, see *op. cit.* pp. 161 and 290.
[3] *Cal. Anc. Corr. Wales*, p. 163. The payment to the abbot was *in plenam satisfactionem extente quam Rex ei facere tenebatur pro situ abbatie sue de Coneweye in quo Rex de novo construxit castrum et villam de Conwey* (E 372/136, rot. 33).
[4] According to Walter of Guisborough, the king and queen had been at York for the translation of the remains of St. William and consecration of Anthony Bek as Bishop of Durham on 9 January, after which the king set out for Wales *ut terram illam et stabiliret et ordinaret* (*Chronicle*, ed. H. Rothwell, Camden Soc., 1957, p. 222).
[5] Powicke, *Henry III and the Lord Edward* ii, p. 722. The presence at court of the abbot of the king's other Cistercian foundation lends colour to the likelihood of a similar ceremony having taken place at Maenan.
[6] The evidence is inferential, being derived from the record of payments for shipping the king's pavilions from Conway to Maenan and back on 26–27 March and moving them about while they were there (*pro portagio dictorum papilon' de loco ad locum apud Maynan*), E 101/351/9, para. 63. The confirmatory Bull of Honorius IV (24 April 1285) shows that constitutionally Maenan was a new foundation of the king's to which the former abbey of the princes was united (*Littere Wallie*, p. 182).
[7] For such fragmentary remains as have come to light, see Hist. Mon. Comm., *Caernarvonshire* i, pp. 1–2. Attention should also be drawn in the present context to the grant of protection for one year made at Macclesfield to Walter of Hereford, the Vale Royal master mason, during the same week as Master James of St. George was instructed from Macclesfield to proceed to Maenan to conduct the conveyance of the site (*Cal. Pat. Rolls 1281–92*, p. 75); 9 carpenters sent at the same time from Macclesfield to Aberconway *per preceptum Regis* (*Archaeologia* xvi (1806), p. 35) may also have been destined for Maenan.
[8] *Littere Wallie*, p. 47; *Cal. Close Rolls 1279–88*, pp. 407–8.

king of all further responsibility for its rebuilding.[1] Its cost may possibly be another of the items concealed under the head of 'divers other places' in Louth's account of moneys expended by the Wardrobe between March 1282 and November 1284.[2] If so, it would follow that these initial works at Maenan were subject to the supervision of the master of the works, who as already noted was personally cognisant of the site from the moment of its transfer to the abbey. Though the main account is lacking some supplementary details are known from other sources. Thus a visit of the king and queen to Maenan on Sunday, 8 October 1284,[3] possibly marking the dedication and occupation of the new buildings, was the occasion for paying £53 6s. 8d. (80 marks) for finishing certain works in the new abbey church and constructing a bakehouse and brewhouse,[4] and £6 17s. 10d. for the purchase of such necessaries as boards, shingles, nails and iron.[5] Shortly afterwards £100 was paid to the abbey by way of compensation for damages sustained in the war.[6] An undated payment belonging to the years 1284–6 is of £7 8s. 10d. for the making, probably at Chester, and carriage to Maenan of glass windows, with their ironwork, a gift to the abbey from the king.[7] A statement in the Aberconway Chronicle that he gave the monks 'large funds for new buildings'[8] probably refers to a number of additional endowments,

[1] *Littere Wallie*, p. 47. The Cistercian *Consuetudines* laid it down that before a colony was sent to a new site certain specified buildings must be provided, so as to enable the monks to live forthwith in accordance with the Rule ('nec tamen illuc destinentur donec locus . . . domibus . . . aptetur: oratorio, refectorio, dormitorio, cella hospitum et portarii; necessariis etiam temporalibus ut et vivere et Regulam ibidem statim valeant observare', —*Consuetudines*, secunda sectio, cap. xii, *Nomasticon*, 215). The assumption is that all these buildings had been provided by the king, though mostly no doubt in temporary form, by October 1284. Legal arrangements for the appropriation to the abbey of its former conventual church, henceforward to serve as a parish church for the new borough, had been concluded some months earlier; it was constituted a perpetual vicarage in the gift of the abbot, who was to present two English chaplains and one Welsh, the latter on account of the language difficulty (*propter idiomatis diversitatem*) (*Cal. Welsh Rolls*, p. 287). Inquiries were also to be instituted (June 1284) as to whether the abbey's former cemetery at Conway had ever received episcopal consecration, as if so its appropriation for other uses would require apostolic sanction (*Littere Wallie*, p. 108). For the adaptation of the abbey church, see Royal Commission, *loc. cit.* p. 39.
[2] Cf. Dolwyddelan, above p. 44.
[3] E 101/351/12, 'Pro passagio domini Regis et Regine et eorum familiarum de Maynan usque Abbercon' vj.s.' The stop at Maenan and subsequent passage down river to Conway fall into place in a royal tour which in the two months preceding 10 November also included stays at Chester, Hope, Denbigh, Caernarvon, Criccieth, Harlech, Bere and Aberystwyth. Works were in progress at most if not all of the places named, and the tour looks as if it was planned as the king's farewell inspection before his departure from Wales and the seasonal stand-down at the onset of winter. It was to be ten years before the rebellion of Madoc brought Edward back to keep Christmas in his new castle at Conway.
[4] E 101/351/15 (Alms Roll), 'Abbati de Aberconwey ad quedam opera perficienda in ecclesia apud Mainan et pro constructione unius pistrine et unius bracine de elemosina Regis'; against a duplicate entry on the keeper of the Wardrobe's 'necessaries' roll (E 101/351/9) is written *et sic quietus est Rex de translacione Abbacie de Aberconewey*. The abbot and convent of Cymmer also received a gift of £5 from the king *ad quedam opera sui monasterii perficienda* in October 1284 (E 101/351/15).   [5] *Ibid.*
[6] *Littere Wallie*, pp. 95–6. If the record is complete, compensation totalling £1733 13s. 4d. was paid out at Chester in November 1284 in settlement of 104 claims for war damage to churches. Most of the sums were quite small, but Bangor Blackfriars, Basingwerk and Conway Abbeys and St. Asaph Cathedral each received £100, Valle Crucis Abbey £160, and the Bishop of Bangor £250; the Hospitallers were awarded £95, Cymmer Abbey £80, Strata Florida Abbey £78, Bangor Cathedral £60 and Strata Marcella Abbey £43 (*Littere Wallie*, passim).
[7] E 372/131, rot. 26, '. . . et in fenestris vitreis operatis ad abbaciam de Maynan unacum ferramentis et cariagio earundem de dono Regis, £7 8s. 10d.' The glazing, like the similar gift to the Rhuddlan Dominicans in 1277 (above, p. 27, note 6) recalls Edward's grant of £200 towards the glazing of the windows of Westminster Abbey in 1285. In 1281 the windows of the exchequer in Dublin castle were glazed by Brother Robert of Chester, *vitrearius* (E101/230/13); in 1284 Simon le Verrer of Chester made glass windows for the king and queen's chamber at Caernarvon (E 101/351/9) and for the queen's chapel at Overton, Flints. (E 101/351/15).
[8] 'The Register and Chronicle of the Abbey of Aberconway', *Camden Soc.* xxxix (1847), p. 13.

recorded on the Welsh Rolls,[1] whose income could be used for that purpose, and to other sums specifically assigned to the abbot for the works of the monastery.[2]

The provision of quarters for the king and queen, the construction of the wardrobe and accommodation for its clerks, the moving of the abbey, all these were subordinate to the main task of building at Conway an entirely new castle and walled town of unsurpassed strength. Preparations for this were begun within days, if not hours, of the king's arrival. Already by 17 March Sir Peter of Brampton, who had been in charge of the diggers at Flint in July and August 1277,[3] was on his way to Chester to recruit 200 woodcutters (*coupiatores*) and 100 diggers; he was now ordered to hurry them to Conway, if necessary paying their journey wages out of his own pocket.[4] Next, on 30 March, Master Richard the Engineer was despatched to the Chester Wardrobe to arrange with William of Perton for the purchase of the tools and gear needed to cut the rock ditches and for the recruitment of masons and quarry hands;[5] he was then to go on to Newcastle-under-Lyme with orders to Edmund of Lancaster's bailiffs there to provide the king with smiths and other workmen and also to assist with the carriage of products essential for the Conway works.[6] It was no doubt as a result of his negotiations that supplies of iron, steel, nails and tin for both Conway and Harlech appear normally to have been sent carriage-paid from Newcastle to Chester, whence shipment to Wales was charged separately.[7] Two letters survive from the clerk of the works, John of Candover, begging Perton to expedite the despatch of these materials to Conway.[8]

Though the earliest 'particulars of account' are no longer extant, the speed with which the works were prosecuted during the first two years of building may be gauged from the fact that already by November 1284 a sum of £5819 14s. od. had been issued by the keeper of the Wardrobe to John of Candover and Master James of St. George specifically for the works of the castle and town of Conway.[9] An important part in their direction appears also to have been played by Sir John de Bonvillars,[10] a knight of the king's household and a kinsman and deputy of Otto de Grandson, who at the end of 1283 received expenses for going to Wales 'to supervise the king's

---

[1] *Cal. Welsh Rolls*, pp. 290, 291.

[2] As, for example, a debt of 200 marks due to the king from the Bishop of St. Asaph, but paid instead to the abbot for the works (*ibid.* p. 291). For details of the demolition of the church at Maenan in 1539–40, and conveyance of its roof and building stones by water to Caernarvon for use in rebuilding the Justice's hall there, see Edward Owen, 'The Fate of the Structures of Conway Abbey, and Bangor and Beaumaris Friaries', *Y Cymmrodor* xxvii (1917), pp. 70–114.

[3] E 101/485/19. [4] *Cal. Chancery Warrants* i, p. 8. [5] *Cal. Anc. Corr. Wales*, p. 265. [6] SC 1/13/152.

[7] For the full text of the writs of 30 March and details of the supply and transport of metal products needed for the works, see A. J. Taylor, 'The Prelude to Construction', in *Studies in Building History*, pp. 121 ff.

[8] Both probably of the summer or autumn of 1283; for their text, and for details of John of Candover, afterwards treasurer of the Agenais, see *op. cit.* p. 128.

[9] E 372/130, rot. 5*d*. Conway is also amongst the places named, along with Chester, Hope, Rhuddlan, Caernarvon, Criccieth, Harlech, West Wales and *alia diversa loca*, as receiving a share of £9414 4s. 11d. issued by the keeper for building wages between March 1282 and about the end of 1284 (E 372/136, rot. 33). Edwards, 'Castle-building in Wales', *Procs. Brit. Acad.* xxxii, p. 70, n. 1, considers it was probably a substantial one; but the very large specified Conway assignment of over £5800 already referred to, by itself larger than any previous recorded expenditure on a single castle within a comparable period, seems on the contrary to suggest that Conway's claim on this 'omnibus' figure is more likely to have been relatively small. See also below, p. 81.

[10] *Alias* 'de Bevillard' (cf. A.J. Taylor, 'Who was 'John Pennardd, leader of the men of Gwynedd'?', *Eng. Hist. Rev.* xci (1976), pp. 79–97).

castles there'.[1] His personal concern with the Conway works is evidenced by explicit references to tasks carried out by his authority or commission. Thus amongst many payments made on 29 September 1286 one of £25 to Master Henry of Oxford for completing the carpentry work of the hall and the king's *camera* and making the other 'houses' in the castle was said to be made *per preceptum domini J. de Bonouill'*, while work done by Master Henry on the staircase to the king's apartment and on an 'oriel' in the middle of the castle was 'assigned' to him jointly by Bonvillars and James of St. George.[2] In or before June 1284 the keeper of the Wardrobe and others with him spent three days at Conway for the purpose of surveying the works and paying the workmen,[3] and in October provision was made for the permanent garrison. This was to consist, besides the constable and his household, of thirty fencible men, of whom fifteen were to be crossbowmen, and the others to include a chaplain, an 'artiller', a carpenter, a mason and a smith, and such janitors and watchmen as should be needed.[4] Sir William de Cicon, who had served in the same capacity at Rhuddlan until the previous May,[5] was appointed first constable.[6]

The accounts of Richard of Abingdon,[7] who was chamberlain at Caernarvon until January 1286, show that in the third building season, covered by the accounting period November 1284–November 1285, a further £3313 1s. 2d. was paid out, bringing the specified cost of the works to date to £9132 15s. 2d. Expenditure during this phase included £472 10s. 4d. paid for the construction *ad tascham* of a portion of the town wall and its ditch.[8] That the portion in question must have included the long northern stretch of the wall facing what is now Mount Pleasant and Town Ditch Road, and that some of this length had been built to battlement level by the time of the termination of Abingdon's account, is clear from an entry in the 'particulars' roll of the following year;[9] it is clear also, from an examination of the walls

[1] 3 December 1283, 'Johanni de Byueillard militi eunti in Walliam ad supervidendum castra domini Regis ibidem precepto Regis, pro suis expensis eundo, morando et revertendo . . .' (E 101/351/12; the amount is torn away). In 1286 Louth accounted for £200 paid to Bevillard for the works in Wales by the hands of the Lucca merchants (E 101/352/2). Bevillard was probably Otto de Grandson's brother-in-law; at the time of his death in 1287 he was the justiciar's personal deputy in North Wales, being succeeded in that capacity by Otto's brother William. He was from Bonvillars near Grandson, on Lake Neuchâtel.
[2] '. . . eidem Henrico pro fractura graduum camere Regis in castro predicto et pro oriolo in medio castro factis ad tascham predicto Henrico traditam per dominum J. de Bonouillar' et Magistrum Jacobum' (E 101/485/28). Five hundred handbarrows obtained at Conway in 1286 for £5 3s. od. and sent to Caernarvon for the works there are stated to be bought by Bevillard, while another 17 were bought by Master James (*ibid.*).
[3] E 101/351/12.   [4] *Cal. Welsh Rolls*, p. 292.
[5] *Littere Wallie*, ed. J. G. Edwards, p. 186.
[6] *Cal. Welsh Rolls*, pp. 291–2. Like Bevillard, Cicon appears to have been introduced to the king's service by Otto de Grandson (13 November 1276: '. . . Willelmi Cykun nuper venientis ad nos in nuncium a partibus transmarinis ad partes Angl' ex parte Ottonis supradicti', Liberate Roll 52); in the summer of 1277 he served as a knight in South Wales under Payn de Chaworth (E 101/3/13); he continued to hold the constableship of Conway until his death in 1310/11 (SC 6/1211/4). The castle of Cicon, now entirely destroyed, is in the Jura, 15 miles north of Pontarlier.
[7] E 372/131, rot. 26.
[8] '. . . in quadam parte muri circumcingentis villam de Conewey et fossato eiusdem ville factis ad tascham CCCC.lxxij.li.x.s.iiij.d.' (*ibid.*).
[9] E 101/485/28, 29 September 1286: 'to John Flauner, for work done in Master Richard of Abingdon's time in battlementing a stretch of the wall facing towards the north and for daubing the same battlements, by 'task' assigned to him by Master James, £2'. Flauner worked at Flint (1281) and Hope (1282) (above, pp. 21, 39) and presumably he is the John Flauner of Boulogne (John le Flauner Bon') who in 1278 was paid for two boatloads of hard Boulogne stone for building a 'cistern' for the queen at Westminster (E 101/467/7/7(7)).

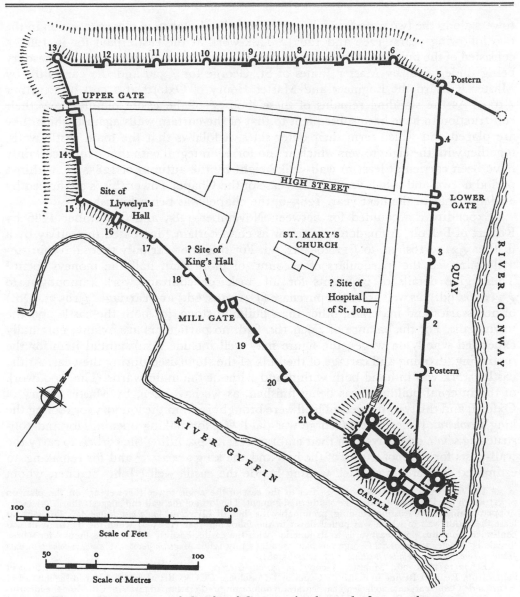

Fig. 5. The Town and Castle of Conway in the early fourteenth century.

themselves, that this first section to be constructed was not limited to the long
stretch facing northwards but included, at the one end, the line of walls and towers
sloping down on either side of the Upper Gate to the former margin of the Gyffin
stream and, at the other, the lower 12 feet or thereabouts of the spur wall running
out to the water's edge of the main river. A continuous line of defences was thus
initially provided between the site's natural boundaries, the building of the walls and

towers along the two waterfronts being left to be undertaken in close succession in the two following years (1286 and 1287).[1] Task-work at the castle paid for in 1284–5 consisted of the building of the hall and the king's and queen's chambers, the masonry being undertaken by Master James of St. George for £320 and the carpentry by Master Richard the Engineer and Master Henry of Oxford at a cost of a further £100.[2] As the standing remains of these 'houses' of the castle plainly show their construction to have been subsequent to that of the curtain walls against which they are placed and which form their outer sides, it follows that the main castle walls, together with the eight towers which are uniformly integral with them, must certainly have been carried at least to wall-walk height by the autumn of 1285, i.e. within a period of two-and-a-half years. In the case of the Chapel Tower this is confirmed by evidence that in the next year, 1285–6, the chapel was being furnished.[3]

Expenditure accounted for between November 1285 and September 1286 by Robert of Belvoir, Abingdon's successor as chamberlain,[4] increased the outlay by a further £2152 16s. 3d. to £11,285 11s. 5d. For this one year only there have fortunately survived the 'particulars of account' of more than half the moneys spent.[5] These give details of payments for all 'task' or contract work (amounting to £731 16s. 9d.), as well as for the purchase (£315 19s. 6d.) and carriage (£105 3s. 5¾d.) of necessaries and materials, other than building stone, for both the castle and the town walls. For the balance of £999 16s. 6½d. no particulars are extant; nominally expended wholly on wages, the figure may well include a substantial item for the quarrying, dressing and cartage of the bulk of the stone used during the year. At the castle, work was in hand both within and without the main wards. The woodwork of the internal buildings was being finished, as we have seen, by Master Henry of Oxford, and thirty-two sheets of lead were brought in from the foundry for roofing the king's *camera*. James of St. George was paid £64 for making openings for and constructing seven doorways with their embrasures; for providing the corbels to carry the wall-posts for the roof trusses of the hall and the king's *camera*;[6] and for remaking an estimated six perches of thick walling beside the castle well.[7] John Flauner, whom

[1] The first work terminated some 27 feet to the east of the angle tower ('Tower 15' on the plan on p. 51) which marks the west end of the southern alignment. The form of the wall end suggests that it originally stopped against a pre-existing building, presumably the 'hall of Llywelyn' (*aula que dicitur Aula Principis*), at least the south wall of which was pulled down in the following year (1285–6) when the Town Wall was continued from this point eastwards to its junction with the castle. Possibly this was the 'house' for whose 'breaking' Master James of St. George was paid 5s. 0d. (7 July 1286: *Magistro Jacobo pro quadam domo per ipsum fracta que erat ubi murus ville est situs, v.s.*, E 101/485/28).

[2] E 372/131, rot. 26: 'Magistro Jacobo de sancto *Gregorio* cementario facienti cementariam aule et camerarum Regis et Regine in castro de Conewey ad tascham, CCC.xx.li.; Magistro Ricardo ingeniatori et Henrico de Oxon' carpentario facienti carpentariam domorum predictarum ad tascham C.li.' For the identification with James of St. *George*, see *E.H.R.* lxv (1950), p. 444, n. 7. As noted above, an additional £25 was paid to Master Henry for carpentry task-work on the royal chambers in 1286.

[3] E 101/485/28, 8 September 1286: 'W. de Herlawe clerico pro quodam imagine per ipsum empto apud Cestriam pro capella in castro de Conewey, v.s.'   [4] E 372/136, rot. 28.

[5] E 101/485/28, from which unless otherwise stated the contents of this and the two following paragraphs are drawn.

[6] Some of these corbels survived the reconstruction of the castle roofs in 1346–7 and may be seen both in the hall and in the apartments in the inner ward; for details, see the *Official Guide* (1956), pp. 17–18 and 23–24.

[7] The whole entry reads 'Magistro Jacobo de sancto Georgio pro fractura et factura vij hostiorum in castro et pro auultis eorundem, et pro corbellis aule et camere Regis, et pro quodam muro facto et reficiendo et pro operibus factis ad tascham ibidem ad estimacionem vj perticat' grossi muri iuxta puteum in castro, ut patet per litteram suam, Lxiiij.li'.

we have previously encountered at Flint and at Hope,[1] made 142 arrow-slits (*archer'*) both at the castle and in the town, receiving £8 5s. 8d., or 1s. 2d. each, for them, and worked 250 dressed stones, at 25s. the 100, to provide voussoirs for the doors and windows in the castle and in the towers of the Upper Gate and Mill Gate. He also, on Master James's commission and at a cost of £10, carried out the cutting of the rock below the castle adjoining the river postern (*pro cissura cuiusdam rupis subtus castrum per commissionem Magistri Jacobi iuxta posternam versus magnam Rupem in aqua*), adjacent to which, for another £14, he built a 48-foot length of wall, 10 feet high by 3 feet thick, together with a turret and other works.[2] Nearby, but a little farther upstream, John Francis[3] and his fellow masons were engaged in building a tower standing out in the water, which was linked to the castle by a wing wall of which the remains can still be seen running down the rock below the south-east corner turret. Altogether £104 was spent on this in 1285–6, £12 for 4 feet *de opere Maaso* (?) *super turrim in aqua ibidem sita*, £30 for 12 feet *de opere Croyse super eandem turrim*, and £62 for building 15½ feet of the wall *versus aquam*. Meanwhile at the west end of the castle John of Bedford, one of the masons named at Hope in 1282, and Henry de Forneys, a carpenter, had been paid 34s. 7d. for making the outer drawbridge towards the town, and Robert Fleming and William of Launde, masons, 33s. for two small walls built in the ditch between the castle and the apartment (*camera*) of Master James of St. George.[4]

This same year, 1285–6, witnessed the building of the whole southern stretch of the town walls, comprising the twin-towered Mill Gate and eight lengths of wall and six towers[5] spaced more or less equally on either side of it. The major part of the work, probably begun in February 1286[6] and completed by the following September at a cost of £389 13s. 8d., was in the hands of a group of mason contractors headed by John Francis,[7] with whom were associated William Seysel,[7] Roger of Cockersand, Peter of Boulogne (*de Bonon'*), Jules (*Gillottus*) of Chalons,[7] John of Sherwood and Robert of Frankby.[8] Their 'tasks' were broadly of two kinds, the straightforward building of curtains and open-gorged towers to a routine pattern (*opus cursabile*), and

[1] Above, p. 50, note 9.
[2] These works were obliterated by the construction of Telford's bridge and approach road in 1825–6. Flauner's cleft in the rock can be clearly seen in the 'North East View of Conway Castle' by S. and N. Buck (1742), with his wall and turret flanking the steps which led up from the Water-gate and into the East Barbican. The *magna rupis in aqua*, though no longer an island, provides the eastern abutment for Telford's suspension bridge (1826), Stephenson's tubular bridges (1848) and Fitz Simon's span bridge (1958).
[3] See Appendix III, p. 128 below.
[4] If, as seems probable, the reference is to the ditch on the west side of the castle, in which Benarth Road now runs, it follows that the master of the works' accommodation must have occupied a site on or near the eastern end of the present vicarage garden, i.e. between the castle and the wardrobe (see below, p. 55, n. 4). Here presumably was the headquarters office of the *operaciones Regis in Wallia;* it may be noted that when, ten years later, the Exchequer at Westminster called for reports on the state of the works at Beaumaris and Caernarvon, it was from Conway that James of St. George and Walter of Hereford both dated their replies (below, pp. 88 and 106).
[5] Viz. those numbered 16 to 18 and 19 to 21 on the plan on p. 51.
[6] Payment was made for carts removing earth from the foundation of the wall (*de fundamento muri*) between 3 February and 14 April.
[7] See Appendix III, p. 128 below.
[8] From Frankby in the Wirral. Previously employed at Flint, 1279–81 (C 47/2/2, 17), where he was a burgager (Exch. Subsidy Rolls, 242/52) in 1292 and where he was killed at the time of the rising of 1294–5 (Chanc. Inqs., 56, no. 17); employed on task-work at Harlech in 1288–9 (E 101/501/25, no. 63).

the addition thereto or separate erection of special features (*opus extra cursum*). In the first category was the erection of five 'common form' towers, two to the west and three to the east of Mill Gate, at a cost of £126 11s. od. (141 feet of *opus cursabile*, i.e. a round average height of 28 feet per tower, at 16s. per foot, £112 16s. od.; plus battlements, £12 10s. od.; plus 'daubing'—i.e. limewashing or rendering—the battlements, £1 5s. od.). The six adjoining lengths of wall (*panni muri*), three immediately west and three immediately east of Mill Gate, cost £117 (98 feet of *opus cursabile*, i.e. an average height of 16 feet 4 inches per length, at 20s. a foot, £98; plus battlements, £18; plus 'daubing' the battlements, £3). The easternmost length of all (*pro quodam panno muri prope castrum*) was achieved at an inclusive cost of £7 15s. 8d. Twelve privies (*pro xij cameris forinsecis de opere extra cursum*), the remains of which can still be seen projecting from the section of wall next west of the Mill Gate, were constructed for £15. For the twin-towered Mill Gate itself, which was adjacent to and probably formed part of the king's wardrobe, John Francis and his associates were paid £118 7s. od. (main work—*pro opere turrium garderobe Regis*— excluding fireplaces and windows, £53 11s. od.; plus additional work—36 feet '*de opere extra cursum super duas turres gemellatas ad portam versus molendinum*' between first-floor level and the leads—£47; plus battlements, £7; plus 'daubing' of battlements, 16s. od.; plus three fireplaces and six windows *operatis in eadem garderobe et in turres januarum predictarum*, £10). In addition John Flauner, besides providing the dressings (as mentioned earlier) for the doors and windows and making the arrow-slits, built 30 feet of chimney work *ad portam australem et ad turrim rotundam*,[1] *viz. Garderobe aule Regis* for £4 10s. od. The dressings for the great gate arch (*pro cissura petrarum ad magnam januam in muro de Conewey versus austrum et molendinum*) were worked by John Bargas for 25s. od. and two lintels (*usser*') cut for two doors in the flanking towers for 11s. od. Thus the whole stonework of the Mill Gate was achieved for approximately £125. There would in addition have been the cost of the timber-framed chamber occupying the full width of the building at first-floor level, as also of the great double-leaved doors, construction of which probably followed on in 1286–7; the corresponding doors and chamber at the Upper Gate were executed by Master Laurence of Canterbury in 1285–6 (*factura magne porte et pro factura camere super portam versus Carnaruan*) for £15 10s. od. Such a figure, with the added cost of the necessary lead and iron work, must have brought the total cost of the Mill Gate to approximately £150. This again, however, would be in respect of constructional work only; the cost of the stone must be reckoned additionally in terms of the wages paid for quarrying and cutting it.

To complete the southern enclosure it was still necessary to close the gap left in front of the 'Prince's Hall' and thereby link the eastern termination of the 1284–5 work to the western end of John Francis's work of 1285–6. This was done by extending into a full *pannus muri* the short return already built beside the south-west angle tower (Tower 15), piercing the extension with three windows to give light to the hall behind it, and at the appropriate spacing erecting a wall-tower (Tower 16)

---

[1] I.e. the more southerly of the Mill Gate towers, which is a three-quarter round on plan (Hist. Mon. Comm. *Caernarvonshire* i, fig. 63).

whose uniquely irregular plan[1] was devised to overcome and contain a variation that had been allowed to arise between the alignment of the 'second period' work to the west of Tower 17 and the short run of earlier work east of Tower 15. The whole operation was assigned as a separate 'task' to Philip of Darley (*de Derle'*), who executed the masonry work involved for £31 10s. 0d. (*pro operacione xxvij pedum fact' ad tascham super murum in* [*? recte 'et'*] *turrim versus le Giffin et novam cameram elevatam*,[2] £27; *pro iij fenestris factis ad tascham in eodam panno*, 30s.; battlements, £3).

Operations were also in progress in 1285–6 on the wing wall and tower jutting out into the river at the end of the waterfront towards Deganwy (*turris rotunda in mari de Conewey . . . propinquiori le Gannou*). For £7, or 13s. 4d. a foot, Philip of Darley, Alan of Bucknall (*Bokenhale*), William of Thornton and Thomas of Roche cut the facing stones (*petrarum circumquarum turris*) for 10½ feet of the tower's height, and John Bargas, for £8 6s. 8d., those for a further 12½ feet.[3] For 28s. Bargas also dressed the voussoirs and jamb stones (*vousur' et tibiis*), still partly remaining to-day, of the postern in the wing wall itself. Meanwhile at the top of the town the diggers were at work on the Town Ditch. William Barber and Richard of Roding were paid £6 16s. 0d. for 4 perches made by the north-west angle tower (Tower 13) (*pro iiij perticatis in fouea muri de Conewey, scilicet ad cornar' muri*), and Walter of Roding, William of Launde, William of Macclesfield, Simon of Gedling, Robert of Wirral, Richard of Kingston and Thomas Picard £16 16s. 0d. for 8 perches made in front of the Upper Gate section (*versus occident'*).

Activity was not, however, confined to the castle and the walls and ditches. Within the town itself work was in hand on a number of projects. During September, cartloads of shingles were being brought in for roofing the king's hall,[4] to which repairs and alterations costing 30s. had been carried out by Jordan of Canterbury, a son of Master Laurence,[5] while timber for its porch was supplied by another carpenter, Henry of Chester. Repairs were also being undertaken at the hall of the justiciar, Otto de Grandson, where new passages (*aluris*) and other unspecified works were in the hands of carpenters whose names[6] suggest they may have come over with others like Master James, John Francis or Jules of Chalons; for a fireplace made in one of the rooms in Otto's hall (*in quadam camera in aula domini Otonis*)

[1] Hist. Mon. Comm. *Caernarvonshire*. i, fig. 65.
[2] The reference is probably to the first-floor chamber in Tower 16, which is approximately level with the ground floor of the *Aula Principis*.
[3] These entries are probably to be read as implying that, as a protection from the water, the tower was faced with dressed ashlar blocks. It stood immediately at the end of the surviving wing wall, where some of its bonding stones are still visible with a fallen remnant of the tower itself nearby. The date of its fall is unknown; it was still standing in *c*. 1600, being shown in a drawing of that period (*Arch. Cambrensis* xcvi, 1941, plate facing p. 168).
[4] Early fourteenth-century references speak of the King's Hall as being both *iuxta cimiterium* and *iuxta castrum* (SC 6/1170/4); it must therefore almost certainly have stood on the ground at present occupied by the vicarage garden.
[5] '. . . pro reparacione magne aule et cuiusdam paneterie iuxta parvam aulam in eandem magnam aulam et pro operibus in eadem factis ad tascham'.
[6] Michael de la Verdenoye, Bertotus Cokel, and Brodulphus. The Chillon accounts of 1257–8 show that Peter of Savoy's master-carpenter was at that time a *Magister Rodulfus carpentarius* (M. Chiaudano, *La Finanza Sabauda nel Sec. XIII* Turin 1933–8, i, pp. 10–11); *Rodulphus carpentator* also occurs at Gruyères (cant. Fribourg) in 1277 (J. J. Hisely, 'Monuments de l'histoire du Comte de Gruyère', *Mem. et Docts. publiés par la soc. d'histoire de la Suisse Romande* xxii, vol. i, Lausanne, 1867, pp. 67–8).

on Master James's orders in the time of Richard of Abingdon, John Flauner was paid 16s. A third building named is the Hospital of St. John, for the masonry work of which John Francis and his associates received £3 in September 1286.[1]

The Conway 'particulars' of 1285–6 are not only invaluable as a record of building achievement, capable for the most part of being set against the visible evidence of structures which still stand much as their builders left them. They also preserve much detailed information as to the quantities of materials, and arrangements for their carriage, needed to sustain the progress of the works. This may be summarised as shown on the opposite page. These figures reflect no more than part of the supply organisation required for one castle for one year. They take no account, for example, of the immense quantities of building stone and lime for mortar, all of which had to be prepared and carted to the scene of operations, nor of the measures needed to ensure the presence of adequate supplies of money for wages and other payments.[2] When we recall that in this same year the corresponding figures for materials supplied for the works at Caernarvon amounted to £151 5s. 6½d., for those at Harlech to £125 17s. 5¾d., and for their carriage to £535 8s. 8½d. and £285 2s. 5d. respectively,[3] we are made aware of the extent and complexity of the supply problems to which the king's works in Wales must have given rise.

The following season, represented by an accounting period running from Michaelmas 1286 to 12 October 1287 and by the further expenditure of £1990 9s. 0d.,[4] must have seen the Conway works completed in all essentials. While no details of the year's operations have been preserved, we may reasonably suppose them to have included, as the principal single item, the construction of the eastern stretch of the town walls with its twin-towered Lower Gate and four flanking towers. There must have been substantial building at the castle also, including perhaps the masonry of the watch turrets on the four eastern towers and perhaps the final structural work and crenellation of other towers as well. After 1287 expenditure dropped markedly— to less than £240 in 1287–8 and less than £19 in 1288–9.[5] For the 1290 and 1291 seasons no central expenditure is recorded. A final figure of some £155 in the period Michaelmas 1291 to Michaelmas 1292 brings the total specified outlay to £13,689 15s. 6¼d., which is furthur increased to £13,730 6s. 11¼d. by expenditure of £40 11s. 5d. incurred by Cicon, the constable, before (and evidently not long before) Michaelmas 1291.[6]

Adding, say, £770 from Louth's general works account for 1282–4,[7] we arrive

---

[1] The records give no clue to the site of Otto's hall; it is clear, however, that its size must have much exceeded that of an ordinary burgage and the plot it occupied may well be that on which Plas Mawr has stood since the later sixteenth century. The site of the medieval hospital is also unknown; but here again there is an inherent probability that it may have been the predecessor of the building known as the 'old college' (cf. Robert Williams, *History and Antiquities of Aberconwy* (Denbigh, 1835), pp. 82–3; Hist. Mon. Comm. *Caernarvonshire* i, p. 67).   [2] On which see *Flints. Hist. Soc. Pubns.* xvii (1957), pp. 40–41.
[3] E 372/136, rot. 28.   [4] *Ibid.*   [5] *Ibid.*
[6] E 372/141. Approximately £22 was for the construction and mounting, probably on the eastern barbican, of two 'engines'; the balance is accounted for by a new granary, a bell for the chapel, a room made over the outer gate, roofing one tower and two turrets, and minor works.
[7] This is an arbitrary, though by no means a negligible, figure. For reasons given above (p. 49, n. 9), it is considered unlikely that Conway can have received a very high proportion of the total of £9414.

CONWAY CASTLE AND TOWN WALLS: 1286

A. Purchase of Materials

Period of Account	Commodity	Source of Supply	Quantity	Rate	Cost
28 Jan.–29 Sept.	Charcoal		19 tons 2 qrs. 6 bush.	1½d. per qr.	£10 0s. 4d.
5 May–29 Sept.	Sea-coal	Whelston in Bagillt (*Holston'*)	524 tons	6d. per ton May–July / 5d. per ton July–Aug. / 4d. per ton September	£13 11s. 6½d.
26 May	Lead	Flint	140 carrats	26s. 0d. per ct.	£182 0s. 0d.
5 May–29 Sept.	Iron	Newcastle-under-Lyme or Chester	90 *summe*, 70 pieces	2d. the piece / 8s. 10d. to 10s. the *summa**	£44 17s. 6d.
28 July–18 Aug.	Steel	Newcastle-under-Lyme	3 barrels	£3 6s. 8d. per barrel*	£10 6s. 0d.
28 July–29 Sept.	Tin	Chester; Boston	500 lbs.		£3 11s. 4d.
26 May	Nails	Newcastle-under-Lyme	125,000	7d. to 6s. 0d. per 1000†	£10 11s. 8d.
	Ropes	Chester	(Unspecified)		£12 2s. 10d.
28 Jan.–8 Sept.	Timber		Shingles, 13,500 / Boards, 11,644	3s. 6d. per 1000 / 1s. 9d. to 3s. 6d. per 100	£12 18s. 8½d.
5 May–29 Sept.	Scaffolding		Poles (*lignis*), 2000 / 'Clayes', 1180	2s. 6d. or 3s. 0d. per 100 / 1d. or 1½d. each	£9 8s. 8d.
	Other items				£6 10s. 11d.
				TOTAL	£315 9s. 6d.

* Including carriage to Chester   † Including carriage to Conway

B. Cost of Carriage

Commodity	Quantity	Shipment	Charges
Sea-coal	524 tons	Whelston–Conway	£42 6s. 4d.
Lead	140 carrats	Flint–Conway	£14 0s. 0d.
Iron	90 *summe*, 70 pieces	Chester–Conway	£2 5s. 6d.
Steel	3 barrels	Chester–Conway	1s. 6d.
Tin	500 lbs.	Chester–Conway	1s. 0d.
Sand	106 tons 16 cwts. 3 qrs.	Deganwy–Conway	£34 16s. 9½d.
Other items			£11 13s. 4¼d.
		TOTAL	£105 3s. 5¾d.

at a round figure of £14,500 as the overall cost of the Conway works, £14,086, or 97 per cent, of it expended in the five years 1283–7.

After the completion of the castle in 1291–2 no further works are recorded at Conway until February 1296, when expenditure of £12 9s. 9d. was incurred on repairs and minor works at the King's Hall in the town, which was now enclosed with a wall. At the same time the king's granary was repaired and a new watermill and leat (*fossatum molendini*) were constructed at Gyffin for a further £8 19s. 5d.[1] Similar small works are recorded in each of the five following years. In 1298 William of Thornton, mason, was paid £3 for quarrying and dressing stone for building a new tower between the castle and the river (*pro quadam turri quam Rex ordinavit de novo fieri inter castrum de Coneweye et aquam*),[2] probably the *turris iuxta posternam* for whose flooring 100 boards and seven 23 foot by 18 inch oak joists from trees newly felled higher up the Conway were supplied by Roger of Drayton, carpenter, in 1313,[3] and whose completion, at an estimated cost of £60, was still being urged in the interests of the greater safety of the castle in 1343.[4]

A seven years' murage grant to the burgesses in 1305[5] is an indication that some work still remained to be done on the town walls. Possibly it was not until now that Towers 5 and 6 were completed to their full height, their upper stages being distinguished by the use of brown rhyolite stone and by arrow loops with original cross oillets, whereas on the remainder of the northern towers, as well as on those on the west and south, the cross form of opening appears to be an adaptation, perhaps made at this same time, of the simple vertical slits which characterised the work of the 1280's. In or about 1313 flooding caused serious damage to the foundations of the eastern wall, facing the river, and the burgesses petitioned for a further grant of murage together with the assignment of £20 a year out of the issues of the town or from elsewhere *pur sauvacion du mur et des tours de la vile qe sunt en grant peril pur les vades de la mier*.[6] The Crown agreed to bear the cost of the works,[7] which are probably reflected in the expenditure between April and October 1315 of £93 15s. 3½d. on the 'repair and emendation of the quay of Conway'.[8] In the following year £6 3s. 5d. was spent on the repair of damage which had been similarly caused to the water-gate and adjoining works at the east end of the castle.[9] The floods of 1313 were clearly something of a catastrophe, and may explain why construction of the 'new tower

---

[1] The mill was built *ad tascham* by Masters Nicholas of Chester and John of London, carpenters. Other carpenters named are Henry of Chester and Richard Weston, with Henry of Flintham and Roger of Winterbourne as masons (E 101/486/9).   [2] *Ibid.*   [3] SC 6/1211/6.

[4] '. . . turris extra posternam dicti castri que stat in magnam salvacionem eiusdem castri et que incepta est et non perfecta' (Emeldon's Survey, E 163/4/42). In all probability it is this tower which is shown protecting the river entrance to the castle in the drawing of *c.* 1600 reproduced in *Arch. Cambrensis* xcvi (1941) facing p. 168. For the location of its foundations, now buried beneath the approach to the new bridge, see *op. cit.* pp. 165–7.

[5] *Record of Caernarvon*, p. 223.   [6] Ancient Petitions, file 188, no. 9365.

[7] *Ibid.* (endorsement). Expenditure of up to £100 'on repairing the king's quay at Conway' was authorised on 13 May 1315 (*Cal. Close Rolls 1313–18*, p. 178), and a further 100 marks a year later, any further costs having to be met by the burgesses themselves (*ibid.* p. 357).

[8] Pipe Roll 1 Edward III, rot. 6d. (Remainder of account of Thomas of Chedworth, chamberlain of North Wales, for 8 Edward II).

[9] '. . . circa emendacionem posterne exterioris castri de Coneweey subtus herbarium versus mare et in emendacione muri circa eandem posternam per maris tempestatem dirutorum, ac eciam aliorum murorum ultra predictum herbarium exaltandorum . . .' (SC 6/1211/7).

Plate 1

A. Rhuddlan Castle

B. Harlech Castle

Plate 2

A. Caernarvon Castle

Crown copyright

B. The Theodosian Wall of Constantinople

Dr Martin Hurlimann

Plate 3

Conway Castle from the south-west

W.W. Harris

Plate 4

National Buildings Record

A. Caernarvon Castle: the Queen's Gate

B. Beaumaris Castle

Plate 5

A. Caernarvon Castle: interior

B. Beaumaris Castle: view from east

Crown copyright

Plate 6

A. Conway: Town Walls and Castle from Old Bangor Road
Watercolour by Moses Griffiths, 1806

B. Conway Town Walls: Towers 6 and 7 in 1957

C. Harlech Castle: Gatehouse from west

Plate 7

A. Conway Castle from south-east
Watercolour by Moses Griffiths, c.1810

B. Conway Town Walls: Towers 6, 7 and 8 in 1960

C. Beaumaris Castle: North Gatehouse from south-east

Plate 8

A. Flint Castle. Drawing by Francis Place, 1699,
showing old course of River Dee, with
Chester (a) and Beeston Castle (b) in background

B. Flint Castle: view from north-east in 1954

C. Rhuddlan Castle: view from across
River Clwyd in 1951

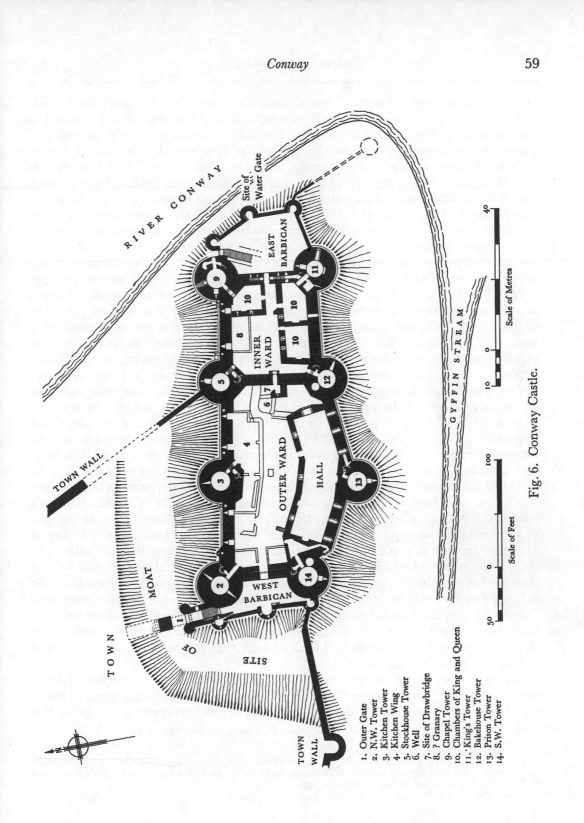

Fig. 6. Conway Castle.

1. Outer Gate
2. N.W. Tower
3. Kitchen Tower
4. Kitchen Wing
5. Stockhouse Tower
6. Well
7. Site of Drawbridge
8. ? Granary
9. Chapel Tower
10. Chambers of King and Queen
11. King's Tower
12. Bakehouse Tower
13. Prison Tower
14. S.W. Tower

outside the postern', evidently then well advanced, was still unfinished thirty years later. After 1316 the recorded annual expenditure on works is generally so small as to suggest little more than maintenance. There is, however, a notable exception in 1325–6 when Robert Power, the chamberlain of North Wales, accounted for an outlay, on unspecified works at Conway, of no less than £139 1s. 8d.[1] Possibly this was the occasion of the erection of the upper part of the 'spur' wall at the Deganwy end of the waterfront. A change-line in the masonry shows that above a height of approximately 12 feet from the ground the build of this wall is secondary, and as the provision of access to its wall-walk involved converting into a doorway one of the arrow-slits in the added upper part of Tower 5, the raising of the 'spur' wall must itself be subsequent to the date of the addition. The expenditure of 1325–6, not otherwise readily explicable, could well have been devoted, in whole or in part, to such an undertaking.

A proportion may also have been applied to making good certain dilapidations in the castle reported in a survey of 1321. This showed that several of the main timbers of the hall roof, and also many of those on the towers and other buildings, had perished through failure of their covering of lead, and estimated that the repairs would require 5 chars 20 lb. of lead; it was no good repairing the woodwork so long as the timber itself was uncovered (*le charpentrie ne poet pas estre bien eymee tantque le meryn soit descouert*).[2] It is doubtful, however, whether anything effective was done at this time. In 1332 Conway, like the other Welsh castles, was reported to be unfit for the accommodation of the king,[3] and in 1343, when the castle was inspected by the Black Prince's officials, the roof of the great hall was found to be completely rotten for want of lead, and could not be repaired for less than £160. The roofs and floors of eighteen chambers in six of the castle's eight towers were found to be in a similar condition 'for want of repair and covering', and required an expenditure of £131 to put them right.[4] The accounts of the chamberlain of North Wales are missing from 1345 to 1352, but the Black Prince's Register indicates that the hall was under repair in 1347 by the direction of the prince's mason, Master Henry of Snelston. Instead of replacing the original trusses he spanned the hall with eight great stone arches, of which one still survives. The architectural evidence shows that these arches were insertions into the thirteenth-century walls, and we learn from the prince's Register that the stone of which they were made came from a quarry near Chester.[5] Upon these arches the prince's carpenters built a new roof which survived until the sixteenth century. Similar arches were inserted to sustain the roofs of the chambers in the Inner Ward, and it is evident that the whole castle underwent a thorough repair at this time.[6]

From 1382 to 1394 Conway was held by Queen Anne, and after her death it was placed under the control of the Clerk of the King's Works.[7] This arrangement lasted apparently until 1401, when, through the treachery of a carpenter, the castle was

[1] E 372/174, rot. 23.   [2] B.M., Add. Roll 7198.   [3] *Cal. Close Rolls 1330–3*, p. 491.
[4] E 163/4/42.
[5] *Black Prince's Register* i, pp. 46, 61.
[6] There is, however, no evidence, either structural or documentary, to suggest that the traceried windows in the Inner Ward were inserted at this time, as suggested by S. Toy in *Archaeologia* lxxxvi (1936), p. 190, and by J. H. Harvey, *Mediaeval Architects* (1954), p. 247.
[7] *Cal. Pat. Rolls 1381–5*, p. 159; *1396–9*, p. 404.

captured and held for some weeks by Welsh rebels.[1] After this the officers of the principality resumed control, and the maintenance of the castle continues to figure year by year in the chamberlains' accounts. The annual expenditure rarely exceeded £10, but in 1437–8 it amounted to the exceptional sum of £77 8s. 8d.[2] No details of the works carried out are, however, preserved.

Lastly at Conway we have to follow the vicissitudes of the group of buildings known as the Prince's[3] or Llywelyn's[4] Hall. The decision to retain these buildings in addition to the castle, the king's hall occupied by the Wardrobe, the hall of the justiciar and the lodging over the Mill Gate assigned to the chamberlain[5]—and the documents leave no doubt that these were all separate premises[6]—must from the first have envisaged a particular user for them, while the careful incorporation of one side of the hall in the new town wall[7] is of itself sufficient to suggest a user of some importance. There can indeed be little doubt that what had been the residence, and continued to be known by the name, of the last native princes of Wales[8] was reserved by the king to provide accommodation in Conway for their intended English successor, for whom separate provision would one day be needed so long as the king might himself require to occupy the royal apartments in the castle. That this was so is borne out by the hall's subsequent building history. First there is the evidence of money spent on its maintenance in four out of the five years following King Edward's sojourn at Conway in the winter of 1294–5.[9] Then in October 1302, eighteen months after the vesting of the younger Edward with the principality and his visit to Conway to receive the homages and fealty of his Welsh subjects,[10] works of some consequence were begun, involving the acquisition of additional land[11] and alterations to the tower adjoining the hall (Tower 16);[12] at the same time the self-contained character of the house and its fitness to accommodate the prince and his suite were emphasised by the addition of a private chapel,[13] for the windows of which freestone from a quarry in Anglesey was dressed at Caernarvon and brought to Conway by water.[14] The works continued intermittently until April 1306, the recorded cost being £48 13s. 11d.[15] Their effect must have been to give the prince within the walls of Conway, as within

---

[1] *Chronicon Adae de Usk*, ed. Thompson (1904), p. 61: 'duobus janitoribus subtilitate cujusdam carpentarij, ad opus suum solitum se venire asserentis, interfectis . . .' It may be noted that a number of Welsh carpenters were employed at the castle in 1395–6 (E 101/487/14).

[2] B.M., Add. Roll 26597 (Chamberlain's account for 1437–8).

[3] E 101/485/28, '. . . iij camere in aula que dicitur Aula Principis' (1286).

[4] E 101/486/9, '. . . pro Aula Lewelini cooperienda' (1296).

[5] E 101/533/7, '. . . pro domibus domini Principis ultra portam de Mullegate apud Conewey pro hospicio Camerarii sibi per Justiciarium assignatis'.

[6] The accounts repeatedly differentiate between repairs of the *domorum domini Regis* and of the *aule Leulini* (e.g. E 101/486/9, where repairs are mentioned to *both* groups of buildings in 1296, 1297, 1299 and 1300).

[7] Above, p. 346.

[8] As to whether it originated under Llywelyn the Great (d. 1240) or Llywelyn ap Gruffydd (d. 1282) there is no evidence. The devotion of the former to the Aberconwy Cistercians makes the earlier date not unlikely.

[9] E 101/486/9. [10] Hilda Johnstone, *Edward of Carnarvon* (Manchester, 1946), p. 62.

[11] E 372/176, rot. 54; E 101/533/7: 'in empcione duarum partium unius burgagii non edificati . . . pro placea aule domini Principis, dicte aule Lewelini, inde amplianda, xx.s.'

[12] E 101/486/23, '. . . pro operacionibus Turris iuxta Aulam Lewelini, pro muris lapideis faciendis et exaltandis cum muro garderobe eidem spectanti'; 27 masons and 11 carpenters are named in the account; 6 tie-beams (*latie*) are provided for the *supremum solarium*, presumably the topmost room of the tower.

[13] This was an entirely new building, the account recording payments to Ralf of Goldstone and Hugh of Derby, masons, *pro muris capelle incipiendis* and to John of Cambridge *querenti fundamentum dictorum murorum*.

[14] E 101/486/23, and SC 6/1170/4. [15] SC 6/1211/2.

the palace of Westminster, a fully appointed privy palace of his own. Only a year later, however, his accession was to make such a separate establishment redundant and the disposal of its buildings merely a question of time. In 1316 the king assented to a proposal to make use of the timberwork of the hall, 'our old hall' as he called it, 'known as Llywelyn's hall' (*quedam vetus aula nostra vocata aula Lewelini*),[1] for constructing what was said to be a much needed storehouse for victuals in Caernarvon castle,[2] whereupon it was carefully dismantled, shipped along the coast and re-erected in its new position.[3] It was perhaps not inappropriate that so historic a relic of the older dynasty should thus finish its days in the reputed birthplace of the new.

7. THE BRIDGE NEAR BANGOR

Edward I's strategy for the encirclement of Snowdonia envisaged a threefold assault on Llywelyn's mountain stronghold. We have seen how on the east the advance from Rhuddlan and Denbigh, led by the king himself, culminated in the capture of Dolwyddelan in January, and occupation of Conway in March 1283. From the south, forces from Shropshire and South Wales, led respectively by Roger Lestrange and William de Valence, joined hands in April to besiege and capture Castell-y-Bere in Meironydd[4] and thereby open the way for a northward advance to Harlech. In the north, the services of the Cinque Ports fleet were used in August and September 1282[5] to effect a lodgement in strength on the island of Anglesey, whence a bridge of boats was built across the fast-flowing strait to a mainland bridgehead near Bangor. The way was thus opened for a central army, led by the king's friend and lieutenant Otto de Grandson and supplied by sea from Chester and Rhuddlan, to land at the appropriate moment within striking distance of Caernarvon and thence through Criccieth and Harlech to complete the encircling chain.[6] The bridge-works (*opera pontis Bangor'*)[7] were cardinal to the whole scheme. As the means of providing the link between the castle works begun at Conway in March, and at Harlech and Caernarvon in June 1283, they may conveniently be considered here.

Planning began to take shape in the early summer of 1282, and the bridge may have been one of the matters discussed with William Marlepas and Laurence of Windsor, two Cinque Port barons from Hastings who were called to the king's

---

[1] Close Roll 133, m. 17.   [2] *Cal. Close Rolls 1313–18*, p. 267.

[3] SC 6/1211/7, 'Johanni de Mere carpentario pro amocione tocius maeremii Aule Lewelini in villa de Conewey et relevacione eiusdem in castro de Caernarvon sumptibus suis propriis ad tascam per convencionem inter dominum Johannem de Grey et ipsum inde factam per breve Regis £14 13s. 4d.'; cost of carts, oxen and men carrying timber from hall to riverside, £2 11s. 1d.; shipment from Conway to Caernarvon, £5; carriage from quay into castle, £1 12s. 7½d.; 53,500 nails *pro eadem aula*, £6 2s. 0d.; Henry le Sclatiere for roofing re-erected building, £8 10s. 0d.; total cost, £38 9s. 0½d. John de 'Mere' is probably the John de More who accompanied the Black Prince to Calais and who in 1347 was appointed carpenter, engineer and keeper of the engines in the castles of Caernarvon, Conway, Beaumaris, Harlech and Criccieth (*Black Prince's Register* i, p. 95).   [4] For works at Bere, see below, p. 75.

[5] Detailed payments for ships and sailors are preserved in E 101/3/26.

[6] The best account of the campaign remains that in Morris, *Welsh Wars*, pp. 176–95.   [7] E 101/4/6.

court at a date which cannot have been later than the end of April.[1] Very soon afterwards orders were sent to Reginald Alard of Winchelsea and another to bring 40 flat-bottomed boats (*escutes*) to Chester for the king's use in Wales. The reply from the Ports was that this was not practicable as the boats were so large and heavy that no ship could hold them, and it would be better for the king to order the bailiffs of the Ports to send carpenters to Chester to make the boats there.[2] This advice was accepted, and on 24 May the warden of the Cinque Ports, Stephen of Penchester, was ordered to select ten or twelve good and strong carpenters, discreet and skilled (*subtiles*) in making these boats (*shutas*) and barges, whom he should cause to set out for Chester with their tools (*attiliis*) so as to arrive there not later than 23 June; he was further to have work started immediately on building two new 32-oared barges, which were to be manned and sent to Wales later in the summer in company with the *servitium debitum* of the Ports. These instructions were conveyed to Dover by the king's clerk, John of Maidstone, who with Penchester's help was also to recruit 200 'strong and agile' men of the Cinque Ports and send them well armed to Denhall (*Danewell*) on the Wirral shore of the Dee; he was to pay their wages for the journey, with those of the carpenters and two crews, out of a sum of 100 marks to be made over to him by the keeper of the exchange in London. He was also to pay for the two new barges.[3] From a surviving fragment of his account we learn that these were each equipped with 4 anchors, one of them being built at Winchelsea at a cost of £46 14s. 10d. and the other at Romney at a cost of £30 1s. 1d.[4] It appears that to start with Penchester obtained 20 carpenters from Sandwich and sent them to build the barges and boats at Winchelsea, but nothing was accomplished and they were paid only 11s. 8d. Subsequently, on the Sunday after St. Barnabas (14 June), 10 master carpenters were sent on their way from Winchelsea to Chester to make the boats there; the journey took ten days and they received £5 between them to cover riding costs and the carriage of their gear, with an extra half-crown for their leader William Martyn 'as he was an old and experienced master'.[5]

Work must soon have been under way, and between 30 July and 9 August the keeper of the Wardrobe recorded the payment, by the hands of Robert FitzJohn,[6] of £3 14s. 11¼d. for poles bought at Chester for making punts or pontoons (*pro lignis emptis . . . ad pontes faciend'*), for their carriage to Burton (Denhall adjoins Burton in Wirral) and for the manufacture of pontoons and 'clays' (*pro factura Clayarum et pontium*).[7] The structure was apparently to consist of linked boats carrying a decking of poles and flat sections wide enough to allow a body of troops to cross in column.[8] Some at least of the fabricated products were ferried across the estuary to Rhuddlan to await shipment to Anglesey, John of Maidstone accounting between

[1] *Cal. Welsh Rolls*, p. 249. See also K.M.E. Murray, *Constitutional History of the Cinque Ports* (Manchester University Press, 1935), Appendix III B, pp. 247–8.
[2] *Cal. Anc. Corr. Wales*, p. 109; the date there suggested is too late, as the letter clearly precedes the orders of 28 May (see next ref.).
[3] *Cal. Welsh Rolls*, p. 251.   [4] C 47/3/48, m. 33.   [5] *Ibid.*
[6] Steward of the household and king's marshal.   [7] E 101/3/29, para. 6.
[8] '. . . naves multas adinuicem coniunctas compositis lignis et coniunctis tabulis super ipsas naues ita quod in fronte vna transire possent .lx. armati' (*Chronicle of Walter of Guisborough*, ed. H. Rothwell, Camden Soc. 1957, p. 219). The width is at once credible and impressive if the figure '.lx.', common to all the surviving texts, is an early copyist's slip for '.ix.'

22 and 30 August for making 500 'clays' in Neston Park[1] and their carriage to Rhuddlan.[2] On 18 August Luke de Tany, the former seneschal of Gascony, was gazetted to Anglesey with orders 'to provide and make a bridge there', the king's barons and subjects of the Cinque Ports in his garrison at Anglesey being simultaneously ordered to provide the ropes and anchors necessary for its construction.[3] Between 16 August and 15 September Ralf of Broughton, formerly king's receiver in West Wales and now receiver for the Anglesey operation, bought 14 ships for use in constructing the bridge, while on 20 August the keeper of the Wardrobe paid out £25 in wages to carpenters going to Anglesey to work there[4]—John of Maidstone's 200 'strong and agile' men from the Cinque Ports. Three days later another 60 carpenters left for the island with Master Richard the Engineer, to be followed in a week's time (30 August) by 100 more under Master Henry of Oxford.[5] Not all of this number were necessarily engaged on the bridge itself, for the base established at Llanfaes, near—perhaps on—the site of the future castle of Beaumaris, must have required the construction of landing stages, huts, cookhouses, stockades and the like.

Of John of Maidstone's accounts for the actual bridgeworks only a single fragment, and that much mutilated, has survived.[6] None of its figures is legible, but payments are recorded for felling timber *ad ingenia et ad pontem*, for hauling timber from the woods to the waterside and transporting it to the bridge, for bringing up from the water the 'clays' that came from the Wirral, and to the men in the two galleys—probably the new ships from Winchelsea and Romney—going to and fro (*sepe euntibus*) between Llanfaes and Rhuddlan and Chester. Finally, perhaps an indication that the task was all but done, there was a distribution of wine to those who had seen it through—a tun to Master Bertram[7] *et R. socio suo*, possibly Richard the Engineer, a tun to the master of the ship called 'La Blithe' of Hastings 'in which the engines were placed', and a tun to the wardens of the bridge (*custod' pontem*) Bartholomew Godard and Robert Pauline,[8] each one a gift from Luke de Tany; in addition there were 87 tuns and 2 pipes for Ralf of Broughton to issue to the rest of the workmen.

Such celebrations were shortlived. By November, whether or not it was completely finished, the bridge was considered to be ready for crossing, and on the 6th Tany led his forces over. The story of how they were ambushed and forced back by the Welsh, only to find a rising tide had added to the hazards of retreat, is well known,[9] and what had started as a triumph ended in disaster. Sixteen knights, their squires with them, were drowned, including Tany himself, young Roger Clifford, the chancellor's two sons Philip and William Burnel,[10] and Walter Jay who had

---

[1] Cf. Parkgate, near Neston: Denhall is in Neston parish.
[2] E 101/3/29, para. 10.   [3] *Cal. Welsh Rolls*, p. 235.
[4] E 101/3/26. This is the naval roll, containing details of the keeper of the Wardrobe's payments for ships and sailors in August and September 1282, and for wages to sailors based at Rhuddlan (£13 18s. 5d.) and Caernarvon and Criccieth (£4 10s. 7½d.) in 1283; the total for the roll, including the four items quoted, is £1404 9s. 10½d.
[5] *Archaeologia* vi (1806), p. 33.   [6] E 101/3/31, m. 2.   [7] Appendix III, p. 126 below.
[8] Both were prominent barons of Winchelsea; cf. Murray, *op. cit.*, p. 247. While Pauline was away on the king's service in Wales his house at la Forde (? Fordwich), Kent, was broken into and robbed (*Cal. Pat. Rolls 1281–92*, p. 91).   [9] Morris, *Welsh Wars*, pp. 179–80.
[10] For a letter of sympathy to Burnel from one of his clerks, see *Cal. Anc. Corr. Wales*, p. 126.

superintended the masons at Flint in the early days in the summer of 1277; so also were 300 infantry[1] and probably bridge-warden Godard as well.[2] For the king the narrow escape of Otto de Grandson must have come as the only good news from a day of otherwise unrelieved catastrophe.[3]

The bridge was evidently not destroyed, and from 23 November to 28 December quantities of 'clays' and stockading continued to be shipped almost without interruption from Rhuddlan to Anglesey, either for the repair or perfecting of the bridge itself or as a stock-pile against the coming build-up on the Bangor side. Cartload after cartload of timber was brought from a wood near St. Asaph to Rhuddlan 'to make brattices to send to Anglesey', and on 4 December Master Henry of Oxford sailed again for the island with a squad of 20 carpenters. Between 28 December and 3 January 1283 the emphasis of the record shifts across to the mainland, and by the latter date the Bangor bridgehead was probably being set up and reinforced. Cargoes of boards from Rhuddlan were now sailing to Bangor and 'clays' were sent there on 14 February for making gangways for embarking the horses.[4] 150 pieces of iron sent by Perton from Chester were made into nails 'for the works at Bangor' and other nails supplied 'for the works of the Bangor bridge'.[5] By midsummer Caernarvon was occupied and the castle works there and at Harlech beginning. The bridge, having served its purpose, was now dismantled to allow uninterrupted passage through the strait to ships bringing supplies for them. Its materials, like those of Rhuddlan's promised palisade, were pressed into service for building the future capital: five boats were engaged, between 14 and 17 July 1283, in carrying timber from the 'bridge of Anglesey' to Caernarvon, where 48 porters unloaded and took it into the castle.[6]

8. HARLECH

Harlech makes its earliest appearance in the records towards the end of April 1283, when a force of 560 infantry led by Sir Otto de Grandson marched there from Castell-y-Bere.[7] Preparations for the building of the new castle must have been begun very soon after their arrival, and it was probably only a week or two later that two panniers containing £100 were sent under guard from Cymmer Abbey to Harlech 'for the works there'.[8] On 21 June, still three days before the first recorded mention of work at Caernarvon, 10 masons and quarriers were despatched from Conway to Harlech with a packhorse to carry their tools on the two-day journey; by the middle of July

---

[1] Thus the Chester chronicle, generally a reliable source.
[2] Murray, *loc. cit.*
[3] '. . . cum magna difficultate evasit dominus Oto de Graunsun', *Annales Cestrienses*, Lancs. and Chesh. Rec. Soc. xiv, p. 112.
[4] E 101/351/9, paras. 1–6, 10.   [5] E 101/4/6.   [6] E 101/351/9, paras. 31–2.
[7] C 47/2/4, 'pacatum domino Othon' de Gradisono ad sustentacionem D. et lx. peditum secum euncium de Castro de Bere usque Hardelach xx li. per talliam'.
[8] E 101/351/9, para. 40. The entry is undated, but other Wardrobe payments are known to have been issued at Cymmer on 14 and 20 May 1283 (*Littere Wallie*, pp. 180 and 193).

half a dozen sawyers, similarly accompanied, and a further 15 masons, had followed them.[1] The king himself was at Harlech from 17 to 20 August,[2] leaving its affairs from that day forward in the charge of five squires of the royal household.[3] Provision to sustain the works up to the end of the season is indicated by the sending of two further consignments of money, one of £100 and the other of £60, from Acton Burnell to Harlech during October.[4] Their continuance in the following season (1284) may be inferred from a record of wages paid to Hugh of Leominster, the future chamberlain of North Wales, as clerk of works for Harlech as well as Caernarvon in the eleventh and twelfth regnal years.[5] Of their extent and cost we have no precise knowledge, but they appear to have been sufficiently advanced by October 1284 to justify the replacement of the squires of the household by a constable with a normal castle establishment.[6] It is not until 1285, in Richard of Abingdon's first chamberlain's account, that we have an explicit record of particular expenditure, £205 1s. 5½d. being stated to have been laid out between 29 April and 4 November of that year on excavating the rock-cut castle ditch (*ad operacionem fossati de rupe ante castrum de Hardelagh*).[7] This is because the cost of the Harlech works was met, throughout their first two years, directly from the Wardrobe, and the amount spent on them, so far as the record goes, is submerged in the total figure, already referred to in connection with Conway,[8] of £9414 issued by William of Louth for the wages of workmen at Chester, Hope, Rhuddlan, Conway, Caernarvon, Criccieth, Harlech, West Wales and elsewhere. It is difficult amidst so many unknowns to estimate what Harlech's share of this figure may have been. Some guidance is, however, afforded by the relative scale of the various works named, and by the entries, scant and fortuitous though they are, of individual amounts stated to have been transmitted from the Wardrobe for the works at Harlech at particular times during 1283. The issues, noted above, of £100 in May of that year, of a further £100 early in October, and of £60 later in October when the season would be drawing to a close, point to a probable summer expenditure of £100 a month,[9] and on that basis it may well be that we should allow a round figure of, say, £1500 for the period prior to May 1285

---

[1] E 101/351/9, paras. 26, 27 and 31. The sawyers were headed by Richard of Mountsorrel; the masons are unfortunately all unnamed.

[2] 'Itinerary of Edward I' compiled by E. W. Safford (typescript in P.R.O.).

[3] John Cosyn, Ebulo de Montibus, John of Gayton, John de Scaccario and Peter of Cornhill, *scutiferi de hospicio regis morantes in municione apud Hardelegh.* John de Scaccario drops out after Christmas 1283; the wages of the remainder can be traced in the Wardrobe accounts down to the date of the appointment of the first constable in October 1284 (E 101 /4/1 and 4/8). John Cosyn, alias John Cosyn de Grandisono, and Ebulo de Montibus were Savoyards closely associated with Otto de Grandson, a connection further exemplified by the successive tenure of the constableship of the castle by the Savoyards John de Bevillard, Agnes de Bevillard and James of St. George from 1285 to 1293 and the presence of Savoyard names among the builders in 1286 (Appendix, II and III).

[4] E 101/351/9, paras. 39, 40.

[5] *Ibid.*, para. 70, 'Hugoni de Leominstr' clerico in partem solucionis vadiorum suorum de tempore quo fuit ultra operarios apud Caernaruan et Herdelawe annis xj⁰ et xij⁰, £15 0s. 1½d.' Details of the quantities of iron, steel and nails sent from the Chester wardrobe by Sir William of Perton 'for the works of the bridge of Bangor and of the castles of Criccieth, Harlech and Caernarvon' in 1283 and 1284 are preserved in E 101/4/6.

[6] *Cal. Welsh Rolls,* p. 291.

[7] £186 14s. 11½d. for wages of quarriers, smiths, hodmen and their guards (*cum custodibus eorundem*); £18 6s. 6d. for iron and steel for their tools (E 372/131, rot. 26d).

[8] Above, p. 49, note 9.

[9] It should be emphasized that no record has survived of issues as such, but only of those happening to involve non-routine expenditure on their transit.

when calculating the total cost of the castle. The relatively lower expenditure in the 1285 season itself would then be explicable in terms of that year having been one of maximum effort at Conway and Caernarvon.

From 1286 onwards the progress of the works can be followed in the series of roughly annual totals of expenditure on wages, 'task' work, carriage and materials recorded on the chamberlain's account of Richard of Abingdon's successor Robert of Belvoir.[1] In the nine-and-a-half months from 30 December 1285 to 15 September 1286 there was an outlay of £1602 18s. 6¼d., the great bulk of it, £1157, on daily and weekly wages; as it happens that for this period, and for this period only, there have also survived copies of all the 'particulars' on which the totals entered on the Pipe Roll were based, we have an exceptionally complete picture of the year's activities.[2] Especially notable is the gradual build-up of the labour force from some 60 men in January to nearly 950 men at midsummer, with a gradual fall again to some 770 at the beginning of September; in terms of wages this called for an expenditure in June of nearly £55 a week. When the work was at its height there were 227 masons, 115 quarriers, 30 smiths, 22 carpenters and 546 labourers and minor workmen.[3] Ships were bringing limestone from Anglesey and Caernarvon, freestone from Egryn (7 miles down the coast to the south), and iron and steel from Chester. The figures for the following year, covering a 14-month period from 15 September 1286 to 9 November 1287, show that the tempo was if anything increased, the total outlay of all but £3357, over £2200 of it accounted for by daily wages, being only £12 short of the combined expenditure on Conway and Caernarvon between nearly identical dates.[4] In the 1288 season expenditure was very much lower, with wages during a 13-month accounting period amounting to only £530; even so the year's total of £914 17s. 2d. is this time more than double the corresponding figure for Caernarvon and Conway together. In the following year, from 26 December 1288 to 26 December 1289, the scale of expenditure increases markedly again, with wages alone accounting for £1850 of a total of £1877. As, however, over £1700 of the wages figure is booked to 'task' or contract items, some of the work, though only paid for in 1289, may have been begun in 1288 or even 1287. In the next full year, to 27 December 1290, payments dropped to the relatively small figure of £221, the major portion, £180, again being in respect of task work.[5]

In all essentials the castle must by now have stood complete, having cost something of the order of £9,500 and taken seven and a half years to achieve. There remained to be constructed in stone only the outermost wall enclosing the castle rock on the north and the now vanished bridge works leading to the main gate.[6] It is possible, by applying the evidence of the records to that of the castle itself,

[1] E 372/136, rot. 28; the principal totals are tabulated in Edwards, 'Castle-building', p. 72.
[2] E 101/485/26 and 27. Besides containing invaluable information in regard to Harlech itself, these accounts are of exceptional interest as being the only surviving set of 'particulars' which is complete for all four main heads of expenditure for a given castle for a given period. They are accordingly given in summary form as an appendix to this chapter (below, pp. 120–125).
[3] For an analysis of the wage payments and discussion of their economic implications, see Edwards, *op. cit.* pp. 73–9.   [4] *Op. cit.* pp. 70–71.
[5] This marks the end of the continuous accounts; minor expenditure totalling only £6 5s. 2d. is recorded for the exchequer year 1291–2 (E 372/138, rot. 25).   [6] Below, p. 72.

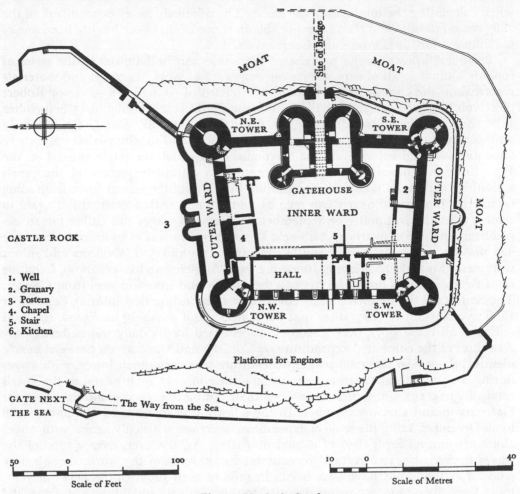

Fig. 7. Harlech Castle.

to suggest a sequence for the main work. Well defined structural breaks in the north, south and west curtains of the inner ward show there was a first stage of building in which the main walls were erected to a width of only 8 feet and a height of approximately 15 feet. It similarly appears that the southern section of the east curtain was not at first built to its full thickness, and the same may be true of the lower part of the northern section also. With the first work in the curtains go the two eastern, but not the two western, corner towers, and probably also the lowest stage of the gatehouse. It is suggested that most of this work belongs to the period 1283–4, and that the cutting of the ditch 'in front of the castle' in 1285 was undertaken not, as used to be thought, as the first operation of all, but in order to protect substantial work already built. If this view is correct, it follows that much of the stone for the first campaign will have been obtained not from the ditch but from the levelling of the site and the ground outside it to the east; the material from the ditch will have helped to provide for the needs of the second work.[1]

Constructional details noted after the resumption of building in 1286 include the dressing of steps for staircases in the towers, reveals for tower arrow-slits (*archer' turrium*) and 200 feet of stringcoursing (*tabellamentum*), the making of the chimney of the lodging of the constable, Sir John de Bonvillars, the provision of wood and thatch for roofing the castle's 'houses' and the purchase of an image for the chapel.[2] Of progress in the 1287 season—in terms of expenditure the most active of all—and in that of 1288 no details have come down to us, but together they must have seen the further growth of the gatehouse and the topmost storeys of the eastern corner towers, and perhaps also much of the work on the outer curtain.

The recent discovery, among accounts hitherto unidentified, of a substantial portion of the 'particulars' of the £1709 16s. 3d. spent on taskwork at Harlech in 1289 has thrown much new light on the final phase.[3] This is shown to have included the following items, here grouped for convenience under the names of the contractors to whom they were assigned:

(i) *Master William Drygda*

	£	s.	d.
N. tower towards sea, 49½ ft. high @ 45s. per ft.	111	7	6
Turret (*garrita*) on same, 19 ft. @ 12s. per foot	11	8	0
Wall between mantlet below same tower and sea	7	0	0
S. tower towards sea, 52 ft. high @ 45s. per foot	117	0	0
Turret on same, 19 ft. @ 12s. per foot	11	8	0
Turret over the way from the sea (*garrita super passum maris*)	[illegible]		
Part of N.E. tower and wall on N. side of great gate (*pro xxiij pedibus in altitudine turris et muri ex parte boriali magne porte*), 23 ft. @ 55s. per foot	63	5	0
For ?14 ft. in height of same tower above the curtain wall (*pro ?xiiij pedibus turris predicte de alto supra murum . . . .*)	[illegible]		

(ii) *Hugh (?) de Wemme*[4]

For 10 feet of S. tower towards the town @ 12s. 2d. per foot	6	1	8

(iii) *John de . . . , John de . . . , Richard . . . and their fellows*

Doubling the thickness of the old wall towards the sea (*veteris muri versus mare spissitudinem dubland' . . .*)	[illegible]		

[1] For details of wall thicknesses, etc., see C. R. Peers, 'Harlech Castle', *Cymmrodorion Trans.*, 1921–2, p. 69 and ground plan. Peers was unaware of the £9414 paid out by the keeper of the Wardrobe in wages for castle works, including works at Harlech, in 1283–4 and thought the cutting of the ditch in the following year must be the earliest work.

[2] See Appendix II.

[3] Now E 101/501/25, no. 63. The document is in a fragmentary and blind condition and can be read only with the greatest difficulty. It is possible to make out paragraph totals amounting to not less than £1189 out of the known enrolled total of £1709 16s. 3d., but the substance of many of the paragraphs can no longer be recovered.

[4] A Maurice de Wemme is named next but one to William of Drogheda in the list of Caernarvon burgesses in 1298 (*Bull. Bd. Celt. Stud.* ix, p. 240).

(iv) *Richard of Radwell,*[1] *Robert of Eccleshall*[2] *and John Clifford*[3]

	£	s.	d.

Building up the thick wall on the old wall towards the sea, from the one tower to the other (*pro cymentar' et elevacione grossi muri super veterem murum versus mare . . . de una turri ad aliam*)   100   7   6

Battlementing the same wall, building a look-out (*garrita*) on it,[4] and making voussoirs for the windows in it   25   0   0

Making a new kiln in the castle   2   6   0

(v) *Robert of Frankby*[5] *and Reginald of Turvey*[6]

Building 18½ feet of the S. stair turret of the gatehouse (*pro cyment' et elevacione xviii ped' et di' grossi muri garrite australis ultra magnam portam*) @ 13s. 4d. per foot   12   6   8

Building the battlements of same turret   2   0   0

Building walls of new hall, chapel, pantry and kitchen   70   0   0

Repairing window in inner room on W. side of top floor of gatehouse (*in camera interiori versus occident' in stagio superiori ultra magnam portam*)   10   0

(vi) *William of Thornton*[7]

Making the fireplace in one of the top rooms on S. side of gatehouse   8   0

(vii) *'Breynford'*[8]

Making a window in the same room   15   0

(viii) *Albert de Menz*[9]

Dressing freestone details, including chimney stacks and mullions (*columpne*) for windows of hall, pantry and kitchen   12   12   9

(ix) *Robert de . . .uldon'*

Building the wall at the bottom of the moat below the mantlet (*pro muro facto in fundamento fossati . . . . mantell'*)   5   13   0

[1] From Radwell in Felmersham, Beds., burgage-holder at Caernarvon in 1298 (*ibid.*, p. 239); probably to be associated with Nicholas de Radewell who in 1316 was clerk of works at Beaumaris (*Arch. Camb., Original Docts.*, 1877, pp. xix ff.) and Adam de Rodewell who in 1309 was one of four Bedfordshire masons sent to Caernarvon to help Henry of Ellerton after the death of Walter of Hereford (Exch. L.T.R. Mem. Roll 79, rot. 111). Adam and Richard of Radwell were both working at the palace of Westminster in 1307 (Lethaby, *Westminster Abbey and the King's Craftsmen*, p. 185).

[2] Served as sheriff of Merioneth in 1295-6 (Breese, *Calendars of Gwynedd*, p. 68).

[3] Employed at Builth (*Cal. Anc. Corr. Wales*, p. 250) and in 1281 on the Great Tower at Flint (E 101/674/23); burgess of Flint in 1292 (E 179/242/52).

[4] This is the only evidence now surviving for the Harlech curtains having been embellished with *échaugettes*, all trace of these having been destroyed by the restoration of continuous parapets; at Rhuddlan, breaks in the masonry at wall-top level show that there was originally a corbelled-out turret at the centre of each curtain.

[5] Employed at Flint in 1279 (C 47/2/2, no. 17); burgess of Flint in 1292 (E 179/242/52).

[6] Probably to be associated with the Henry of Turvey employed at Hope in 1282 (above, p. 39, note 7).

[7] Burgess of Conway before 1295 (*Caerns. Hist. Soc. Trans.* viii, p. 10); employed on Conway Town Walls in 1285-6 (E 101/485/28) and on the new tower between Conway Castle and the river in 1298 (E 101/486/9).

[8] 'Breyford', mason, was employed at Flint in 1280-1 (E 101/674/23).

[9] See Appendix III, p. 128 below.

	£	s.	d.
(x) *Ralf de Ocle*[1]			
Building the path from the sea to the castle, with the wall (enclosing it) (*pro passu de mare usque castrum et pro muro . . . . . .*)	124	15	11
(xi) *Nicholas de Newingham*[2] *and Ralf of Radwell*			
Dressing 171 corbels[3] for the two turrets on the great gate and the two turrets on the towers towards the sea, viz. 138 @ 8d. each and 33 @ 1s.	6	5	0
Battlementing curtain wall between great gate and N.E. tower	15	0	0
(xii) *John the Carpenter*[4]			
Making 423 joists at 10d. each	17	12	6
Roofing the S. tower towards the town	22	0	0
(xiii) *William the Plumber*[5]			
Covering with lead the roofs of the gatehouse and the two towers towards the sea	35	6	8
For 30 carrats of lead for these works and for roofing the kitchen, hall, chapel and pantry	10	10	0

The sum of £1710 paid for task work at Harlech in 1289, less than £800 of it represented by the foregoing extracts, is challengingly high. For the other castles the nearest comparable totals are only £893 at Conway in 1285 and £757 at Caernarvon in 1287, while in the latter year the 'task' payments for all three buildings together amount to only £1405. Most probably the explanation of Harlech's exceptional figure is to be sought in the departure to Gascony, in or about November 1287, of the master of the works, Master James of St. George.[6] Conway at the time of his going was virtually finished. At Caernarvon, where an intended first stage had probably been attained[7] and where the vastness of the conception left no possibility of its early realisation under his own or any other direction, his departure coincided, significantly enough, with a drop in expenditure from £1379 in the year ending

[1] Employed in 1286 at Conway (E 101/485/28) where he had 2 burgages (*Caerns. Hist. Soc.* viii, p. 9). He was also in the king's service in Galloway at the time of the siege of Caerlaverock in 1300 (*Liber Quot.* p. 268), and was with Master James of St. George at Linlithgow in 1302
[2] A Philip de Newenham appears among the masons at Hope in 1282 (C 47/2/3).
[3] As at Conway the corbels were used to carry the turret parapets. On the gatehouse turrets the full complement of 100 still remains in position; on the seaward turrets a few have been destroyed in the loss of the original chimney stacks.
[4] Probably John of Maghull, master carpenter at Aberystwyth in 1283 (above, p. 13, note 10); in 1290–1 bailiff of Conway, of which he was a burgess (*Caerns. Hist. Soc.* viii, p. 9, n. 22).
[5] Probably the 'Master William the Plumber of Lichfield' who was working at Flint in 1281–2 (E 101/674/23) and who may be inferred to have roofed the Great Tower there, assisted by a William of Stoke, in 1286 (C 47/3/52, no. 31); named as 'Master William, king's plumber', at Rhuddlan in 1283 (E 101/351/9).
[6] *Cal. Anc. Corr. Wales*, p. 120. The fact that his expenses (£5, not 5s. as in the *Calendar*) were authorised by William de Grandson indicates a date after the death in August 1287 of John de Bonvillars, whose place as deputy justiciar Grandson appears to have filled; John of Havering, the acting justiciar, went to the king at Bordeaux early in November and Master James may well have been of the party. If the seven years 'protection' granted to him in December 1280 (*Cal. Pat. Rolls 1272–81*, p. 418) was related to a contract of service for an equivalent period, it is worth noting that it is just at this time that it would have expired.
[7] See below, p. 85.

September 1287 to less than £160 in the fifteen months following. Harlech, however, was a project smaller in compass and altogether simpler and more compact. By the autumn of 1287 its full achievement must have been sufficiently nearly in sight to allow of the remainder of the work being left in other hands.[1] In such circumstances it would be reasonable to suppose that many of the major items paid for in 1289 may have been 'assigned' as 'tasks' by Master James before he went away; and if, as is possible, he only returned from France with the king in the latter year, we can perhaps see why some of the chief remaining operations, notably the completion of the gate towers and entire construction of the two western towers, had to be placed in the control of a master brought over from Ireland. Despite his absence, Master James remained ultimately responsible for the works at Harlech. He continued to receive his fee as master of the king's works in Wales, and his appointment in July 1290 to the constableship of the now finished castle was a fitting reward for his outstanding services.

Additional work was undertaken following the siege of the castle during the rising of 1294–5. As soon as the rebellion was over, Robert of Standen, St. George's successor as constable and one of Otto de Grandson's deputies as justiciar, built 'by order of the king a wall of stone and lime around the rock adjoining the castle and constructed a new gate-tower towards the sea'.[2] The 'way from the sea' had been built *ad tascham* by Ralf of Ocle before 1290. The new gate-tower is presumably the small water-gate at the foot of it, built perhaps in replacement of an earlier and simpler entry; the rest of the work is represented by the remains of the wall which in places still bounds the northern limits of the site. The cost of Standen's additions is unrecorded.

Two further works complete the building history of the castle. In 1306 £4 6s. 5d. was spent on a new bakehouse of 'cruck' construction (. . . *in duobus grossis lignis tortis dictis Crokkes*, each 25 feet long).[3] In 1323–4 Robert of Helpston built stone piers and arches for an elaborate bridge. There were two piers: one, 20 feet by 17 feet and standing 40 feet high, cost £20; the other measured 16 feet by 23 feet, stood 60 feet high and cost £23; the higher pier carried a gateway and the springing of two arches. The freestone required was cut at Caernarvon and transported '80 leagues' by sea to Harlech at a cost of £1 13s. 0d., while John of Audley, carpenter, was paid £10 18s. 4d. for making two turning bridges and removing into the castle the wood of the old bridge.[4]

[1] Harlech was no doubt one of the 'king's castles in Wales' for which 200 shields of the royal arms were made and sent from Bordeaux in 1287–8 ('. . . pro CC targeis factis apud Burd' de armis Regis per preceptum Regis nunciante domino Othone de Grandissono ad mittend' in Walliam ad municionem castrorum Regis ibidem, £31 1s. od.'). Such shields were commonly displayed on castle walls and battlements. Thus at Rhuddlan in 1304 100 rounded boards (*bordis curuis*) were bought to make 'targes' for Gillot's Tower and the gate towards the Clwyd, and 100 ledges (*legiis*) provided to support them (E 101/486/15). There is similar evidence from Newcastle upon Tyne (1296) and St. Briavel's (1314). A Windsor inventory of 1330 includes '29 targes bearing the arms of England' (SC 6/753/8).

[2] '. . . et misis et expensis quas predictus Robertus statim post eandem gwerram sedatam posuit per preceptum Regis in quodam muro de petra et de calce circa quandam rupem castro predicto contiguam et in quadam porta in castro predicto versus mare ad modum turris de novo construenda' (Exch. L.T.R. Memoranda Roll 76, m. 8d). For further details see A. J. Taylor, 'Harlech Castle: the dating of the Outer Enclosure', *Journ. Merioneth Hist. and Rec. Soc.* i, pp. 202 ff.).

[3] E 101/485/29, where sizes and quantities of other structural timbers, etc., are given in some detail.

[4] SC 6/1214/4.

The architectural history of Harlech Castle in the fourteenth and fifteenth centuries is not well documented. From 1332 to 1372 it was held by Sir Walter Mauny, first of the king, then of the Prince of Wales.[1] Princess Joan held it in dower from 1376 to 1385,[2] when Queen Anne appears to have taken her place.[3] When she died in 1394 the chamberlains of North Wales had consequently had no direct responsibility for the castle for many years, and when it reverted to the Crown it was placed under the control, not of the chamberlain, but of the Clerk of the King's Works.[4] From 1403 to 1409 it was in the hands of Welsh insurgents. After its recovery the prince's officers resumed control, and fairly extensive repairs costing £52 5s. 8d. were accounted for by the chamberlain in 1417–18. They included making a new bridge at the main entrance to the castle.[5] The 'great bridge' was again repaired or rebuilt in 1458–9.[6] From 1461 to 1468 the castle was held by a Lancastrian garrison, but no reference to its capture or subsequent repair occurs in the accounts of the chamberlains of North Wales.

9. CRICCIETH

Criccieth Castle is first mentioned in 1239 and probably owed its establishment to Llywelyn ap Iorwerth; from 1259, if not earlier, it was in the possession of Llywelyn ap Gruffydd and was still held by him at his death in 1282.[7] No details of its capture by Edward I's forces are known, beyond the fact that it was in English hands by 14 March 1283, from which date Henry of Greenford received wages as its constable.[8] Only a few weeks previously, on 20 January, Greenford had been paid for bringing up from Rhuddlan to Llanrwst four cartloads of the king's shields (*targias*); as this was but two days after the surrender of Dolwyddelan, some of the shields were no doubt to be used to mark that castle as the king's.[9] Greenford's early appearance thereafter at Criccieth, the next castle to fall, may point to its capture by a detachment of the king's troops sent on from Dolwyddelan by the old road across the mountains.

Criccieth is included by name amongst the castles upon works at which the keeper of the Wardrobe laid out over £9400 in the years 1283 and 1284.[10] Judging by the ratio of subsequent expenditure to that at the major castles, its share of this figure is not likely to have been large; allowance for some expenditure at this time has none

[1] *Cal. Fine Rolls* iv, p. 340; *Cal. Pat. Rolls 1343–5*, p. 113. In 1343 the castle was inspected by the prince's surveyors, who reported various defects whose repair they estimated at £50.
[2] *Cal. Pat. Rolls 1374–7*, p. 374. Richard Massey had the custody for life from 1376 until after 1391 (*Cal. Pat. Rolls 1388–92*, p. 419).
[3] SC 6/1203/2 includes an account of John de Audeley as 'surveyor of works of Harlech Castle for Queen Anne' from September 1391 to Easter 1392.   [4] *Cal. Pat. Rolls 1396–9*, p. 404.
[5] SC 6/1216/3.   [6] SC 6/1217/3; cf. E 28/30, 12 February 2 Henry V.
[7] For Criccieth's origins, see (Sir) J. E. Lloyd, 'Some notes on mediaeval Eifionydd', *Arch. Cambr.* 1905, pp. 295–302; *History of Wales* i, p. 238.
[8] E 101/4/1, mm. 9, 17, 19. For Greenford, see above, p. 41, note 6. He was succeeded at Criccieth before 6 February 1285 by William of Leybourne, who was thus the second and not as generally supposed the castle's first English constable (C 47/4/2, m. 13; cf. *Cal. Welsh Rolls*, p. 296, where 'Gul(de)ford' is a misreading for G(re)neford').   [9] For the use of 'targes', cf. above, p. 72, note 1.   [10] E 372/136, rot. 33.

the less to be made in any estimate of the extent and cost of the works as a whole. At least part of a sum of £200 recorded to have been sent from Conway to Criccieth between 7 and 12 April 1283[1] may possibly have been issued for use on the works. After 1284 expenditure is recorded as follows:

Period of Account	Wages			Task Payments			Carriage			Necessaries			Total		
	£	s.	d.	£	s.	d.	£	s.	d.	£	s.	d.	£	s.	d.
2.7.1285–25.11.1285[2]	44	3	5½	—	—	—	4	5	4	—		—	48	8	9½
21.11.1286–6.10.1287[3]	30	15	11	—	—	—	11	2	7½	2	4	5	44	2	11½
6.10.1287–29.9.1288	77	2	5½	25	0	0	15	16	7	35	4	0¼	153	3	0¾
29.9.1288–29.9.1289	17	17	2	7	0	8	12	3	10	1	13	6	38	15	2
29.9.1289–29.9.1290	1	15	10	19	14	10	—	—	—		13	4	22	4	0
29.9.1291–29.9.1292[4]	2	18	9		6	5		3	2		5	6	3	13	10
TOTALS	174	13	7	52	1	11	43	11	6½	40	0	9¼	310	7	9¾

In the absence of 'particulars' this expenditure, which even with an addition for 1283–4 is unlikely to have much exceeded £500, cannot be related with certainty to particular parts of the surviving buildings. According to the generally accepted dating these belong almost wholly to the period of the princes, only such relatively minor works as the evident heightening of the gatehouse and rebuilding of the eastern tower being assigned to the period of the English conquest.[5] But the expenditure that has to be accounted for, though small in relation to that at the major new castles, is nevertheless not negligible; it almost certainly exceeded, for example, the combined cost of the complete building of the two western towers at Harlech, each four storeys high and surmounted by a tall battlemented turret (£250),[6] and six entire sections, totalling some 700 feet in length, of Conway Town Walls (£117).[7] Nor has it been denied that there are difficulties in dating a two- or three-period castle so drastically ruined as Criccieth on the evidence of archaeological *minutiae*.[8] It may indeed be that in 1283 the English forces found themselves in possession of a castle that had been severely damaged by the retreating Welsh as well as by their own assault, and that in consequence much of the work done was concerned with the upper parts, now destroyed, of all three of the rectangular towers and with the rebuilding of sections of the outer curtains that have since disappeared. It was no doubt also necessary to build a new hall,[9] and probably an associated kitchen and chamber, in the inner courtyard.

Over £250 were spent on the castle during the reign of Edward II. In 1310–11 £12 5s. 2d. were spent on 'making a tower called Leyburn Tower by taskwork'.[10]

---

[1] E 101/351/9. Criccieth is included, with Harlech and Caernarvon, as one of the castles for the works at which supplies of iron, steel and nails were sent from Chester in 1283 and 1284 (E 101/4/6).
[2] E 372/131, rot. 26d.   [3] E 372/136, rot. 28.   [4] E 372/138, rot. 25.
[5] B. H. St. J. O'Neil, 'Criccieth Castle', *Arch. Cambr.* xcviii (1944), pp. 1–51; Hist. Mon. Comm., *Caernarvonshire* ii, pp. 59–60.   [6] Above, p. 361.   [7] Above, p. 346.   [8] O'Neil, *op. cit.*, p. 15, n. 2.
[9] Apparently at first a timber-framed structure, to support the uprights and infills of which a stone sleeper wall was inserted in 1316 (... *facienti unum murum lapideum subtus postes et parietes aule Regis*, SC 6/1211/9).
[10] SC 6/1211/4.

This tower was named after William of Leybourne, who had been appointed constable of Cricceith in 1284, but which of the towers bore his name it is difficult to say.[1] The roof of the 'upper step of the Mounfort Tower' was repaired in 1312–13.[2] The heightening of the gatehouse, previously supposed to have been one of the adaptations of the 1280's, was begun in 1315, when 29s. 8d. was expended on raising the wall of the 'twin' tower,[3] and completed in the following year at the cost of a further £22 2s. 7d. Of this latter sum £4 18s. 7d. was said to be for raising the masonry of the 'Cistern Tower' and laying new joists on it (*circa . . . cementariam de Cisterne Tour . . . exaltandam, pro gistis de novo super eandem Turrim cubandis*), £14 for cutting and preparing the timber work and £3 4s. 0d. for the lead roof.[4] That the 'twin' tower is the gatehouse admits of no doubt, and the conclusion that the 'Cistern Tower' is synonymous with it seems inescapable, despite its previous indentification as the tower on the east side of the castle.[5] As the castle's only known water supply was the spring-fed stone-lined tank (*cisterna*) in the floor of the gatehouse passage, there is no difficulty in accepting this. It follows that the 'Sister Tour' of Emeldon's Survey (1343)[6] is likewise the gatehouse, and that the 'Great Tower' (*Magna Turris*) of the Survey must be sought elsewhere: most probably it was the South-west Tower, whose dimensions are larger than those of any other in the castle including the gate-tower itself. Of the further expenditure in 1317–19 of £52 no details are preserved.[7]

Only minor defects were reported when the castle was surveyed in 1321, but by 1343 the roof of the great hall, 'Gynnetour', Leyburn Tower and Cistern Tower were all in need of repair, the estimate amounting to £96.[8] In 1404 Cricceith Castle was captured and partly demolished by Owain Glyndŵr.[9] When it was recovered no attempt was made to repair the damage, and it remained an abandoned ruin until modern repairs carried out by the late Lord Harlech and the Ministry of Works.

10. CASTELL Y BERE

Like Cricceith, Castell y Bere was a foundation of Llywelyn ab Iorwerth, being in all probability the castle in Merioneth which according to the chronicle the prince 'began to build for himself' in 1221.[10] Architectural details found when the site was explored in 1851[11] and now preserved in the National Museum of Wales are consistent with a date in the second quarter of the thirteenth century, and the ground-plan exposed in the course of clearance of the site by the Ministry of Works between 1950 and 1960 displays features which are common to other native castles in North

---

[1] The identifications suggested by O'Neil in his article in *Archaeologia Cambrensis* xcviii (1944–5) should be treated with caution.   [2] SC 6/1211/6.   [3] SC 6/1211/7.   [4] SC 6/1211/9.
[5] O'Neil, *op. cit.* p. 9.   [6] E 163/4/42.
[7] E372/164, rot. 35. Particulars of some minor works done in 1320 will, however, be found in SC 6/1287/2(4).
[8] B.M., Add. Roll 7198; P.R.O. E 163/4/42.   [9] O'Neil, *op. cit.* pp. 10–11, 258.
[10] *Brut y Tywysogion, Red Book Version*, ed. T. Jones, p. 221.   [11] *Arch. Cambr.* (1861), pp. 105–10.

Wales.[1] Edward's forces captured Bere by siege on 25 April 1283, and after the departure of the army 5 masons and 5 carpenters remained behind in the castle 'to carry out various works', apparently under the direction of Master Bertram the engineer and his assistant Simon le Counte.[2]

Castell y Bere is not specified as one of the castles on which the keeper of the Wardrobe incurred works expenditure in 1283–4, though a later record shows that he in fact did so. For, long afterwards, in 1306, Walter of Huntercombe claimed that while he was constable of Bere, i.e. between March 1284 and October 1285,[3] he had received £31 from Louth to build a new 'chamber' in the castle; he said he had had the work done, and that the account for it, which he had rendered at Caernarvon, had showed that a further 25 marks was owing to him. The reason he had not been paid was said to be that the account in question had been burned when the Welsh rebels seized Caernarvon Castle in 1295, and Richard of Abingdon who had been chamberlain at the time later testified to the truth of this.[4]

The following further expenditure was incurred on works at Bere between 1286 and 1290:[5]

Period of Account	Wages			Task Payments			Carriage			Necessaries			Total		
	£	s.	d.	£	s.	d.	£	s.	d.	£	s.	d.	£	s.	d.
29.9.1286–29.9.1287	55	11	8½	144	1	0	1	7	8½	5	14	2	206	14	7
29.9.1287–29.9.1288	8	8	8	5	0	0		14	0	5	7	8	19	10	4
29.9.1288–29.9.1289	11	2	3¾	8	13	4	6	16	3		7	6	26	19	4¾
29.9.1289–29.9.1290	5	6	9	—	—	—	1	8	1	2	6	9	9	1	7
TOTALS	80	9	5¼	157	14	4	10	6	0½	13	16	1	262	5	10¾

The high proportion assigned to the period ending Michaelmas 1287 may perhaps reflect works put in hand to meet the threat of Rhys ap Maredudd's rising in the spring and summer of that year. If so, these are likely to have included as their main item the one substantial piece of building in the surviving ruins that can be seen to be a secondary construction, namely the massive curtain walls erected to enclose the former open area and rock-cut ditch in front of the southern apsidal tower, which from its isolated and commanding position may have been the *camera* of the princes.

In Madoc's rising of 1294 the rebels laid siege to Bere and the king ordered the mounting of an expedition to relieve the castle, 'whose safety we desire with all

[1] Particularly the irregular shaped enclosure, and two apse-ended towers similar to those at Ewloe, Dinas Bran and Castell Carn Dochan.

[2] C 47/2/4, which gives many details of preparations for the siege and of masons and carpenters engaged therein. For Master Bertram see below, Appendix III. Simon le Counte, who, as *Countevilla cementarius*, is named at Hope in 1282, was paid continuously as Master Bertram's assistant from 25 March 1283 to 1 May 1284 (E 101/4/1, m. 19); he was possibly a son of the Master John le Counte named among the masons at the Tower of London between 1274 and 1277 (E 101/467/6(3) and 467/7(2)); he died and was buried at Caernarvon in October 1284 (E 101/351/9, m. 11).

[3] *Cal. Welsh Rolls*, pp. 284, 302.

[4] '. . . eo quod rotuli scaccarii in quibus hoc plenius continebatur in dicto castro de Carnaruan in guerra Wallensi combusti fuerunt' (Exch. L.T.R. Memoranda Roll 76, rots. 11 and 47).

[5] Pipe Roll 136, rot. 30.

our heart'.[1] The outcome is unknown. All that is certain is that, in contrast to the other Merioneth castles of Harlech and Criccieth, Castell y Bere makes no further appearance in the accounts.[2] When the castle well was excavated in 1952 late thirteenth-century pottery was found in association with charred timbers probably from the roof of the well-house. Thus evidence both archaeological and documentary points to the probable destruction and abandonment of the castle in 1294–5.

11. CAERNARVON

Caernarvon was the ancient centre of Gwynedd, and its occupation by Edward's forces, probably in May of 1283, following as it did on the death of Llywelyn in battle and the successive investment of his brother's remaining strongholds of Dolwyddelan, Criccieth, Bere and Dolbadarn, was the culminating act of the war. Thereafter Dafydd's own capture and execution merely gave finality and legal form to Edward's total victory over the last Welsh prince of Wales and lord of Snowdon.[3]

Caernarvon Castle was conceived and commissioned, probably even while these events were still in train, as a building which would be at once the memorial and symbol of past greatness, a worthy witness of present victory, and the viceregal centre of a new order already being planned[4] and soon to be promulgated in the Statute of Rhuddlan. Though we have no means of knowing how much still remained at this time of the ruins of Roman Segontium, the old Caernarvon, there is nevertheless evidence that the Welsh had not ceased to associate them with an age-old antiquity. Thus the twelfth-century writer of the *Hanes Gruffydd ap Cynan*, in speaking of the new castles and strong places built in Gwynedd by Earl Hugh of Chester during the reign of William Rufus, could choose to describe the castle of Arfon as being erected 'in the old city of the Emperor Constantine, son of Constans the Great'.[5] Already in 1086 Earl Hugh's cousin, Robert of Rhuddlan, was holding North Wales of King William at farm for 40 pounds,[6] and by retaining and incorporating the motte of Hugh's own castle within the walls of the greater

---

[1] Morris, *Welsh Wars*, p. 252, quoting *Parl. Writs.* i, p. 264.
[2] E 101/486/9 (1295–1301); SC 6/1211, 1212, 1213 *passim* (1304–30).
[3] *Princeps Wallie et dominus Snaudonie* was the style David used in letters issued from Llanberis (i.e. Dolbadarn) as late as 2 May 1283 (*Littere Wallie*, ed. Edwards, pp. 75, 77); E 101/351/9 has several references to the search for David, his capture, guarding and eventual execution. The precise date of the capture of Caernarvon by the English is unknown: Hugh of Leominster accounted for wages paid to knights and squires *in municione de Kaernarvon* between 1 April and 11 June 1283 (E 101/4/1), but if, as is likely, *municio* here has the sense of 'attacking force' as well as that of 'occupying garrison', the entry cannot be read as necessarily implying capture by the earlier date.
[4] Caernarvon's selection as the centre of the new administration was foreshadowed in a preliminary draft of the Statute (see W. H. Waters, 'A first draft of the Statute of Rhuddlan', *Bull. Bd. Celt. Studies* iv, 1929, pp. 345–8).
[5] *The History of Gruffydd ap Cynan*, ed. Arthur Jones (Manchester U.P. 1910), pp. 132–3; for date of composition, see *ibid.* 18–25. 'In the old city' is not strictly correct, but the difference was a matter of only 700 yards: see sketch-map showing position of Earl Hugh's motte-and-bailey in relation to the Roman fort in R. E. M. Wheeler, *Segontium and the Roman Occupation of Wales* (1924), p. 14.
[6] D.B. i, f. 269.

castle now to be begun King Edward at once perpetuated the work of the Norman forerunner and emphasised that here was not new gain but due reconquest.[1]

The king, however, must have been aware of the traditions of the remoter past also, the traditions which still linked the 'gaer in Arfon' with imperial Rome: for, whatever may have been the validity of the identification, there is no reason to doubt the veracity of the record that what was believed to be the body of Magnus Maximus, 'father of the noble emperor Constantine', was found at Caernarvon in 1283 and reburied in the church on Edward's own orders.[2] He was thus not insensitive to Caernarvon's claims to be an immemorial repository of imperial power. Nor, indeed, in his sojournings in Wales can he have failed to become acquainted with the romance of Maxen Wledig, with its tale of how long ago that same Emperor Maximus had dreamed of journeying from Rome to a land of high mountains, and coming to a river flowing into the sea, and seeing facing the land an island; and of how in his dream he had seen a great fortified city at the mouth of the river, and a great fort in the city, the fairest man ever saw, and great towers of many colours on the fort; and in its hall a chair of ivory, and the image of two eagles in gold thereon.[3] To all this the castle which Edward now began to build at the mouth of the river Seiont and opposite the island of Anglesey was plainly intended to give substance, to be both the fulfilment of the tradition and the interpretation of the dream. It is thus that Caernarvon bears an outward appearance so different, seemingly so deliberately and consciously different, from those others of its contemporaries that we have considered hitherto and to the castle at Beaumaris yet to be begun. The difference consists chiefly in the choice of polygonal instead of the more usual round towers or turrets, and in the prominent patterning of the walls with bands of differently coloured stone. For the former there were few, and for the latter no English precedents. Banded masonry was not uncommon in medieval Italian architecture, but for its use in conjunction with polygonal towers there was one celebrated precedent: the tile-laced Theodosian wall of Constantinople, the first Constantine's own city (Pl. 2b). The resemblance seems too striking to be fortuitous, and argues for the presence in Edward's circle of someone who was not merely familiar with Villehardouin's famous description, but who had seen the defences of the eastern capital with his own eyes and could instruct the architect as to the characteristics to be reproduced.[4]

[1] The Norman motte survived little altered until the late nineteenth century and is shown in a photograph of *c*. 1870 printed in *Antiquity* xxvi (1952), plate IVb; it still accounts for the high ground of the castle's upper ward and on the south and east is revetted by the glacis that supports the Edwardian curtains.

[2] *Flores Historiarum* (R.S.) iii, p. 59: 'Apud Kaernervan, corpus Maximi principis, patris imperatoris nobilis Constantini, erat inventum, et rege jubente in ecclesia honorifice collocatum.' Cf. M. P. Charlesworth, *The Lost Province* (Cardiff, 1949), pp. 27–30, where it is pointed out that Nennius had made reference to an inscribed tomb of Constantine at Segontium.

[3] *The Mabinogion*, ed. T. P. Ellis and John Lloyd (Oxford, 1929) i, pp. 133–50. For the vogue of the Mabinogion tales in the thirteenth century see J. E. Lloyd, *History of Wales* ii, p. 692; the historicity of the Maxen legend is discussed *ibid*., pp. 92–3.

[4] For the walls of Constantinople, see A. M. Schneider, 'The City-Walls of Istanbul', *Antiquity* xi (1937), pp. 461–8; for the description of the city as the Crusaders saw it in 1203, G. de Villehardouin, *La Conquête de Constantinople* (ed. Edm. Faral), Paris, 1938–9 i, p. 131. A possible eye-witness was the king's knight Sir William de Cicon, who in 1283 was constable of Rhuddlan Castle but was shortly to be appointed as first constable of Conway. His arrival in England from abroad at the end of 1276 (above, p. 50, note 6) closely coincided with the recapture by the Greeks earlier in the same year of the Cicon fief of Karystos in Euboea, where a branch of the family had become established in the early years of the Latin empire of Constantinople. For the

Nor were imperial symbols of a more obvious character omitted: for it was intended that one of the principal towers of the castle should be crowned by a triplet of turrets each bearing an eagle, and it can hardly have been accidental that the tower thus distinguished was almost certainly the one designed for the accommodation of Sir Otto de Grandson both as constable of Caernarvon and as first justiciar of Wales.[1] In such ways, it would seem that the new building was intended from the outset to recall Caernarvon's legendary past and to exemplify it in the architectural forms of the imperial power with which that past was associated; and in such terms, its builder must have been commissioned to develop the project and raise a castle that might indeed be acclaimed 'the fairest man ever saw'. Caernarvon's distinctive treatment is thus seen to have had its origin in royal policy, in the same way that policy may be supposed to have directed the choice of the city of the emperors to be the birthplace, in April 1284, of the first royal child to be born in Wales since the deaths of the two last princes of Gwynedd.[2]

The building works were probably begun early in June 1283. The first recorded reference to them is the order of 20 June, already noted in another context,[3] to transfer to Caernarvon the timber palisading previously allocated for the town defences of Rhuddlan. In administrative charge of the whole operation, which was envisaged from the first as embracing the construction of the walled town as well as of the castle, was a household knight, Sir Eustace de Hache, with his clerk John of Dunster as the first clerk of works.[4] As early as 24 June a 'task' payment of 10s. was made by Dunster for the digging needed to prepare the site of the 'new moat' (*Pro fossura et apparatu noue mote de Caernaruan*), presumably the great ditch along the north

Cicon pedigree, see F. I. Dunod de Charnage, *Mémoires pour servir à l'Histoire du Comté de Bourgogne*, Besançon 1740; for their holdings in the Levant, J. Longnon, *L'Empire Latin de Constantinople*, Paris 1949; for the capture of Karystos, Steven Runciman, *The Sicilian Vespers*, Cambridge, 1958, pp. 177, 178. It is also a most curious fact that Caernarvon, like Constantinople, should have had its own Golden Gate. As a variant name for the West or Water Gate of the walled town this now only survives in its Welsh form of Porth yr Aur, but its antiquity is testified by a reference in 1524 to the repair 'of the kee by the gate called the Gildyn yeate' (E 101/488/26); it looks as if we may have here the echo of a still earlier time when the idea of the parallelism between Edward's re-creation of 'the old city of the Emperor Constantine' in Arvon and the buildings of Constantine's own city of New Rome on the Bosphorus was a known and accepted thing.

[1] For evidence that there were originally three eagles, borne out by references of 1322 and 1330 to the 'Turris *Aquilarum*' (E 101/16/27 and 18/19), see Sir Llewelyn Turner's edn. of D. W. Pughe's *History of Caernarvon Castle* (Caernarvon, 1889), p. 19; Thomas Pennant believed that one of them was Roman and was brought by Edward from Segontium. C. L. Kingsford, 'Sir Otho de Grandison, 1238?–1328', *Trans. Royal Hist. Soc.*, 3rd Ser. iii (1909), p. 127, points out that the lords of Grandson themselves claimed to spring from an imperial stock.

[2] For a different view see Hilda Johnstone, *Edward of Carnarvon* (Manchester, 1946), pp. 16–17. But if there had not been an element of intention about the choice of Caernarvon, where the available buildings were still of a relatively temporary character, one might have supposed it would have been easier for Queen Eleanor to have remained behind at Rhuddlan, where her last child the Princess Elizabeth had been born in August 1282. Instead, the Easter festival was kept with high ceremony at Caernarvon, the king's and queen's robes being sent for specially from London (*Robinetto Cissori pro duobus haken' conductis ad cariandum robas Regis et Regine de London' usque Caernaruan pro festo Pasche*, 20s.), only sixteen days before the prince's birth.

[3] Above, p. 31, note 11.

[4] 'Eustachio de Hache, Militi, deputato custodi ultra opera et cariagia necessaria ad constructionem castri et ville de Carnaruan' (E 101/351/9; unless otherwise noted this, the keeper of the Wardrobe's 'necessaries' account, is the source used in the present paragraph; for other extracts covering the earliest phase of the Caernarvon works see J. G. Edwards, 'Edward I's Castle-building in Wales', pp. 43–5, and A. J. Taylor, 'The birth of Edward of Caernarvon and the beginnings of Caernarvon Castle', *History*, New Series xxxv, pp. 256–61). For Sir Eustace de Hache see G.E.C., *Complete Peerage* vi, pp. 387–9; the reference to John of Dunster as his clerk is in E 101/351/12.

side of the castle or *mota castri* of a later record.[1] Already by the middle of July existing houses were being demolished to make way for the bank and ditch defence of the new town, 20 men being employed for five days in taking away their timbers (*portantibus meremium de domibus prius factis de Carnaruan et prostratis pro fossat' ville ibidem faciend'*). By the following spring some of the new earthworks were ready, and in April and May 1284 payments were being made for great quantities of turf brought in from the fields and used to revet them. From 30 July 1283 onwards the excavation and earth-moving works were directed by Master Mannasser de Vaucouleurs, whom we have previously encountered at Hope, and whose notable service at Caernarvon the king rewarded in October 1284 with a gift of the where-withal to provide himself with a new cart.[2] As at Builth and Conway and elsewhere, one of the first tasks was the building of a timber stockade (*brettach'*) to enclose the whole site of the works.[3] The earliest buildings to be erected within its protection, again as at Conway, were timber-framed structures put up by 42 carpenters for the immediate housing of the king and queen: no less than eight chambers and accompanying buildings were ready to accommodate them by the time the court arrived from Conway on 12 July, and once again a lawn was prepared for the queen.[4] Amongst innumerable details recorded before the end of 1283 we read of millstones shipped from Conway for the new Caernarvon mill, of wood being felled to make a cellar, and of 25s. paid to Nigel the goldsmith for brass used in making a great *balista* in the castle. Perhaps most remarkable of all is the amount of information given about the immense quantities of timber used in the early stages of the works. The main port of shipment was Liverpool, whence even before June was out 20 shiploads had arrived at Caernarvon with cargoes assigned 'for the building of the new castle and town' (*ad constructionem castri et ville tunc inceptum*),[5] while others came in from Rhuddlan, Conway and the dismantled bridge near Bangor. Many ships were engaged, their masters hailing from places as far away as Calais and Boulogne, Dublin and Wexford, Plymouth and Swansea, Yarmouth and Hythe; the tonnage they carried—e.g. 8, 12, 14, $18\frac{1}{2}$, 24, 40, 60, 80, 150—was no less varied.[6]

As at Conway, however, the activities echoed in the 1283–4 account were merely the preliminaries and incidentals to the main task. This was the setting out of the new castle itself, the rock cutting, the foundation laying, and the first crucially formative stages of wall-and-tower building that were to set the pattern of the whole structure. There seem good grounds for supposing that for about a twelvemonth

---

[1] Below, p. 89.

[2] 'Magistro Mansero de Vaucolurs, Magistro Ordinatori fossatorum apud Carnaruan, de dono Regis ad unam carectam sibi emendam, £6 13s. 4d.' (C 47/3/21, no. 11). See Appendix C, III.

[3] Besides the palisading diverted from Rhuddlan, Perton was instructed on 23 July 1283 to send all the *bretaschias* and timber at Chester to the king at Caernarvon (*Cal. Anc. Corr. Wales*, p. 205).

[4] Improvements made in time for the royal return in the following spring included the insertion 'in the king and queen's chamber' of 9 glass windows made by Simon le Verrer of Chester.

[5] A privy seal mandate sent from Rhuddlan to Chester on 24 June instructed Perton to despatch a suitable clerk or *vallet* to Liverpool to arrange the loading of the king's timber ordered to be brought to Caernarvon and to stay and see it shipped (*Cal. Anc. Corr. Wales*, p. 205); E 101/351/9 shows that the duty was assigned to Thomas le Charun and lasted for nearly 2 months (expenses for 58 days at $4\frac{1}{2}$d. a day).

[6] It is expressed in terms of so many tuns of wine, e.g. *Ade de Dundalk, marinario, habenti in naue sua maeremium ponderis 50 doliorum vini, percipienti pro fretto nauis sue pro pondere 12d., per manus Magistri Henrici de Oxon*, 50s.

from July 1283 this first creative thrust in what was to be Caernarvon's long evolution may have been the most important of all the works then in progress in Wales. We know that for the earliest works of the castle and town of Conway sums amounting to over £5800 were issued by the keeper of the Wardrobe to their clerk, John of Candover, and their master, James of St. George, and expended between March 1283 and November 1284.[1] Unfortunately we do not know how much was similarly issued to the clerks of the Caernarvon works, John of Dunster, Hugh of Leominster[2] and Roger Cosyn[3] and spent there during the corresponding period, June 1283 to August 1284, when works payments specifically allocated to Caernarvon first begin to be recorded.[4] What, however, we do know is that Caernarvon was one of the works that benefited during those early months from the sum of nearly £9500 issued by the keeper of the Wardrobe for Welsh castle works generally. And, just as it has been previously suggested that Conway with its separately recorded allocation of £5800 is unlikely to have drawn heavily on the general total also,[5] so now it is suggested that Caernarvon, with no similar record of an allocation of its own, is likely to have absorbed by far the biggest single share of the omnibus figure, a share at least proportionate to the specified outlay on Conway. This at any rate is what we should expect in view of the scale of the building and the importance attached to the castle as the future residency of the new justiciar, who besides being the king's lieutenant was also one of his closest personal friends.[6] Moreover it is a fact that on the one occasion in this early period when evidence has survived to allow us to draw a direct comparison between moneys used for the works of the two castles individually, Caernarvon's allotment was as high if not higher than Conway's.[7] It would therefore seem not unreasonable to postulate a sum of at least £5000 as Caernarvon's share of the £9414 expended by the keeper of the Wardrobe on the Welsh castles in 1282 –1284.[8] That preparations for building in stone were being made as early as

[1] Above, p. 49.

[2] Named as having been *ultra operarios apud Caernaruan et Herdelawe* (Harlech) in the 11th and 12th years, i.e. for part of 1283 and 1284 (E 101/351/9); also as *clericus noster operacionum nostrarum Snaudon*' (C 62/67).

[3] Named as *clerico existenti ultra operarios apud Caernaruan* in the 12th year, i.e. for part of 1284.

[4] Enrolled totals of Caernarvon expenditure between 1284 and 1301 are tabulated in Edwards, 'Castle-building', p. 71.

[5] Above, p. 49, note 9.

[6] For the closeness of the relationship and interesting comment on Otto's special concern with the Welsh castle works, see Kingsford, *op. cit.*, pp. 129 and 133. In the absence of any formal record of the grant of the constableship of Caernarvon to Otto it must be presumed to have been one of the matters the king 'more fully enjoined upon him by word of mouth' when he left him to keep the land of Wales in 1284 (*Cal. Close Rolls 1279–88*, p. 273); it was not until May 1290, when he was about to leave England for Acre, that he 'surrendered to the king the castle of Karnarvon, which the king had committed to him' (*Cal. Welsh Rolls*, p. 325). That the grant of the castle to John of Havering in 1284 (*ibid.* p. 291) was made in his capacity as Otto's deputy is clear from the fact that Otto himself received £100 a year 'for keeping the castle of Caernarvon' (E 101/352/12, p. 8ᵛ) in addition to the £1000 a year paid him 'for keeping the land of Wales' (E 101/352/1).

[7] Writs of privy seal dated Leominster, 8 December 1283, authorising William of Perton to issue 200 marks (£133 6s. 8d.) for Conway and £200 for Caernarvon, the latter figure to include any advance issued by Perton on his own initiative (*Cal. Anc. Corr. Wales*, p. 206); this was only five days after the return to court of Sir John de Bonvillars from visiting Wales *ad supervidendum castra domini Regis ibidem* (E 101/351/12; and see above, p. 342 note 1), which would suggest that the sums authorised may reflect assessments he had brought back as to the needs of the respective works.

[8] A figure of £3000–£3750 is suggested in the account of the castle by the Royal Commission on Ancient Monuments (*Caernarvons. Inventory* ii, p. 129); but the greater scale of the castle, as well as what must have been the relatively much higher cost of transporting and dressing its building stone, make it difficult to believe that Caernarvon's initial expenditure could have been so much the lower of the two.

August 1283 is indicated by orders issued on the 13th of that month for the sheriff of Shropshire and Staffordshire to provide 30 good masons and cause them to come to Caernarvon without delay,[1] while grounds are given below[2] for believing that Caernarvon may likewise have been the destination of 20 Yorkshire masons who about this time were posted in the first instance to Rhuddlan; by the following April shipments of stone were already being made from the quarries in Anglesey.[3] It is the greatest misfortune that so few details of this vast outlay of castle-building expenditure should have come down to us, for it is all stated to have been wholly assigned to workmen's wages and all in all, in terms of modern labour costs, must have represented something of the order of £5,000,000.[4] In the case of Caernarvon the loss is doubly tantalising, because here we also lack anything corresponding to the 'particulars' which survive for both Conway and Harlech, and are thus left entirely without information as to the identity of the principal masters employed in the formative stages of the work.

With the commencement of the enrolled accounts of the chamberlains of North Wales in August 1284, direct though still all too limited information as to the progress of the works becomes available.[5] The first account, running from 21 August 1284 to 18 November 1285, records expenditure of £3040 5s. 6½d.[6] At least £1818, or more than half of the total, was devoted to the construction of the town wall, the commencement of work on which during the week beginning Monday 9 October 1284 may conceivably have been timed to coincide with a formal presentation by the king of the borough's charter;[7] £1575 of this was accounted for by wages paid directly to masons, quarrymen, smiths and labourers, £151 by payment for a part of the wall (the Exchequer Gate perhaps?)[8] built under contract, and £92 for necessaries and tools purchased 'for the works of the wall round the town'; in addition a high proportion of £440 recorded as being spent between January and October 1285 on bringing stone, freestone, coal and timber to Caernarvon by water should no doubt also be reckoned against the cost of the wall, bringing the cost of the whole structure to something like a round figure of £2100. The form in which the accounts have survived in the two cases precludes a detailed comparison of costs with those for the Conway wall, but having regard to the much smaller extent of the Caernarvon

[1] *Cal. Chancery Warrants*, p. 12.   [2] P. 95.
[3] E 101/351/9, 'pro uno batello conducto ad querend' petram apud Angles' et ducend' apud Carnaruan per quinque vices, pro qualibet vice tam pro fretto nauis eiusdem batelli quam pro cariagio et discariagio eiusdem, 3s. 6d.,—17s. 6d.').
[4] A round multiple of 100 was based on the ratio of a thirteenth-century building craftsman's average wage of 4d. for an average 10-hour day to a 1952 building trades worker's prevailing rate of 3s. 4d. an hour, or 400d. for a 10-hour day, and was necessarily approximate. The amounts today (1985) would be at least five times as great, and the figure of £5m can be regarded only as the minimum modern equivalent of the £9414 spent on castle works in 1282-4.
[5] E 372/131, rot. 26, 136 rot. 28, 138 rot. 25, tabulated in Edwards, 'Castle-building', p. 71.
[6] Including a small item for watching services omitted from the figures given by Edwards, *loc. cit.*, but accepted as a legitimate works charge originally.
[7] The Flint, Rhuddlan, Conway and Caernarvon charters were witnessed at Flint on 8 September (*Cal. Welsh Rolls*, p. 289); the king returned to Caernarvon on 10-11 October (*Cal. Pat. Rolls 1281-92*, p. 136); the grant of Master James of St. George's life pension of 3s. a day, together with one of 1s. a day to Master Richard of Chester, was enrolled at Caernarvon ten days later (*op. cit.* p. 137); the first reference to individual burgesses of the new borough is in June 1285 (*op. cit.* p. 177).
[8] Cf. the estimated cost of building the Mill Gate at Conway *ad tascham*, above, p. 54; purchase of cloth for the exchequer 'over the gate of Caernarvon' was accounted for by Robert of Belvoir as chamberlain, i.e. in or after January 1286 (*Cal. Anc. Corr. Wales*, p. 121).

enclosure (10 lengths, 8 towers, 2 twin-towered gateways, as against Conway's corresponding 26, 22 and 3) there is no reason to suppose it may not have been substantially completed for the amount stated and within the thirteen months ending in November 1285. At the same time much work was undertaken on the construction of the quay and on forming the King's Pool (*stagnum Regis*) or mill-pond to the east of the town, over £121 being spent on workmen's wages for this latter operation between May and November 1285. The quay appears at first to have been an embankment of earth and timber, the carpenters and sawyers working on it between 21 August and 4 March 1285 receiving wages amounting to £76; the earth was obtained by completing the excavation of the ditch on the north and east of the castle (*fossato castri, fossato contra castrum, fossato circa castrum*) begun in the previous year, close on £70 being spent on carting the material from the one site to the other; a further £22 was spent on the purchase and carriage of timber.

With regard to the castle itself, it seems clear that this must have been the source from which, from 9 October 1284 onwards, the requisite labour was made available for building the town wall. In other words the masons and quarriers whose wages of £1575 appear for the next year in relation to that work on the chamberlain's account, will be those who had hitherto been employed upon the work of the castle under the financial and administrative control of the keeper of the Wardrobe. Mason work at the castle must thus already have reached a level at which building operations could be safely and conveniently suspended while the emphasis was shifted to the enclosing of the town. The prolonged pause involved is likely to have left its mark in the structure, and horizontal changes of masonry approximating to the lower passage floor levels in the south and east fronts of the castle may well bear witness to it and indicate the general height to which the building had risen by the time the masons were withdrawn to begin work on the town wall; this, when built, brought the whole combined outer circuit of castle and town defence up to an approximately common level.[1] Meanwhile the castle works did not come wholly to a standstill. No less than £319 was paid in wages to the *fossatores* for their labours in excavating material from the castle ditch for use at the quay, and more than £27 to plumbers, smiths, watchmen, etc. Stone, timber and sand were brought by land for use at the castle at a cost of £140 between January and October 1285, and a like proportion of the £440 expended on materials brought by water is probably assignable to the castle also. Amongst the latter we know that 14 loads of lead were bought and sent to Caernarvon by the constable of Bristol Castle at a cost of £31 7s. 8d. 'to roof our buildings in the same castle'.[2] Taken in conjunction with a note of the purchase of boards, shingles, nails and glass windows, also in 1285, this suggests that some part of the castle, possibly the three lower storeys of the Eagle Tower, was nearing completion.

In each of the two succeeding years, ending September 1286 and 1287 respectively,

---

[1] The structural development of the castle is examined at length in Hist. Mon. Comm. *Caerns. Inv.* ii, pp. 127–30; indications of the first general pause are described *op. cit.* p. 129. A projecting stone set on the north-west face of the North-east Tower (*Antiquity* xxvi, Plate III(*a*)) was to give a siting point for the alignment of the adjacent length of the town wall (similar siting stones were set on each of the towers of the northern stretch of Conway town walls, also building in 1284): it therefore precedes the building of the town wall and indicates a minimum height to which the outward walls at the eastern end of the castle had been carried by October 1284.   [2] Liberate Roll 62.

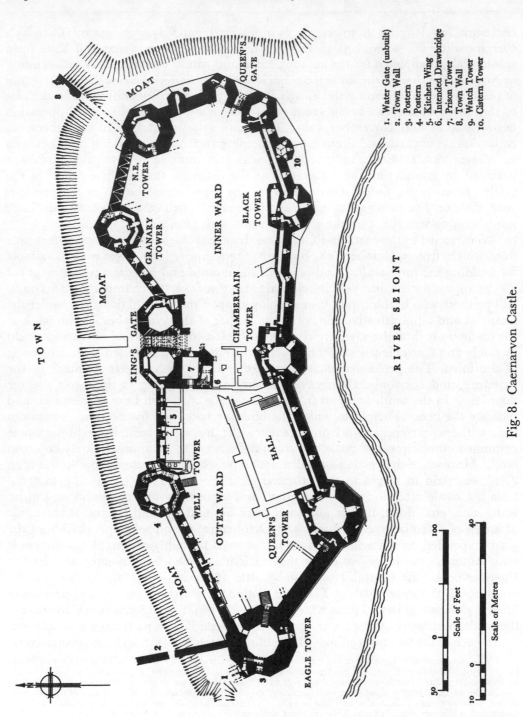

Fig. 8. Caernarvon Castle.

1. Water Gate (unbuilt)
2. Town Wall
3. Postern
4. Postern
5. Kitchen Wing
6. Intended Drawbridge
7. Prison Tower
8. Town Wall
9. Watch Tower
10. Cistern Tower

TOWN

MOAT

MOAT

MOAT

MOAT

QUEEN'S GATE

N.E. TOWER

GRANARY TOWER

INNER WARD

BLACK TOWER

KING'S GATE

CHAMBERLAIN TOWER

WELL TOWER

OUTER WARD

HALL

QUEEN'S TOWER

EAGLE TOWER

RIVER SEIONT

Scale of Feet

Scale of Metres

wage payments still amounted to over £1000; the pace was slackening, however, and at £1773 and £1379 the recorded annual totals of expenditure were very far below the 1284–5 outlay of £3040. Thereafter the scale of the work dropped to an altogether lower level, accounting for totals of only £156 in 1288, £170 in 1289,[1] £50 in 1290 and £42 in 1292. If we accept the £5000 suggested as a reasonable estimate of expenditure on the Wardrobe 'wages' account for 1283–4, and include £300 for the Caernarvon items specified on the Wardrobe 'necessaries' account for the same period,[2] the total outlay for the 9¼ years June 1283 to September 1292 amounts to a round figure of £12,000, rather above £2,000 of which has to be assigned to the construction of the town wall, quay and mill-pool, and probably the justiciar's court-house in the south-west angle of the town also.

In a building where work was to be resumed on a major scale some three years later, and was thereafter to continue intermittently for more than thirty years, it is exceedingly difficult to say how much of what we still see had actually been achieved in these first nine seasons. The evidence of the structure itself, interpreted in the light of an original memorandum describing how part of it stood in February 1296,[3] suggests that: (i) the whole external southern façade and east end of the castle from the Eagle Tower round to the North-east Tower had been built at least to the floor levels of the lower wall passages (i.e. to an average height of some 30 feet above external ground level), and perhaps, if we are right in relating the changes of masonry near the courtyard floors of the southern towers to a first suspension of work in 1284–5, to a rather higher level (which in the north-east sector would include all the banded exterior faces of the Queen's Gate and North-east Tower); (ii) the Eagle Tower had been built as an occupiable apartment of three storeys left temporarily roofed in at that level; and (iii) at least a start had been made on the four northern towers and curtains fronting the castle ditch, though the walls may not yet have reached the heights of 12 feet to 24 feet at which they were said to stand at the beginning of the 1296 season.

At the end of September 1294 the Welsh rose in general revolt. Caernarvon was captured and sacked and in the six months it remained in their hands the rebels did grave damage both to the castle and the walls. The testimony of the chroniclers that they not only set fire to the town and castle 'so recently most lavishly built by the king' but also set about demolishing the town walls[4] is borne out by clear references in the records to the rebuilding of what they had thrown down as well as to irreparable losses resulting from the fire.[5] In terms of the king's works the rising

---

[1] During this year, according to *Cal. Pat. Rolls 1281–92*, p. 302, Otto's brother and deputy, William de Grandson, and his fellow knight Sir Richard Fukeram, stayed in Wales 'to fortify' the castle. The wording of the original, however, *qui in municione castri Regis de Karnaruan moratur* (Pat. 16 Ed. I., m.4), need imply nothing more active than residence with the garrison establishment. A letter from Grandson to Burnel, the chancellor, dated to the last ten days of May 1290 and printed in *Cal. Anc. Corr. Wales*, pp. 118–21, shows that one of his functions was to audit and approve a miscellaneous account of the chamberlain.

[2] E 101/351/9.   [3] Below, p. 381.

[4] 'Villam et castrum de Karnervan combusserunt' (Trevet, *Annales*, ed. Eng. Hist. Soc., 1845, p. 333; '. . . ceperuntque castrum de Karnarwan quod rex noster dudum sumptuosissime construxerat, demolientes muros . . .' (*Chron. Walter of Guisborough*, Camden Third Series, 1957, p. 250).

[5] 'In reparaciones et emendaciones muri ville Regis de Carnaruan per Wallenses in guerra Wallie prostrati' (Pipe Roll 146, rot. 24; Adam of Wettenhall gave formal testimony that the rolls and memoranda and everything he had pertaining to his office as comptroller to Robert of Belvoir (chamberlain 1286–95) had been

had a twofold outcome, leading first to the initiation, in April 1295, of an entirely new castle at Beaumaris in Anglesey, and secondly to the resumption, from June 1295 onwards, of major building at Caernarvon itself. The castle at Beaumaris, as we shall see later, was entrusted to Master James of St. George. At Caernarvon both the wall repairs and the ensuing phase of constructional work on the castle were entrusted to Master Walter of Hereford, a mason previously employed by the king at Vale Royal Abbey in Cheshire.[1]

The 'works of Caernarvon' began on Sunday 5 June 1295, with 70 masons led by Richard of Radwell[2] and Richard of Weldon,[3] 18 quarriers employed under John of Wytgraue (Whitegreave, Staffs.) and John of Lewes in a quarry across the water in Anglesey, 8 carpenters led by Peter of Derby and Philip of Ewyas,[4] 8 smiths led by Ralf Smith and William of Wirral, 175 labourers from Warwickshire led by Adam of Overton and William Butler, with Stephen Clerk and 8 other 'clerks' as gangers and keepers of the workmen (*vintenariis custodientibus operarios*): altogether 288 men with a total week's wage of £23 5s. 11d.[5] More masons were needed, however, and before the end of the week orders were sent to the justiciar of Chester 'to cause 100 suitable masons experienced in such work as the king is engaged upon at Kaernaruan to be chosen in the town of Chester and in other parts within his bailiwick, and to cause them to come with their tools to Kaernaruan without delay, there to do what Edmund the king's brother shall enjoin upon them, as the king needs masons for his works there at once'.[6] Five days later, on 16 June, Edmund of Lancaster sent an urgent request from Caernarvon that the chancellor 'should with all speed procure from all parts up to 100 stonecutters to come to Caernarvon to Master Watier de Ambresbury, who is there to repair the castle and walls of the town'.[7] As a result of these steps the combined strength of masons and quarriers increased in the third week (June 19–26) to 136 and in the fourth (June 26–July 3) to 212. For most of the period of the detailed account,[8] which does not continue after 10 July, the men engaged (apart of course from the quarriers in Anglesey) are simply described as working 'at Caernarvon'; but from the second week onwards the 8 to 15 carpenters are explicitly stated to be working 'in the castle', in the fourth week the 160 masons are said to be working 'in the castle', and in the fifth and last week 140 labourers are described as working 'in the castle and elsewhere' (*in castro et alibi in opere*). No mention is made of the town walls, and it is probable that the whole of the work accounted for in the first four weeks, when there was a steady upward curve of

burned by the Welsh (Exch. K.R. Mem.Roll 70, rot. 53*d*); Belvoir made a similar claim (*ibid.*); in 1309 Richard of Abingdon (chamberlain 1284–6) testified that the Welsh had burned many exchequer rolls in Caernarvon Castle (Exch. L.T.R. Mem. Roll 79, rot. 73); and cf. above, p. 76, note 4.

[1] For his previous career, see above p. 205.   [2] See above, p. 70, note 1.
[3] Cf. Thomas of Weldon, employed at Rockingham Castle in 1276.
[4] The latter had formerly been employed at Vale Royal, where he is named among the masons (*Ledger-Book*, pp. 201, 207, 208, 212) and probably also at Flint.
[5] E 101/486/8. The account is badly preserved and the figures here given amend those printed in Salzman, *Building in England*, p. 35. Others named in the course of the four succeeding weeks are: *Masons*: Richard de Kinton (Kineton, Warw.), Richard de Skerington (Sherington, Bucks.) and William of Norton; *Quarriers*: John de Douwebrigg (Doveridge, Derbys.): *Labourers (fossatores)*: Richard of Flintham and William of Aslockton (both S. Notts.), Nicholas of Radway (adjoins Kineton, Warw.); *Clerk*: Walter.
[6] *Cal. Close Rolls 1288–96*, p. 413.
[7] *Cal. Anc. Corr. Wales*, p. 150; as in the past, they were to be recruited through the sheriffs.
[8] E 101/486/8.

expenditure (£23 5s. 11d., £24 4s. 3d., £35 0s. 7d., £45 7s. 7d.), was in fact castle work.[1] Only in the fifth week, ending 10 July, when the labour force shows a sudden drop from 549 to 266 and expenditure falls correspondingly to £21 18s. 7d., can we reasonably infer a withdrawal of manpower to the wall repairs; it is from 10 July, moreover, that the enrolled account dates their commencement.[2] The total recorded expenditure from 5 June to 10 July was £170 10s. 4½d., of which £149 16s. 11d. was for wages.

Masons and quarriers need smiths to shape and sharpen their tools. On 30 June instructions were issued at Conway for the chancellor to send letters for the recruitment of 'six good master smiths, each with five or six good yeomen, in the county of Chester or Stafford, so that there shall be 30 or 40 in all, and send them to Caernarvon to Master Walter of Hereford, keeper of the works there'.[3] Three days later the selected men were already on their way, with their expenses paid and a boat hired to take their gear from Chester to Caernarvon.[4] On 10 July letters of protection for one year were ordered to be prepared for Master Walter of Hereford, 'staying on the king's service in Wales',[5] and on the 17th arrangements were made for the immediate delivery from the Exchequer at Westminster to Hugh of Leominster, appointed chamberlain of North Wales as from 10 July,[6] of the necessary financial provision, viz. £100 for the maintenance of the quay at Caernarvon, £400 forthwith for the works of Caernarvon, and £200 per month in August, September and October.[7]

It is clear that for military reasons very high importance was attached to the prosecution of the works at both Beaumaris and Caernarvon. On 1 October a privy seal letter was addressed jointly to their respective masters, James of St. George and Walter of Hereford, stressing that the king was determined that both castles should be made defensible by Martinmas and ordering every available workman to be used to achieve this.[8] Statements were to be sent to London by return showing to what extent the king's aim was likely to be realised and how much additional money would be required to meet it. At the end of January 1296, when every conceivable means was being sought to provide revenue for the coming military demonstration against Scotland, it was ruled that the works in Wales and the painting of the king's chambers at Westminster should be the only permitted exceptions to a general embargo on

[1] The particulars are in respect of wages only, which for the five weeks 5 June–10 July amount to £149 16s. 11d.; details of a balance of £20 13s. 5½d. assignable to carriage and materials are lost, but may be inferred from the total figure of £170 10s. 4½d. expended by Walter of Winchester, as *clericus operacionum Wallie* (E 36/202, f. 42), on the 'repair and amendment of the walls of the town of Caernarvon' (E 372/158, rot. 48). Consistently with this description Edwards, 'Castle-building', p. 71, assigns the whole wages expenditure to 'Town Wall'; but this is difficult to reconcile with the explicit references to masons, carpenters and labourers working *in castro*.

[2] E 372/146, rot. 24, where the dates given point to a similar overlap or change-over period when the wall works were finishing, with the wall account terminating on 18 September and the castle account opening on 11 September.   [3] *Cal. Chancery Warrants*, p. 63.

[4] E 101/14/7. The six masters were Thomas and William of Cheadle, William of Stone, John of Preston (? Preston on the Hill, Cheshire), Simon of Hooton and Alexander Page; with their 30 *valletti* they were allowed 40s. for their journey from Chester to Caernarvon.   [5] *Cal. Chancery Warrants*, p. 63.

[6] *Ibid.*, p. 132; he also discharged the functions of clerk of the works (*assignatus ad soluciones faciendas operariis apud Carnaruan operantibus*, E 36/202, f. 40) as he had previously done in 1283–4.

[7] *Cal. Chancery Warrants*, p. 75.

[8] E 159/69, rot. 38; for full text, see A. J. Taylor, 'Building at Caernarvon and Beaumaris in 1295–6', *Bull.Bd. Celt. Studies* xv, p. 62.

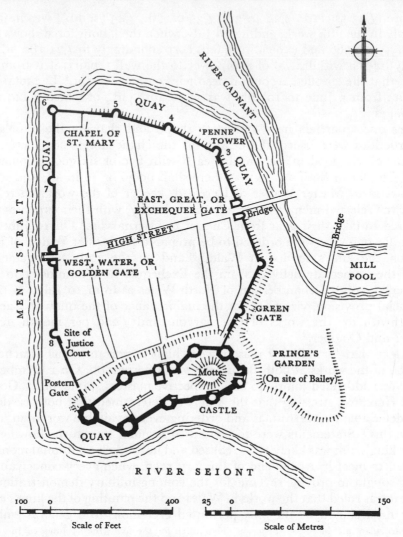

Fig. 9. The Town and Castle of Caernarvon in the early fourteenth century.

royal building operations.[1] Further funds would be sent as quickly as possible after the state of the works had been ascertained,[2] and on 13 February letters were again sent to Master James and Master Walter asking them to supply such information as would enable the Exchequer to make suitable provision for the season that was now imminent.[3]

In their reply, addressed from Conway on 25 February,[4] Walter of Hereford

---

[1] Instructions on behalf of the king by Sir John of Droxford, keeper of the Wardrobe, to the deputy treasurer, barons and chamberlains of the Exchequer: . . . *derechef de cesser de totes maneres de oueraignes sanue le oueraigne de Gales e les peintures des chaumbres de Wesmoster deuisees* (E 159/69, rot.11d). This reference is due to the kindness of Dr. E. B. Fryde and Mr. C. N. Johns.

[2] *Ibid.* rot. 11d.   [3] *Ibid.* rot. 24; text in Taylor, *loc. cit.* p. 63.

[4] E 101/5/18, no. 11, printed *in extenso* in Edwards, 'Castle-building', pp. 79–80.

and Hugh of Leominster reported that at Caernarvon the repairs to the town walls had been completed (*totaliter expediti*) by 10 September; the recorded cost, £1024 18s. 11½d.,[1] is more than half that of their original construction and suggests that considerable sections of the walls had had to be built afresh. The next eleven weeks, from 10 September to 27 November, had been devoted to further building work at the castle. Thenceforward, during the thirteen weeks up to the time of writing the masons were engaged in dressing freestone, and a fluctuating number of carpenters, smiths, quarriers, minor workmen and boatmen in fetching stone in readiness for the coming season and other specific tasks. Many materials needed for the works had been bought, as had a variety of provisions for the victualling of the castle. For all this, as well as for the wages of the garrisons at both Caernarvon and Criccieth, only £100 had been received since the beginning of November, with the result that payments were now more than £400 in arrear. Nevertheless they had decided, after having already put off the start for lack of money, to resume work on the walls of the castle on 26 February with every man they could get, and they would be glad to learn the Exchequer's pleasure as to this and other matters. The letter concludes with a memorandum to the effect that rather more than half of the north curtain wall fronting the castle ditch (*circa motam castri*) had by this time already been carried up to a height of 24 feet, with the remainder standing to 12 feet and a beginning also made on the four northern towers. The near certainty of considerable mason work having been in progress at the castle for five weeks in the summer as well as from September to November makes it likely that a relatively higher proportion of the structures so defined may belong to 1295, and a correspondingly smaller proportion to the period before 1292, than has hitherto been supposed.[2] Between 7 August and 18 December 1295 £17 19s. 9d. had also been expended on rebuilding the damaged or destroyed 'king's houses beside the castle'.[3]

The king's determination that nothing should be allowed to interfere with the works was reiterated on 7 May, when the Barons of the Exchequer were instructed by word of mouth on the king's behalf to see to it that the operations at the two castles should not fail for want of funds and that the auditing of the accounts should be done with the same end in view.[4] In the outcome £4393 13s. 7¼d., or an average

---

[1] E 372/146, rot. 24, giving 18 September as the terminal date.

[2] *Antiquity* xxvi, pp. 25–28, where the interpretation of the 1296 memorandum is discussed in detail; and Hist. Mon. Comm. *Caernarvonshire* ii, p. 129.

[3] E 372/146. Particulars of this expenditure are preserved on E 101/486/9, showing the principal items to have been as follows: (i) *The King's Hall*, i.e. the hall of the justiciar's court, standing on ground north of the Eagle Tower now occupied by the Assize Court and former County Gaol, £4 12s. 4d. (including £2 16s. 8d. to Master John of London, carpenter, for preparing the main timbers in the woods near Conway, 5s. for building the gable in stone, 14s. 2d. for straw thatching for the hall and its two chambers); (ii) *The Knights' Chamber* (*Camera Militum*), 16s. 3d. (11s. 0d. for timber, 5s. 3d. for thatch); (iii) *Kitchen, Bakehouse and Stable*, £4 13s. 5d.; (iv) *Granary*, timber and shingles for which were brought from Beddgelert (Bethkelard), £3 13s. 9d.; (v) *Hand-mill*, built at task by Henry de Ryhull, 11s. 8d.; (vi) *The King's Garden*, dug and hedged (*defossato et sepe claudendo*) for 24s.; (vii) *Buildings at Exchequer Gate* (*pro domibus Porte Scaccarii de Carnaruan*), evidently likewise of timber, £1 17s. 4d.

[4] E 159/69, rot. 85d. 'Ces sunt les paroles qe Richard de Lue dit as Barouns del Escheker de par le Rey al Escheker a Loundres le Lundi procheyn apres la seinte Croyz: . . . . . . Item qe le Lieutenant le Tresorier e les Chaumberleins aident par leur descrecion de partie de deniers pur les oueraignes de Carnaruan e de Beaumareys issint qe les oueraignes ne se defacent. E qe a plustost qe om peut bonement oyr la counte, facent venir les Clers et les autres qi sunt chargees des oueraignes auantdites meme (?) qe les oueraignes ne se defacent'. Thanks are due to Dr. E. B. Fryde and Mr. C. N. Johns for drawing attention to this passage also.

of nearly £1100 a year, was spent specifically on the castle works at Caernarvon between 11 September 1295 and 28 September 1299, and much progress, probably on both the north and south fronts together, must have been achieved.[1] Then, for the five years 1299–1304, major constructional work entirely ceased. Its suspension at this time can only be related to a withdrawal of labour and resources to meet the calls of the Scottish war, and a chance record of the payment of wages to Master Walter of Hereford at Carlisle in October 1300[2] may well reflect his having left Caernarvon for the north at least a year earlier. Between 1299 and 1301 only minor expenditure is recorded,[3] from November 1301 to Michaelmas 1304 none at all. In all, a further £5678 had been added since June 1295 to the suggested total of £12,000 for the period 1283–92.

In the first half of 1304 Master Walter was still actively engaged in Scotland. But by the end of September the works at Caernarvon were resumed under his direction as *magister singularum operacionum constructionis*, with Henry of Ellerton as his *submagister*.[4] Their wages were 7s. and 4s. a week respectively, and both lost no time in petitioning for the payment of substantial debts still due to them for their work on the castle in the years before 1301.[5] Two other petitions presented by Master Walter to the prince's council at Kennington in 1305 refer to the progress and administration of the works. To the first, requesting that the lord prince would appoint and ordain that these should be prosecuted more quickly, it was merely answered that the prince would take counsel; to the second, asking that Walter should be allowed to hold his free court for his workmen at the castle, as he had done under both the king and the prince hitherto, assent was given, and with it confirmation of his right to redress breaches of their contracts and agreements.[6]

The first request is explained clearly enough by the figures of expenditure. In the full year from Michaelmas 1304 to Michaelmas 1305 the total outlay at Caernarvon amounted to only £699 8s. 9d.,[7] compared with an average of nearly

---

[1] For the apportionment between the two sides, see Hist. Mon. Comm., *Caernarvonshire* ii, p. 130: if, however, as has been suggested above (p. 81, n. 8), the earliest expenditure (and consequently the initial progress on the southern façade) was appreciably greater than the figure adopted by the Commission, a higher proportion of the 1295–99 expenditure will have been applied to the works of the north front.

[2] E 101/357/5.

[3] The largest item, £44 4s. 10½d., was for the erection of a new barricade round the unfinished castle (*in operacionibus unius noui gerioli faciend' circa castrum*); £6 os. 2d. was paid for the wages and materials of a smith (Reginald of Bath) and his mate for work done in the castle between September 1300 and May 1301; and 28s. wages were paid to a mason left in charge for 12 weeks after the other masons had ceased work. Also £38 11s. od. was spent between April 1298 and November 1301 on constructing a quay on the west side of the town (*inter murum ville et aquam maris*); this was a timber work, directed by Master Adam of Chellington and Roger of Eccleshall, Thomas Woodwall (*Wodewale*) and Richard of Rowley, carpenters, and nine named *operarii minuti* (particulars on E 101/486/11).

[4] E 101/486/1, on which, unless otherwise noted, this and the following paragraphs are based. These are the 'particulars' of payments made for the works of the castle by Thomas of Asthall, chamberlain of North Wales, in the 52 weeks from 4 October 1304 to 26 September 1305.

[5] SC 8/275/13741 and 13748. Ellerton claimed £30 15s. 5d. *pur les oueraignes qil ad fet en le Chastel de Karnaruan taunt com le dist Chastel fut en la mayn le Rey*, i.e. before 7 February 1301, the date of the bestowal of the principality of Wales on Edward of Caernarvon, and Hereford asked similarly for £131 6s. 0½d.; a third petition (13747) was from 'Henry de Aynesham, maceoun', for £19 5s. 0¼d. due to him from the time when he was engaged on the works. All were ordered to be paid forthwith (Maitland, *Memoranda de Parliamento*, pp. 147, 208, 209, and Liberate Roll 33 Edward I, C 62/81). A grant of property in the West Riding by Master Henry de Eynesham, mason, to Monk Bretton Priory in 1322 is printed in *Yorks. Arch. Soc., Record Series* cvii, p. 121.

[6] *Record of Caernarvon* (Rec. Comm., 1838), p. 220; cf. Hilda Johnstone, *Edward of Carnarvon*, pp. 96, 97.

[7] SC 6/1211/2.

£1100 a year between 1295 and 1299. At the peak of the season, in July 1305, the maximum number of masons employed at the castle was 75 and of minor workmen 117, numbers which are seen in perspective when we recall the 225 masons and 550 labourers recorded at Harlech in July 1286[1] or the 400 masons and 2000 labourers required at Beaumaris in 1296.[2] Even taking all categories together, only 150 to 200 men were employed in the summer and 70 to 100 in the winter months. Until mid-November, and again from May to September 1305, stone was being regularly brought from three quarries by water, viz. the 'black stone' (*petra nigra*) quarry, the freestone quarry and the quarry for lime-burning stone, hired boats as well as the prince's barge and the prince's 'long boat' being used for the purpose. The quarriers stopped work only at Christmas and Whitsun and for ten weeks from late February to early May; the mason-layers (*cubitores*) were laid off most of the time from mid-November to the end of April, but except for the Christmas and Whitsun holidays at least 22 (more generally 30 to 40) mason-dressers were employed in every week of the year. At the beginning of May 1305, just when the numbers on the pay-roll are about to rise in a fortnight from 74 to 176, 7d. is spent on buying a horn for the works, no doubt to be used morning and evening in sounding out the regulation hours of labour.[3]

The accounts throw no direct light on where in particular in the castle the masons were working, but 'task' payments of £22 to Philip the carpenter for joisting a three-storey tower called 'Beleestre',[4] with a chapel on each of its floors, and of £20 to Matthew of Silkstone, carpenter, for the joisting of two other towers, each with chapels, show that the building of the inward-facing parts of the three southern towers was one of the operations being undertaken. At a cost of 20s. Matthew made a crane (*ingenium*) for hoisting the joists and other heavy timber and 8 lbs. of grease were bought to lubricate it. It may be that the 7½ loads of lead, costing £17 10s. 0d., to fetch which the prince's long-boat made two separate 16-day return voyages to Chester in 1305, were for the roofing of these towers. Two timber bridges provided for the castle at this time for £8 6s. 8d. were possibly the drawbridges of the two main gates.[5] Meanwhile other works were in progress without the walls, principally the construction of a dam to the millpond (*caput Stagni*), the building of a swans' nest in the middle of it (*nidum cignorum in medio eiusdem stagni*) and the making of a sluice for the new mill under the bridge outside the East Gate (*sclusa pro nouo molendino sub ponte extra portam de Caernaruan*). These were treated as a separate operation, with their own clerk of works (William of Knapton) and viewer (John of Pilley), and were in hand all through the year 1304–5 with David *fossator* as *magister operacionis stagni* and

[1] E 101/485/26.   [2] E 101/5/18, no. 11.

[3] A hornblower (*sufflator cornu*) was paid 1d. a week at Caernarvon from Easter to 15 July and Michaelmas to Christmas 1319, and again from 6 January to 13 July 1320, *pro sufflacione* (*alias* pulsacione) *cornu operacionum* (E 101/486/29 and 487/2).

[4] A satisfactory explanation of this name has yet to be advanced. As with Gillot's Tower at Rhuddlan and others elsewhere (Appendix C, III, 7 and note), the possibility cannot be overlooked of its being the name of a mason-contractor associated with the tower's original building. Contemporary forms, viz. Belester (1279) and Belestre (1306), for Bellister, near Haltwhistle, Northumberland, point to the most likely toponymic; John Beleyter, named with others concerned in shipping stone from Anglesey to Harlech in 1286 (E 101/485/27) could well have been the mason-contractor.

[5] SC 6/1211/2, printed *Bull. Bd. Celt. Studies* i, pp. 256–75.

Roger of Eccleshall as *magister nidi cignorum*; total costs were £65 9s. 7¾d.[1] Consultation with the prince's Council is suggested by the payment of expenses to a man going from Caernarvon to London *pro quibusdam negociis Principis dictas operaciones tangentibus*.

In the following year, Michaelmas 1305 to Michaelmas 1306, perhaps as a result of Master Walter's petition, expenditure was a little higher—£707 12s. 8¼d. on the castle, and £38 1s. 11¼d. on other works. In contrast, however, to the complete 52-week 'particulars' for 1304–5, all that has survived of its successor is a single fragment giving these totals on the dorse, and, on the face, part of the wages paid to masons and layers during the 31st week, i.e. that beginning on Sunday 1 May 1306.[2] Enough of the paragraph remains to show that including the master and sub-master as many as 65 masons and not fewer than 9 layers were then employed at the castle, with another 4 layers engaged on 'the bridge'.[3] For the seasons of 1307, 1308 and 1309 no 'particulars' have survived at all; but there is no reason to suppose expenditure, though probably diminishing, was not still continuous.[4] When yearly figures become available again in the 1310 season those for Caernarvon amount to £469.[5] From this it would seem fair to allow for sums of the order of £600, £550 and £500 having been spent in the three intervening years, giving a total of approximately £3100 for the five years 1304 to 1309.

Early in 1309 Walter of Hereford died, and on 13 February the king sent letters to Master Henry of Ellerton referring to this and expressing the strongest interest in the furtherance of the works and his full confidence in Master Henry's loyalty and ability; he was therefore directed to carry on until such time as Asthall, the chamberlain, should be able to come to North Wales to explain the king's wishes more fully by word of mouth and fittingly reward him for his devoted services.[6] As the king was informed that several skilled masons and layers would be needed in the coming season, the sheriff of Bedford was being ordered to send to Master Henry at Caernarvon four reportedly experienced men (*in huiusmodi ministerio probatos ut dicitur*), namely Adam de Rodewell,[7] Walter Yep and Richard and John Broy.[8] The

[1] Detailed particulars are on E 101/486/16.
[2] E 101/683/15, recently added from unidentified miscellanea.
[3] Probably the bridge leading to the Exchequer Gate; they are named as *cubitores Pontis*, with *Pons* as a separate marginal heading. A fragment of the chamberlain's account for 34 Edward I (E 101/533/7) also refers to locks made at this time for the gate of a new postern in the town wall between the castle and the justice court.
[4] On the Pipe Roll of 5 Edward III (E 372/176, rot. 56d.ij) Thomas of Asthall, chamberlain of North Wales from Michaelmas 1302 to October 1312, accounted for £2040 13s. 3¾d. expended in the 34th and 35th years of Edward I and 1st year of Edward II (i.e. Michaelmas 1305 to Michaelmas 1307) ('on the purchase of divers necessaries and the wages of workmen for the works of the castles of Caernarvon, Beaumaris, Conway, Criccieth and Harlech; and on the Pipe Roll of 4 Edward III (E 372/175, rot. 44d) for £3383 10s. 3¼d. expended on the works of the same castles in the 1st to 5th years of Edward II (i.e. Michaelmas 1307 to Michaelmas 1312). Against the combined figure of £5424 3s. 7d. only £2961 15s. 6½d. is covered by surviving 'particulars', distributed as follows: (*a*) Caernarvon 1305–6. £745 14s. 7½d.; 1309–12, £1423 12s. 10d. (SC 6/1211/3–5); (*b*) Beaumaris 1309–12, £557 14s. 0¼d. (*ib.*); (*c*) Conway 1309–12, £15 16s. 5d. (*ib.*); (*d*) Criccieth 1309–12, £43 14s. 11d. (*ib.*); (*e*) Harlech 1309–12, £175 2s. 8¾d. (*ib.*). The drop in Caernarvon expenditure from some £745 in 1305–6 to a suggested £600 in 1306–7, with a continuing fall to £440 in 1310–11, may perhaps have been due to Walter of Hereford having taken some of the king's masons and carpenters to London in 1306 to build the new quire of the Greyfriars' church there for the queen (above, pp. 205–6).   [5] SC 6/1211/3.
[6] E 368/79, rot. 111, printed in full in *Caerns. Hist. Soc. Trans.* ix (1948), p. 17.
[7] For Adam, Nicholas and Richard of Radwell, see above, p. 362, n. 1.
[8] ? from Brogborough (Broybury, 1363) in Ridgmont, Beds.

accompanying writ to the sheriff orders him to distrain the four to find sureties that they will set out for North Wales on the king's service and remain in the works at Caernarvon, where they are to be employed according to their seniority and experience.

During Ellerton's first three full years as master of the works, from Michaelmas 1309 to Michaelmas 1312, a further £1424 was expended.[1] The major proportion, £1290, was devoted to the castle; no details have survived, but most of the work in progress at this time is likely to have been on the northern towers and curtains. The chamberlain's accounts do, however, give some particulars of what was being done on the town wall and elsewhere. There were payments in each year, amounting in all to some £14, *circa operacionem* (or *emendacionem*) *giri muri ville*, perhaps to be interpreted as a renewal of the wall-walk; the next wall-tower northwards from the Exchequer Gate, described variously as the *turris Penne*[2] and *turris iuxta scaccarium versus mare*, was rebuilt and roofed at a cost of £8 18s. 11d.; £13 13s. 1d. was spent on further work to do with the new mill-pond; and £1 7s. 2½d. was applied to the reconstruction of the fore-gate which eighteenth-century engravings show standing on the bridge in front of the Exchequer Gate proper.[3] A claim for £2 18s. 8d. spent on providing a toll-house nearby was disallowed. A new stable, bakery and brewhouse were made for the Justice Court at a cost of £7. The next two years, to Michaelmas 1314, saw expenditure of £853 11s. 9d. 'on the works of some of the towers and walls of the castle',[4] with further totals of £468 7s. 11d. to January 1316[5] and £530 13s. 1d. to May 1317[6] respectively. A main operation at this time was the addition of the uppermost storey to the Eagle Tower possibly as yet with only the first of its three turrets.[7]

It appears that the works were now carried on, apart from one short interruption in the summer of 1319, until at least October 1327 and not as was previously thought only until 1323.[8] These ten years saw a further outlay of

[1] SC 6/1211/3-5. Ellerton's appointment as Hereford's successor at Caernarvon at the full daily rate of 2s. followed soon after the latter's death; in 1318 his duties were extended and he became 'master and surveyor' of the king's works at all castles in North Wales.

[2] An isolated payment in April 1317 for 40 boards bought *pro Pennetour cooperienda* (E 101/486/29, m.29) probably refers to this tower and not, as has been supposed, to one of the towers of the castle, where apart from this reference the name would be unknown. As with the *tour de Beleestre* and 'Gillot's Tower' at Rhuddlan (above p. 383, n.4), the name is probably that of the tower's builder or rebuilder: a mason named John Penne was a principal contractor with John Francis for the supply of freestone for Beaumaris in 1296 (E 372/158, rot. 48).

[3] In 1310 it is *quedam porta extra magnam portam ville*, in 1311 *quedam Barbecana lapidea extra portam ibidem pro munitione eiusdem.*   [4] E 372/172, rot. 6d, m.2.   [5] *Ibid.*

[6] SC 6/1211/7-9; in addition, £79 was spent in 1316-17 on works on the quay, and £41 on the mill pool and the town bridge.

[7] For details, based on E 101/486/29, see C. R. Peers, 'Caernarvon Castle', *Cymmrodorion Trans.* (1915-16), pp. 15-17. The 1316-17 account's mention of the affixing of a single stone eagle suggests a single turret; when the three turrets were complete there was an eagle on each.

[8] For the figures for the years 1304-23 as known hitherto from the chamberlains' accounts in the SC 6 and E 101 series, see J. G. Edwards, 'Castle-building' (1946), pp. 50-52. Except for the 1304-5 figure of £633 19s. 4¼d., which is for castle works only, all the sums given are inclusive of expenditure on specified works in the town; adding the figure of £65 9s. 7¾d. recorded for such expenditure in 1304-5, we obtain £3563 14s. 8¼d. as the previously known total for all Caernarvon works after 1301. This covered five periods, viz. (*a*) November 1301 to October 1304, (*b*) Michaelmas 1305 to Michaelmas 1309, (*c*) Michaelmas 1312 to Michaelmas 1315, (*d*) May 1317 to Easter 1319 and (*e*) June 1323 onwards, in respect of which either the accounts were missing or the works themselves suspended. The intermittent character of the extant accounts raised, as the author of 'Castle-building' suggested, 'the reasonable presumption that if accounts had been

£2546[1] which, combined with the figures previously given,[2] advances the estimated total cost of the Caernarvon operations to approximately £26,590. If, in addition, we allocate to Caernarvon a major share of the £714 spent on North Wales castle works during the chamberlaincy of Nicholas Acton in 1329–30,[3] and allow for the probability of something having also been spent in the intervening season of 1328 by John Chiverdon, who died in 1329 without having rendered any account, the final figure will not be less than £27,000.

Week-by-week particulars which survive for parts of the years 1316–17[4] and 1319–20[5] give a picture of the resources and effort deployed in the later stages of building. During the 30 weeks from 4 October 1316 to 1 May 1317 average monthly expenditure was £48; the labour force averaged 97, never (apart from Christmas week when all but the master, clerk of works and foreman were laid off) dropping below 73 and once reaching 115. The average number of masons was 24, with the proportion fairly evenly divided between bankers (*cementarii*) and layers (*cubitores*); during January and February the layers were employed at task rates as dressers (*batrarii*), working 1100 to 1500 feet of stone a week between them at six feet a penny. Generally there were also 35 to 40 quarrymen at work in three quarries, one on the outskirts of Caernarvon (*ad finem ville*), one near Bangor referred to variously as 'Aberputh' (Aberpwll) or 'Pont Meney', and one in Anglesey.[6] The masons' names

extant in an unbroken series, we might well have found that the work had been proceeding—equally quietly but also equally steadily—during the years that are now blank to us'. The rightness of this suggestion has since been substantiated through Dr. R. A. Brown's discovery, on the Pipe Rolls of 12 Edward II (164) and 1–5 Edward III (172–6), of the enrolled 'remainders' of the accounts of Thomas Asthall (chamberlain 1302–12), Thomas of Chedworth (1312–15), Edward Dynieton (1317–19), Robert Power (1323–27) and Nicholas Acton (1329–30), and through the recent identification of E 101/683/15 as part of Asthall's missing works payments roll for 1305–6. The result is that '(*a*)' above remains a gap, making it almost certain that no work to speak of was done at Caernarvon while Walter of Hereford was in Scotland; for '(*b*)' we have the recorded figure of £745 14s. 7½d. and estimated figures of £600, £550 and £500 for 1306–9 allowable within Asthall's now known average annual expenditure of £807 on all North Wales castle works in those three years; for '(*c*)' we have recorded total figures of £854 4s. 10d. for 1312–14 and £482 10s. 6½d. for 1314–15; for '(*d*)' we have a recorded total figure of £663 10s. 8¼d.; and for '(*e*)' the figures are (i) June 1323 to Michaelmas 1324, £365 9s. 0¼d. (£230 castle, £135 quay); (ii) Michaelmas 1324 to Michaelmas 1325, £238 18s. 8¼d.; (iii) Michaelmas 1325 to Michaelmas 1326, £297 17s. 6d.; and (iv) Michaelmas 1326 to October 1327, £117 3s. 3d. (castle £79, quay £38). It would also seem reasonable to allow Caernarvon not less than £250 of the £714 0s. 2¼d. recorded as spent on the works of the castles by Nicholas Acton between March 1329 and August 1330. His successor Adam Withiford spent a further £51 17s. 5½d. at Caernarvon between 16 September 1330 and 15 March 1331 (E 101/487/8), while an account for £144 15s. 1d. spent by John Ellerker between February and September 1339 (E101/487/10) could well imply that the works had continued at least intermittently until that year. Taken together, these additional sums, recorded and estimated, raise the earlier figure of £3564 for the post-1301 combined works at Caernarvon to one of £9471 16s. 6½d. For the interruption of work at the castle in the summer of 1319, see n. 7, p. 387 below; for delays in the settlement of the chamberlains' accounts at Westminster and in their enrolment on the Pipe Rolls, see W. H. Waters, *The Edwardian Settlement of North Wales in its administrative and legal aspects 1284–1343* (Cardiff, 1935), pp. 66–67, 76–77.

[1] £246 of this is assigned to the quay works and £12 to the bridge, leaving an annual average of some £228 spent on the works of the castle.

[2] 1283–92, £12,000; 1295–1301, £5678; 1304–9, £3100; 1309–12, £1412; 1312–17, £1853.

[3] E 372/175, rot. 50*d*, m. ii.

[4] E 101/486/29.   [5] E 101/487/2.

[6] Not only stone but also timber, mostly from the Conway valley, was still coming to Caernarvon by water. In February 1317 £4 was paid for shipping 198 pieces of assorted timber from the hall and other buildings of the late Prince Llywelyn at Aberffraw in Anglesey for general use in the works (*in grosso pro operacionibus*) of the castle. At the same time a 20-ton boat, fully equipped (*cum toto attilio*), called the *St. Mary* of Caernarvon, was bought for £10 'for the works of Caernarvon castle and for fetching supplies for the castles generally from Ireland and elsewhere'.

are given, and insofar as they may be taken to throw light on the districts from which their holders were drawn it is of interest to record them here.[1] The presence of at least four Yorkshire names,[2] coupled with the connection of an earlier Caernarvon master, Henry of Eynsham, with Monk Bretton,[3] suggests the possibility that the 20 Yorkshire masons sent to the king at Rhuddlan in the summer of 1283[4] may have been allocated collectively to Caernarvon and that a nucleus of them may have maintained a continuing association with the works there; the further fact that three of them are East Riding names, one of which, Cottingwith, actually marches with an Ellerton that lies equidistant from the great church buildings of York, Pocklington and Howden and was itself the seat of a Gilbertine priory, points to this as being perhaps the likeliest of the many possible Ellertons and Allertons to have been Master Henry's own place of origin or previous employment.[5]

During the next period for which we have detailed figures, October 1319 to Michaelmas 1320, average monthly expenditure was only £21 and operations were evidently on a generally reduced scale; the maximum labour force in any one week was 51.[6] For reasons explained below,[7] all work on the castle had been in suspense

---

[1] The following list corrects and amplifies that given in *Ars Quatuor Coronatorum* xlv (1932), Appendix I: John de Acton (? Cheshire), Henry and Walter de Carwardyn (Carden, Ch.), John de Chedd (unidentified), Ranulf de Chesterton (u.), John de Cotyngwk (Cottingwith, Yorks. E.R.), Hugh de Crauene (Craven, Yorks. W.R.), Richard de Crichurch (? Christchurch Priory, Hants.), Henry de Elreton (? Ellerton, Yorks. E.R.), Henry de Euredon (Everdon, Northants.), Richard Franceis, Adam de Gerston (? Garston, Lancs.), John and Robert de Grene, John Hauel or Hawel, William de Hayford (Heyford, Oxon.), Peter de Hereford, John and Walter de Hope (u.), John de Ingham (Lincs.), Walter de Karleton (Carlton, u.), Thomas de Leye (u.), Roger de Neth (Neath Abbey, S. Wales), Thomas de Runston (nr. Caerwent, S. Wales), William de Sauvey (Seavy, Yorks. E.R.), William de Scaldebek (? Yorks.), John de Skeyuok (Ysceifiog, Flints.), Robert de Staneston (u.), Henry, John and Robert de Stoke (prob. Staffs.), Adam de Stone (Staffs.), Nicholas de Swynemor (Swine Moor, Yorks. E.R.), Gilbert de Teruyn (Tarvin, Ch.), Thomas and William de Vaureal (Vale Royal Abbey, Ch.), John de Walyngford (Wallingford, Berks.), Robert de Weldon (Northants.), Simon de Wynde (? Windsor, Berks.), Peter de Wynwyk (Winwick, Northants.).
[2] Craven, Cottingwith, Swine Moor and Seavy; Carlton and Scaldebek may also be Yorkshire names.
[3] Above, p. 90, n. 6.   [4] C 62/59.
[5] *The Place-Names of the East Riding of Yorkshire*, Eng. Place-Name Soc. xiv, pp. 237, 238 and 248.
[6] Five of the nine mortar-carriers (*falconarii*) were women; cf. Builth, above, p. 5.
[7] Early in 1318 William of Shalford, burgess of Caernarvon, clerk of the castle works, petitioned the king for consent to rehabilitate the then derelict west gate of the town (*turris nostra que vocatur Watergate . . . in maximum periculum ville nostre predicte confracta*) and to construct in it a residence for his own use (*quod ipse in eadem turri domos pro ut sibi expedire viderit sumptibus suis propriis construere et dictas domos inhabitare ac libere tenere possit*); after inquisition by 12 burgesses of Caernarvon, Conway and Beaumaris permission was given (C 143 [*Inq. ad quod damnum*]/129/19). The sequel appears from a memorandum presented to the king's Council at York by the chamberlain of North Wales, Henry of Shireoaks, on 5 November 1319 (SC 6/1287/2, no. 8). Shireoaks said that when he came to Caernarvon to take up his appointment in the previous June, Shalford, was then about to build his house ('*primes quant le dit Chambrelent vint as dites parties le dit William auoit aucunes maisons affaire en la ville de Caernarvan*'); and that in order to get the work done Shalford simply diverted money, men and materials from the works of the castles, those of Beaumaris as well as Caernarvon apparently being brought to a halt ('*le dit William . . . fist les Ministres de la dite tere retenir les deniers le Roi en lours meins, sicome il fount uncore, par quei les oueraignes des chasteux cesserent pleinement, tantque ses dites maisons furent parfaites de meryn et de piere taillie por les dites oueraignes des ouerours et des ustiz le Roi et dautres necessoires ordinetes por les dites oueraignes le Roi, auxi bien a Beaumareys come a Caernaruan, a grant damage notre seigneur le Roi et arrerissement de ses oueraignes auantdites*'). We thus have the exact date, July—October 1319, for the early fourteenth-century alterations to the Water Gate (cf. plan in Hist. Mon. Comm. *Caernarvonshire* ii, p. 153) as well as the correct explanation of the hitherto puzzling cessation of the castle works at the height of a summer building season. Shalford pushed his quarrel with Shireoaks to the extreme of violence: '*le dit Chambrelent ad este souent enprisonez par le dit William de Shaldeford, ses gentz vileinement batuz et defolez en son office et en son houstel et il meismes et ses dites gentz menacez destre murdrez, coupez les bras et les chambes et lors corps ruez uttre les murs de la ville, issint que le dit Chambrelent ne nul des soens puis queux vindrent celes parties porroient le Roi seruir sicome ils deuereient, a damage et despit notre seigneur le Roi qi le dit Chambrelent enuora illeoqs por li bien et loiaument seruir*'. This personal feud was a manifestation of a more far-reaching administrative

since 14 July 1319, and for the next thirteen weeks the only wages entered on the account were Master Henry of Ellerton's own;[1] during the interval one Walter de Kauk executed a contract for digging and dressing 175 blocks, each 2 feet 6 inches by 1 foot 6 inches by 1 foot, for which he received £1 6s. 3d.,[2] but no other payments are recorded. The works were resumed on 8 October and a week or two later a certain John of Clitheroe travelled to various parts of the country to try to attract masons to Caernarvon for the king's service;[3] as, however, in the ensuing months the number of *cementarii* and *cubitores* together never exceeded 18, ten at least of whom were at Caernarvon in 1316–17 and were therefore not newcomers, the tour may not have achieved the results expected of it.[4] The main, if not the only work now being done at the castle was on the upper part of the King's Gate and its flanking towers. In March and April 1320 Thomas the smith wrought five iron cramps 'for reinforcing and holding together (*simultenendis et afforciandis*) the great stones over the gate carved as a statue of the king (*ad ymaginem Regis talliatis*)'; then, as now, the stonelayers were using string (*una pecia de lynecorde*) for setting out their courses. Another smith, Hova by name, made a dozen iron spikes to prevent birds sitting on the statue's head (*xij pikes ferri pro defensione capitis ymaginis Regis ne aues supersedeant*). In May and June Thomas and Hova were engaged together in making hooks, bars and staples for the large upper windows of the towers.[5] Thirty miles away, in Nant-Conway, there was much activity felling and preparing timber for the great hall over the gate; in June Walter 'le Bordhewer' of Llanrwst was paid 20s. for 12 big joists, each measuring 18 feet by 2 feet by 1 foot 6 inches, and in August a further 33 were provided; in October came 5 huge beams (*grossis wyures*) and in December 6 more, each 32 feet long and 18 inches square, with yet another 72 joists, 8 wall-posts (*corbelle*) and 3 laces (*laquei*). It would seem that here would have been much of the material needed to frame both floor and roof of the six-bay room which the

conflict between justiciar and chamberlain, for which see Waters, *op. cit.*, chapter III, esp. pp. 54–7. The works account shows that shortly after Shireoaks complained to the Council Shalford was removed from the clerkship, the three last entries of his pay, though subsequently allowed, being struck through and cancelled *quia sine warranto;* on 6 January 1320 William Menerel, who up till then frequently appears as a main contractor for supplying stone from the 'black' quarry, was appointed by the justiciar as 'clerk to supervise the king's works at Caernarvon in the place of William of Shalford' (E 101/487/2).

[1] E 101/486/29, mm. 31–33.   [2] E 101/487/2.
[3] 'Johanni de Clederowe eunti in diversis partibus Anglie pro cementar' lucrand' ad opus Regis, viz. pro operacionibus castri predicti, per xij dies, capienti per diem ij.d., xxiiij.d.'
[4] Names appearing for the first time in the 1319–20 account are Richard de Bech (? Waterbeach, Cambs.), Thomas de Blackburn (Lancs.), Geoffrey de Carlisle (Cumberland), John de Charthous (? Hinton Charterhouse, Som.), William de Elreton (? Ellerton, Yorks. E.R.), Robert and William de Helpeston (Helpston, Northants.), Ralf de Keleby (Keelby, Lincs.), Geoffrey de Lichfield (Staffs.), Roger de Mackeszey (Maxey, adj. Helpston, Northants.), Madoc ap Ior, William de Rosse (Ross on Wye, Herefs.), Henry le Rotour, John de Wemme (Wem. Salop.), Roger le Zocke. No less than seven of these, viz. Beach, Ellerton, R. and W. Helpston, Maxey, Ross and le Rotour, are already named in the two weeks preceding John of Clitheroe's tour.
[5] The account also throws interesting light on other tasks undertaken by the smiths; they not only forged the masons' hammers and punches and ground and sharpened their chisels, but also made the little metal drawing instruments used by the master of the works, receiving a bonus because of the fine craftsmanship involved (. . . *operanti diversa minuta ferramenta necessaria ad opus Magistri operacionum per ij dies, capienti per diem quia subtil' vj.d.*); they also worked the metal parts required for the great crane or windlass built for the works (*pro magno ingenio constructo pro operacionibus . . . vocato Wyndeys*), the inclusion amongst which of *lxxx de grosso spik'* possibly points to their providing it with cogs for geared wheels (cf. the *garlewynd* used for raising timber at Ludgershall in 1342, Salzman, *Building in England*, p. 325); the machine had a lifting chain or hawser (*una cabula vocata Hauceour*) controlled by a guyrope (*Gwyrop pro cabla magni ingenii operum gubernanda*).

completed north wall shows to have been intended; yet the hall was never finished, and when Sir William Emeldon came to survey the state of the castle in 1343 no one could say what it would cost to do the work that was still wanting.[1]

It was not only the hall above the gate, but also the gate itself and a tower adjoining it, which the surveyors of 1343 reported had been begun and left unfinished, showing that when work finally came to a halt in about 1330 the gatehouse as a whole must have been structurally in much the state in which it remains at the present day.[2] The 'gate towards the prince's garden', the present Queen's Gate, was evidently also much as we see it now, with the whole rearward part of its flanking towers and intended inner gateway and portcullis barely begun; here also there was still so much to be built that no estimate of cost could be ventured. Even the Eagle Tower, otherwise finished, still required the completion of five chimneys at an estimated price of £3 apiece. The Well Tower, too, still required much work: four storeys had been ordained but only three built, so that the woodwork of these was rotten for lack of proper roofing. The surveyors said it would cost £200 to build the stonework of the additional storey (including, presumably, the tower's surmounting turret) and provide stone arches which they recommended for supporting the requisite new floors; carpenters' services would amount to £12, plumbers' to £2.[3] Other repairs estimated to amount in all to £46 10s. were recommended for the Tour de Baner (Queen's Tower), Eagle Tower, Gyntour (? North-east Tower), Blaketour (? Black Tower) and Prisontour (? Granary Tower).[4]

The surveyors reported on the towers they could see, finished and unfinished. Thus they mention the one of the two rearward towers of the King's Gate, that to the west, because it was already partly built, but say nothing of that to the east because though plainly intended it had not been started. Unfortunately they also make no reference to buildings against the curtains, and we have no certain knowledge of how far these had or had not been built in the later stages of the work. That the Great Hall in the outer ward was completed seems clear from sixteenth-century references to its repair;[5] similarly it is clear that the kitchens were built, though possibly not to the scale indicated by the springing arch stones on their northern wall. On the other hand the buildings in the inner ward, for which provision was made by bondings and dripstones on the northern curtains and towers, were almost certainly never begun, and the question arises as to the purpose they are likely to have been intended to serve.

The answer can perhaps be sought in a comparison of the plan of Caernarvon with that of Conway.[6] Making all necessary allowances for physical differences of site,

[1] Exch. Misc., 4/42. The Caernarvon section of the survey is printed in Peers, 'Caernarvon Castle', pp. 70–71.
[2] 'Item quod porta castri predicti, et quedam turris iuncta dicte porte, ac quedam aula supra portam predictam, que sunt incepte et non perfecte, quarum perfectionem nesciunt estimare' (*ibid*).
[3] It was not until 1891–2 that the top of the Well Tower was completed and the turret built at a cost of £600; see Sir Llewelyn Turner, *Thirty-one Years' Work in the Repair of Carnarvon Castle; what can be done with fourpences* (Caernarvon, 1902), pp. 13–14.
[4] Of the single towers only the Granary Tower has a deep basement with access from above by trap-door, as in the Prison Towers at Conway and Harlech.
[5] E.g. E 101/488/26 and 28.   [6] Figs. 6 and 8.

for the presence at Caernarvon of the pre-existing motte, and for the main water approach being in the one case from the east and in the other from the west, there is a striking similarity in the arrangement of the two castles, a similarity close enough indeed to argue that their general plan was the product of a single mind. One detects in the disposition of the main components of Caernarvon a nearly exact repetition of the layout of corresponding features at Conway. Thus each castle has an outer ward towards the west, containing on its south side the Great Hall and on its north the kitchen wing; in each case this outer ward is entered from the west; and as at Conway the western towers on either side of the gate are most likely to have comprised the residence of the constable, so, as has been suggested earlier, the Eagle Tower over the corresponding gate at Caernarvon (where it had to be a water gate) was similarly planned to house the constable: here, however, he was to be none other than Sir Otto de Grandson, first justiciar of the new regime, and his tower house was designed on a scale appropriate to his viceregal rank, with direct connection (provided for but never built) to the Justice Court across the ditch to the north. As at Conway, so at Caernarvon the outer ward's eastern side was planned to subserve the needs of the inner ward beyond it: at Conway the dividing wall is a fully battlemented curtain pierced by a narrow passage and fronted by a rock-out ditch and drawbridge, virtually cutting the castle in two to give isolation and security to the royal apartments to the east; at Caernarvon the same division was planned and provision was still being made to give effect to it in the 1320's in what must have been the last piece of permanent building to be begun in the courtyard, namely the so-called 'Prison Tower' at the back of the King's Gate. For this tower was designed to form the north side of a passage which was to be even more strongly defended than its Conway counterpart, by double portcullises as well as by the corresponding drawbridge, against approach from the western and outer to the eastern and inner ward of the castle. This can only mean that at Caernarvon as at Conway the eastern ward was planned as the real heart of the whole construction and was always intended—and still intended so long as building work went on— ultimately to contain the private apartments of the king or prince. Thus it was for these royal chambers that the junctions and roof-lines were left on the walls from the King's Gate to the North-east Tower, and it was to give them direct access from outside the walled town that the high Queen's Gate was built: as the counterpart of the high entrance to the inner ward from the Water Gate at Conway, it was perhaps conceived in relation to an approach planned to lead up from a tidal inlet of the Seiont at the mouth of the east castle ditch. The outstanding point of difference between the two plans lies in the position of the King's Gate at Caernarvon which, though the main gate from within the borough, does not as at Conway lead primarily into the outer ward. But nor, if the projected arrangement had been completed, would it have led directly into the inner ward either, but into a vaulted gate-hall placed centrally between the two and in all probability to be heavily barred against both. No doubt there were considered to be advantages in the case of the capital of the principality in having a great ceremonial entrance from within the walled town giving access—with suitable safeguards—to either half of the castle; and nowhere in

Britain were the safeguards of a castle entrance so highly developed as those of the King's Gate at Caernarvon.

Lacking only the top and turret of the Well Tower and the full intended height of the curtain to the west of it, the castle must by 1330 at latest have been to all outward appearance a finished building; and if we allow for weathering, and the loss of finials and eagles and sculptured heads, it must already have worn very much the aspect that meets the eye to-day. Its builders had indeed achieved 'as fair a castle as man ever saw', for Caernarvon has architectural qualities which rank it high among the medieval castles of Europe. Because of this it is important, before we conclude this account of its building, to examine afresh what evidence there may be for attributing its design to an identifiable officer of the works. At one time it was customary to regard Master Walter of Hereford as the architect.[1] This ascription rested in the last resort on the misdating to 1288-9 of the 'particulars' of 1304-5, in which Master Walter is described as 'master of all the works of construction', as indeed he then was.[2] When, however, we come to review his claims to have controlled the earliest, formative stage of the work and thus conceivably to have been the master principally responsible for the whole plan and architectural treatment of the castle, even indirect documentary evidence is wanting. There are, it is true, considerations not cited before which could be held to favour such a claim. One is the fact that Hugh of Leominster, who besides being chamberlain was clerk of works at Caernarvon in the years from 1295, had also acted as clerk of works there in 1283-4; in a neatly ordered world this would suggest that Hereford might similarly have been master mason at the earlier date. But against this has to be set the fact that Hugh of Leominster's earlier clerkship extended to the Harlech as well as the Caernarvon works, and no one has ever supposed the master of the former to have been any other than Master James of St. George. A second consideration is that, just as in July 1295 Master Walter received letters of protection for one year 'staying on the king's service in Wales',[3] so in September 1283 he received a year's protection which can likewise only have related to some Welsh assignment.[4] But this is not to say that the earlier service was also necessarily to do with Caernarvon: it is more likely to have been related to the king's re-erection of Conway Abbey.[5] Nowhere in the surviving records, and one thinks especially of the very detailed Wardrobe 'necessaries' rolls for 1283-4,[6] is there any reference, direct or indirect, to connect Hereford with the works of the castles, although as we have already seen one of these records provides much circumstantial information about the beginnings of Caernarvon. Nor before 1295 is he described otherwise than as *magister cementarius abbatie Vallis Regalis* or *magister operis cementarie ecclesie abbath' de Valle Regali* in any record yet examined.[7] It is true that the wages rolls corresponding to the large Wardrobe works payments of 1282-4 are lost and that, could they be recovered, they might be found

[1] E.g. Peers, 'Caernarvon Castle' (1916), p. 7; W. Douglas Simpson in *Trans. Anglesey Ant. Soc.* (1928), p. 35; J. H. Harvey in *B.A.A. Journ.* (1941), p. 24; and the present writer in *Trans. Caerns. Hist. Soc.* (1948), p. 16 and tentatively in *E.H.R.* (1950), pp. 441-2.
[2] See *Antiquity* xxvi, p. 33, n. 31.   [3] *Cal. Chancery Warrants*, p. 63.
[4] *Cal. Pat. Rolls 1281-92*, p. 75.   [5] Above, p. 47, n. 7.
[6] E 101/3/29 and 351/9.   [7] E.g. C 47/4/5, f. 42ᵛ; E 101/352/24; Plea Roll 106, m. 22*d*.

to show a temporary association of Hereford with the works at Caernarvon; nevertheless the only ground for entertaining such a hypothesis remains the fact of his having been appointed to direct those works when they were resumed in very different circumstances eleven or twelve years later at a time when the king was no longer directly concerned with the building of Vale Royal. And that such an association, had it occurred, could only have been temporary, is shown by the fact that as soon as the chamberlain's accounts begin the works of Caernarvon, just as much as those of Conway, Criccieth and Harlech, are the king's works in Wales for the direction of which wages and robes were issued to Master James of St. George alone.[1]

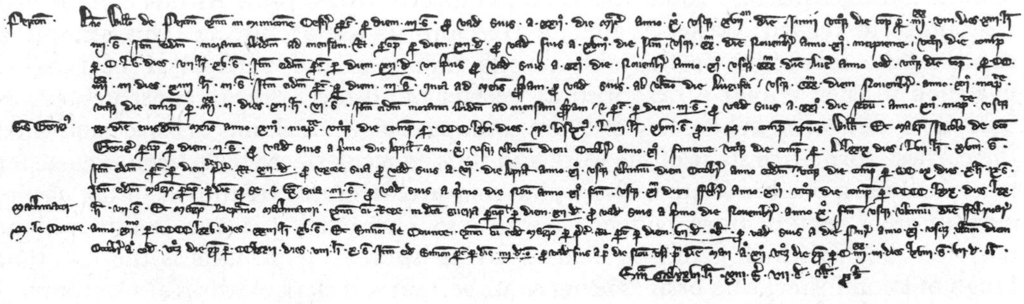

Fig. 10. Extract from the Keeper of the Wardrobe's Roll of Wages in the 10th and 11th years of Edward I (E 101/4/1), recording payments to the officers of the works in Wales.

It happens that a record has survived which gives information of the first importance in this connection. This is the entry, placed perhaps somewhat unexpectedly towards the end of a long roll of wages of knights and squires,[2] of payments made by the keeper of the Wardrobe to four of the chief officers of the works during the same period as he was accounting for the £9414 paid in wages to the workmen themselves and their masters (*cementariorum, carpentariorum, fossatorum . . . et eorum magistrorum*); it is thus the record of the pay of those who were in effect the masters of the masters at the time Caernarvon was begun (Fig. 10). The officers named are Sir William of Perton, Master James of St. George, Master Bertram and Simon le Counte. Master Bertram, paid 1s. a day from 1 November 1282 to 29 February 1284, the probable date of his death at Caernarvon, is styled *machinator* and may have been mainly concerned with the construction of the king's engines, as he was earlier at the Tower of London; Simon le Counte was his assistant.[3] Sir William of Perton, who heads the list, was throughout this period in charge of the Wardrobe office at Chester[4]; through him, as we noted earlier, moneys for both the Caernarvon and the Conway works were being issued in December 1283. From the outbreak of the war on 22 March to 17 June 1282 and again from 31 August 1283 to 20 November 1284 he received a wage

---

[1] E 372/31, rot. 26*d*.   [2] E 101/4/1, m. 19.
[3] For Master Bertram, see also p. 28 and Appendix III, and for Simon le Counte, p. 76, n. 2 above.
[4] E.g. C 47/35/2, where he is named in March 1283 as *clericus garderobe domini Regis apud Cestriam*.

of 3s. a day as living *ad mensam propriam*; during the intervening fourteen months he was following the king, receiving accordingly only 1s. a day as one provided for *ad mensam Regis*. Master James of St. George drew a salary equivalent to a daily wage of 2s. Since 1 November 1280 the amounts had been debited on the masons' account for Flint Castle, the principal work then in progress;[1] but from 1 April 1282 his pay appears next after Perton's as a direct charge on this general Wardrobe wages account, continuing to be paid in this way without a break until, as from 12 February 1285, it passes to the account of the chamberlain of Caernarvon to be explicitly credited to him thereafter as 'master of the king's works in Wales'.[2] It had in the meantime been increased from 2s. to 3s. a day, Master James having since 6 April 1283 been allowed an additional shilling in respect of his wife, an arrangement which the king confirmed in perpetuity at Caernarvon in October 1284 shortly before he departed from Wales.[3] The significance, in the present context, of this record of James of St. George's direct, continuous and highly privileged employment under the Wardrobe organisation throughout the period covered by its keeper's expenditure in 1283–4, lies in its inescapable implication that it was St. George who was the chief professional officer responsible for the whole group of works involved, including from their inception (and not merely from February 1285, when his name first happens to be directly associated with them in a surviving enrolled account) those of Caernarvon. If this be accepted, it seems scarcely possible to doubt that it is principally to him, within the conditions imposed by the site and the terms of the king's and probably Grandson's requirements, that this most remarkable of castles owes its architectural form. It is inconceivable that the initiation of so important and exacting a commission would have been entrusted to any other than the master who, only five years before, had set out for Wales 'to ordain the works of the castles there' and who there is every reason to believe had been doing so ever since with consummate skill and to conspicuous effect. It could well be that the design for Caernarvon was not the least of the good and laudable services which earned him his grant of a pension for life from 1284 onwards.[4] That he must have had able and experienced assistance is not to be questioned. But here again such records as survive point to the probability of his right-hand man having been Master Richard the 'Engineer' of Chester rather than Walter of Hereford.[5]

How far and how closely the final achievement was the realisation of something firmly drawn and visualised in 1283 will always be a matter for speculation. But there is much that points to the steady working out of a fixed plan, consistently adhered to

---

[1] Above, p. 20, notes 9–10.

[2] E 372/131, rot. 26*d*.

[3] E 101/4/1, m. 19; *Cal. Pat. Rolls 1281–92*, p. 137. Other cases of special provision being made for the wives of foreign specialists in Edward I's service include the wife of Simon of Beauvais, the king's surgeon, and Aichina the wife of Francis Accursius, the king's Italian lawyer; for details see *Studies in Building History*, ed. Jope (1961), p. 130, n. 6.

[4] A fuller discussion of the problem of the architectural authorship of the castle, written before the record of St. George's wages from 1.4.1282 to 11.2.1284 had been located, is in *Antiquity* xxvi (1952), pp. 33–4.

[5] A letter printed in *Cal. Anc. Corr. Wales*, p. 164, shows that Master Richard was concerned in the Caernarvon works in 1283–4; the award of a life pension made to him at Caernarvon at the same time as that to Master James of St. George (*Cal. Pat. Rolls 1281–92*, p. 137) is an indication of the value placed on his services. Both he and Master James are named as king's sergeants.

so long as building went on: such for example is the implication of the note of non-fulfilment of plans *laid down* for the Well Tower ('in qua *ordinabantur* quatuor stagie'); such too is the conclusion to be drawn from the Eagle Tower's generous embellishment of turrets, surely no afterthought of days when resources were falling short and buildings for use still to be begun. On the other hand the absence from the upper part of the Cistern, Black, Chamberlain and Queen's Towers of the fourth line of sandstone banding that so heightens the polychrome effect of the Queen's Gate, Watch and North-east Towers looks like a failure to carry this characteristic feature of the original design to its full conclusion on the southern front; so, more certainly, does the omission of the banding from the north front, where its continuance east of the Eagle Tower shows that it was no part of the original design to restrict it to those parts of the castle seen from outside the walled town; similarly the substitution of moulded strings for banding courses on the upper part of the Eagle Tower and the adjoining south-west curtain is plainly anomalous and must have marked a departure from set pattern. All these are variations introduced after 1295 during the regime of Master Walter and Master Henry. Except on the north, however, they are unlikely to have altered the building's intended appearance very radically; nor, except in degree, is the want of the turrets which can be assumed to have been planned to surmount the staircases behind the King's and Queen's Gates. Thus in a word the design that Hereford, Ellerton and Durnford brought gradually nearer to perfection in the thirty-five years after 1295 was in all its essentials the design adopted in the beginning. It is something of a paradox that this most lavishly conceived of all the king's works in Wales, costing probably over £20,000[1] and taking nearly half a century to build, should at the end of it all have still remained unfinished, and have been only once visited by a reigning sovereign from the time of Edward I to that of George V;[2] indeed only with the Investiture ceremony of 1911 did Caernarvon Castle begin to play something of the symbolic role in the affairs of the principality that its founder undoubtedly envisaged for it.

Caernarvon continued, however, to serve until the seventeenth century as the administrative centre of North Wales, and the maintenance of the castle and of the other royal buildings in the town does not appear to have been neglected by the officials whom they housed. In the absence of any accounts for the period of the Black Prince's tenure of the principality it is impossible to say how much was done to make good the defects noted in Emeldon's survey of 1343, but during the reign of Richard II, for which a complete series of chamberlain's accounts survives, expenditure on the upkeep of the castle and other buildings averaged nearly £40 a year. In 1392–3 £20 were spent on building a pier (*columpna*) to strengthen the Banner Tower,[3] and

---

[1] Of the estimated total of £27,000 given above, *at least* £4240 (1284–5, £2566; 1295–1301, £1082; 1304–1327, £592) is assignable to the works of the town walls, the quays, the king's houses, the bridges, the mills and the mill pool.

[2] Henry IV was at Caernarvon in October 1400 (J. E. Lloyd, *Owen Glendower*, p. 33, note 3); Edward II never revisited the place of his birth and his grandson the Black Prince seems never even to have visited Wales (Hilda Johnstone, *Edward of Carnarvon*, p. 62; May McKisack, *The Fourteenth Century*, p. 259); Princess Victoria, the future queen, visited the castle in 1831, the Prince and Princess of Wales in 1868.

[3] SC 6/1215/5. For traces of this pier in the basement of the tower (now the Queen's Tower) see Hist. Mon. Comm. *Caernarvonshire* ii, p. 134.

in 1395–7 £138 were laid out on repairs to the Eagle Tower and other buildings.[1] Some expenditure on the castle, varying from £2 or £3 to nearly £100, also figures in every surviving chamberlain's account of the years between 1399 and 1485.

12. BEAUMARIS

In the thirteenth century the commercial centre and principal port of Anglesey was the Welsh royal manor of Llanfaes near the northern end of the Menai Strait. Here in 1237 Llywelyn the Great founded a Franciscan friary, and under Llywelyn ap Gruffydd (1246–82) the town achieved considerable importance, with burgesses, a ferry across the straits, a harbour and fisheries, and shipmen trading as far away as Liverpool.[2] It was also the local centre of the Gascon wine trade, and in 1283–4 wine cargoes were being trans-shipped from Llanfaes to Conway and Caernarvon.[3] It was the supply base for the bridging operation of 1282 and was visited by Edward I for three or four days in August 1283.[4] The shire status given to Anglesey by the Statute of Wales in the following year would seem to imply that there was then already an intention to establish a castle on the island, and the site on the coast near Llanfaes which Beaumaris was eventually to occupy could very well have been earmarked, if only provisionally, at the time of the king's visit.[5]

The Welsh revolt of 30 September 1294 made itself felt in Anglesey as well as at Caernarvon, and the island's sheriff, Sir Roger Pilsdon, was among its more prominent victims. Anglesey's reoccupation accordingly took a foremost place in the king's plans. So did the construction of the castle that was still needed to put English rule there on the same basis as in the other shires and lordships and provide a permanently defensible foothold readily accessible from the ports of the mainland. The necessary decisions were taken in council at Worcester between 21 and 25 November,[6] and then or very shortly afterwards Sir Henry Latham of Lancashire was ordered to sail in his galley for Anglesey in command of a force of 500 men carried in 12 ships. Pay for this force, amounting to 40 marks (£26 13s. 4d.), was issued to Sir Henry from the Wardrobe at Chester on 7 December. Only the day before, four days' pay, no doubt to cover the time of their travelling to Chester, had been issued for a body of 50 diggers and 21 carpenters.[7] If, as the proximity of the dates and entries suggests, these latter were also to sail with Latham, we may have here a reference to the very first group of workmen to be assigned for the coming

---

[1] SC 6/1215/7–8.
[2] Sir John Lloyd, in Hist. Mon. Comm., *Anglesey* (1937), p. xxxviii.   [3] E 101/351/9.
[4] C 47/3/48; *Cal. Pat. Rolls 1281–92*, p. 72.
[5] There was a Norman earthwork castle at Aber Lleiniog, only 1½ miles on the other side of Llanfaes but its relatively less accessible position would not have commended it to builders for whom use of waterborne supplies was always a prime consideration, nor were there any reasons of sentiment and tradition such as compensated for the expense and inconvenience of retaining the motte-and-bailey site at Caernarvon.
[6] Morris, *Welsh Wars*, p. 245.
[7] Wardrobe Book, E 36/202, f. 33.

operation, an advance party who would perhaps undertake such preliminary site works as the digging of trial holes and the erection of huts to accommodate the larger bodies of men that would follow. The first indication of these comes on 19 February 1295, when William of Dogmersfield and Robert of Rye were sent from Conway to the parts of Chester to seek and bring back 300 diggers, 30 carpenters and 20 masons.[1] Meanwhile, as the book of Wardrobe payments shows, preparations were being put in hand for a second bridging of the Menai. On 7 February £8 were advanced to Master James of St. George at Conway, towards the cost of making 'clayes' and pontoons in the Wirral and buying pitch and other necessaries at Chester.[2] After this he returned from Conway to Cheshire, and on 4 March a Chancery clerk was despatched with an urgent message to him in Wirral, 'or elsewhere where he makes the king's pontoons, to take all the boats he can find in Wirral and elsewhere on the coast to carry the pontoons to the king at Aberconway'.[3] All through March there are many other payments for making pontoons and 'clayes' and for building two barges at Chester; a subsequent inquisition showed that at this time Master James and Master Richard the 'engineer' had between them ordered the felling of over 2300 trees belonging to the abbot of St. Werburgh's and others at Huntingdon, Cheveley, Eccleston, Mollington and Saughall.[4] Side by side with the assembly of the bridge components went preparations for the new building works which would start in earnest directly the main body was across the straits: on 8 April, at Bangor, 'Master St. George' was paid 10s. for tools and accessories, both metal and wooden, which had been made for the masons before leaving Conway.

The crossing took place on or about 10 April, from which date until 6 May the king's headquarters were at Llanfaes. There, on 17 April, Master James received 'by his own hands' a prest of 60s. for necessaries to be provided 'for the new castle', and there at about the same time the king, by verbal appointment, made Walter of Winchester clerk of the new works as also of the repairs shortly to be undertaken at Caernarvon.[5] On the following day Walter received the first of a series of payments which in the course of the next six months were to reach a figure of over £7800, some £6736 of it for the works of 'the new castle of Beau Mareys'. Never before, unless the £5000 suggested for the initial Caernarvon works of 1283–4 is a serious underestimate, had so much treasure been applied so swiftly to one single operation,

[1] Wardrobe Book, E 36/202, f. 35; the same Robert had earlier recruited the 50 diggers.
[2] *Ibid.*; notable as the first evidence of Master James's presence in Wales since his departure for the continent in 1287 (above, p. 363). On the same day, 7 February, he repaid a loan of £20 made to him 'during the time he was constable of Harlech', i.e. 1290–93 (E 101/624/51, p. 17). On 31 March he received a wages prest of £5 by his own hand at Conway and one of 2 marks by the hand of 'Colin' (*per manus Colinhij*), named also as Colin 'the clerk' (E 36/202, p. 79; it would not be surprising if St. George's clerk were a Savoyard, and one wonders whether this may not be the same 'Colin' as the one of whom there are a dozen mentions, all similarly in single-named form, in Philip of Savoy's *Household Roll* of 1271–2, when he was evidently a trusted servant of the count (Chiaudano, *La Finanza Sabauda* (Turin, 1934), ii, *passim*); he is probably identical with the 'Collard', alias *Collard clericus*, who appears several times in the Harlech account of 1286 in company with 'Giletus' (Master Giles of St. George), 'Perottus', Adam Boynard and other probable Savoyards.
[3] *Cal. Chancery Warrants*, p. 53.   [4] *Cal. Inq. Misc.* i, p. 475.
[5] When rendering his account in 1313, the sixth year of Edward II, Walter stated explicitly that he had had no written commission: *monstravit nobis . . . quod cum dominus Edwardus quondam Rex Anglie pater noster ipsum Walterum quondam oretenus deputasset ad soluciones pro operacionibus castri de Beumarreys in Wallia faciendas . . . necnon ad faciendos muros ville de Carneruan dudum in guerra Wallie dirrutos reparari . . .* E 372/158, rot. 48.

and the arrangements for making the money available are accordingly worth tracing.[1] Sums of £100 were issued directly to Walter from the Wardrobe at Llanfaes on 18 April, 30 April and 6 May; on that day the king left Anglesey, and the second May payment, of £666 13s. 4d. (1000 marks), was sent by the constable of Rhuddlan acting on a writ of privy seal (*de parvo sigillo*). Early in June the constable of Conway, Sir William de Cicon, paid Walter half a sum of £1000 lately brought over from the treasurer of Ireland, and on about 20 June a full £1000 was brought from Chester to Llanfaes by William of Doncaster. The next instalment, £600, was paid to Walter at Conway on 13 July;[2] for the king, having made a circuit of South Wales and the March in sixty days, had returned to Beaumaris on 10 July, and when he left a few days later on what was to be the first stage of his last journey from the principality, Walter no doubt accompanied him across the straits. By the beginning of August Edward was back at Westminster and remittances were henceforward sent from the Exchequer in London: £1333 6s. 8d. (2000 marks) on 10 August, another 2000 marks on 3 September, 1000 marks on 2 October and £1400 on 9 October.

Income was matched by outlay, and in the 24 weeks from 18 April to 29 September the bills passed the £6000 mark. In this short summer season the carriage of materials alone cost over £2100, more than the total recorded expenditure on this item at Conway, Harlech or Caernarvon throughout the 1280's. Here most of the stone had to be fetched from a distance by water, which helps to explain the high transport costs and also why Latham's naval force was kept in being till mid-July 'to keep the sea between Snowdon and Anglesey'.[3] In the same period the wages of *fossatores* and minor workmen digging trenches and excavating the moat and also, at the king's order, putting up a barricade round the site of the new castle[4] amounted to no less than £1468 12s. 0d., indicating that their numbers throughout the summer must have averaged something like 1800 men. Similarly masons' wages totalling £1005 and quarriers' totalling £636 point to numbers in these categories of the order of 450 and 375 men respectively;[5] the tonnage of stone quarried and shipped and

[1] Details from Wardrobe Book, E 36/202, ff. 40–63.

[2] On 8 May the king sent a mandate from Llanrug, Caerns., 'to arrest hastily moneys coming from the king's treasury in London to the king in Wales, which are now at or near Chester, as he has heard, and conduct them by good people of Chester to the castle of Rothelan for delivery to the constable to keep safely until further orders' (*Cal. Chancery Warrants*, p. 59). This was presumably the origin of the 1000 marks received from Rhuddlan during that month. Some indication of the apparent priority of the Beaumaris over the Caernarvon works at this time may be inferred from the fact that at the same date and place (Conway, 13 July) as Walter of Winchester, as *clericus operacionum Wallie*, received £600 by his own hand for the former, Hugh of Leominster, as the official assigned *ad soluciones faciendas operariis apud Carnaruan operantibus*, received only £200 for the latter. Not long afterwards Havering, the justiciar, complained to the Exchequer in London that the keepers of the works of Beaumaris, Master James and Walter of Winchester, had kept 650 marks assigned for the works of Caernarvon, with the result that the latter were seriously behind; and he said how dangerous it was for the money for Caernarvon to have to come via Beaumaris, involving a double journey across the water, when it could come quite safely to Caernarvon direct by road: *pur quei, sires, nous vous prioms . . . pur auancer les dites Oeures qe les deners qui serront assignez pour les Oeures de Carnaruan ne soient desoremes enuoyez a Beaumarreys* (E 101/5/18, no. 11).

[3] Besides Latham's own ship, *galia sua propria*, there were barges from Caernarvon and Ireland, three or four in all, with 95 seamen and 20 crossbowmen (details from E 101/353/31 and E 372/158, rot. 48).

[4] '. . . faciencium fossata et motam ubi castrum de Bello Marisco situm est, ac eciam circa quoddam bretagium ibidem faciendum ex precepto Regis . . .'

[5] These are approximations based on the Harlech account of 1286 (E 101/485/27) which besides the wages earned gives the numbers employed in the different categories.

worked and laid by them must have been immense. Of materials other than stone the quantities are itemised in the account, and some details may be given here: 2428 tons of sea-coal, for burning lime; 640 quarters of charcoal; 42 masons' axes; 3277 boards; ropes, cords and chains; 8 loads of lead; 160 pounds of tin; 314 'bends' of iron; 105,000 assorted nails. There must already have been much to see when Edward came back in July to inspect the results of the first three months' work and stayed, not at Llanfaes this time, but at Beaumaris itself; and there, on two summer evenings, in a setting of temporary, thatch-roofed buildings erected 'within the castle',[1] with the great walls and towers laid out and beginning to rise around them, we have a glimpse across the centuries of the king taking his ease after the day's work and listening to the playing of an English harpist.[2]

Just how much may by then have been achieved, and the way in which the building was beginning to take shape, may be judged from a report sent to the Exchequer by Master James of St. George and Walter of Winchester at the end of February 1296 in answer to a similar inquiry to that addressed to Walter of Hereford and Hugh of Leominster in regard to Caernarvon.[3] Throwing light not only on the progress of the works themselves but also on the authority of the Exchequer to control them and on the conditions in which they had to be carried on, this is a document that claims our fullest attention. Freely Englished, it runs as follows:

Conway,
27 February 1296

To their very dear lordships the Treasurer and Barons of the Exchequer of our lord the King, James of St. George and Walter of Winchester send greeting and due reverence

Sirs,

As our lord the king has commanded us, by letters of the exchequer, to let you have a clear picture of all aspects of the state of the works at Beaumaris, so that you may be able to lay down the level of work (*ordiner lestat de loevre*) for this coming season as may seem best to you, we write to inform you that the work we are doing is very costly and we need a great deal of money.

You should know:

(i) That we have kept on masons, stone cutters, quarrymen and minor workmen all through the winter, and are still employing them, for making mortar and breaking up stone for lime; we have had carts bringing this stone to the site and bringing timber for erecting the buildings in which we are all now living inside the castle (*a edifier en chastel la ou nous sumes touz demorrantz ore*); we also have 1,000 carpenters, smiths, plasterers and navvies, quite apart from a mounted garrison of 10 men accounting for 70s. a week, 20 crossbowmen who add another 47s. 10d. and 100 infantry who take a further £6 2s. 6d.

[1] 'in . . . litera pro domibus infra castrum cooperiendo . . .' (E 372/158, in the summer 1295 payments).
[2] 'Ade de Cliderhou (Clitheroe), cithariste, citharizanti coram Rege apud Bellum Mariscum per duas noctes de dono eiusdem Regis per manus proprias apud Bellum Mariscum, xij die Julij,—x.s.' (E 101/14/7).
[3] Above, pp. 380–1; the Beaumaris letter, which is in Norman French (the Caernarvon letter is in Latin), is also in E 101/5/18, no. 11 and is likewise printed *in extenso* in Edwards, 'Castle-building', pp. 80–81. Other documents relating to the financing of the works in 1295–6 are published by the present writer in *Bull. Bd. Celtic Studies* xv, pp. 61–66.

(ii) That when this letter was written we were short of £500, for both workmen and garrison. The men's pay has been and still is very much in arrear, and we are having the greatest difficulty in keeping them because they simply have nothing to live on.

(iii) That if our lord the king wants the work to be finished as quickly as it should be and on the scale on which it has been commenced (*que loevre se perfate vistement ausi come mestier serreit e sicome ele est comencee*), we could not make do with less than £250 a week throughout the season; with it, this season could see the work well advanced. If, however, you feel we cannot have so much money, let us know, and we will put the workmen at your disposal according to whatever you think will be the best profit of our lord the king.

As for the progress of the work, we have sent a previous report to the king. We can tell you that some of it already stands about 28 feet high and even where it is lowest it is 20 feet. We have begun ten of the outer and four of the inner towers, i.e. the two for each of the two gatehouse passages (*si sont comence x tours dehors e quatre dedens, a chescune porte deus pur les alees*'). Four gates have been hung and are shut and locked every night, and each gateway is to have three portcullises. You should also know that at high tide a 40-ton vessel will be able to come fully laden right up to the castle gateway;[1] so much have we been able to do in spite of all the Welshmen (*maugre touz les Galeys tant avoms nous fait*).

In case you should wonder where so much money could go in a week, we would have you know that we have needed—and shall continue to need—400 masons, both cutters and layers, together with 2,000 minor workmen, 100 carts (*charettes*), 60 waggons (*carres*) and 30 boats bringing stone and sea-coal;[2] 200 quarrymen; 30 smiths; and carpenters for putting in the joists and floor-boards and other necessary jobs. All this takes no account of the garrison mentioned above, nor of purchases of materials, of which there will have to be a great quantity.

As to how things are in the land of Wales, we still cannot be any too sure (*de lestat de la terre de Gales nous nensavons uncore si bien nony*). But, as you well know, Welshmen are Welshmen, and you need to understand them properly; if, which God forbid, there is war with France and Scotland, we shall need to watch them all the more closely (*font a duter de tant le plus*).

You may be assured, dear sirs, that we shall make it our business to give satisfaction in everything.

May God protect your dearest lordships.

P.S. And, Sirs, for God's sake be quick with the money for the works, as much as ever our lord the king wills; otherwise everything done up till now will have been of no avail (*tant come ilyad fait uncore poy vaut si plus nysoit fait*).

Already, then, much of what had been built stood 20 feet high and some parts were 8 feet higher still; and as, during the winter, the men had not been on constructional tasks, this must have been the position reached by about mid-November 1295, the date by which the king had required that the castle should be defensible.[3]

---

[1] 'a la porte du chastel'; this follows directly on the mention of the gates, and suggests that 'porte' here means the South Gate rather than the castle dock.

[2] The enrolled account shows that, as for Conway and elsewhere, this was shipped from 'Holston', i.e. Whelston in Bagillt on the Dee estuary.

[3] '. . . nous amerons qe les ouerainnes de Beaumareis e de Carnaruan sespleicassent en teu manere qe les lieus peussent estre defensables entre cy e la seint Martin procheinement auenir' (E 159/69, rot. 4).

What had actually been done becomes clear when we relate the words of the record to the evidence of the structure. Taking first the ten 'outer' towers, these can be seen to be the three more southerly towers of the west outer curtain, plus the two flanking towers of the 'gate next the sea', plus all five towers of the east outer curtain. These ten towers, together with their intervening stretches of curtain wall, in length equivalent to over five-eighths of the whole outer circuit, are characterised at ground level by crossbow-slits whose reveals are of plain ashlar and whose lintels are formed by the ordinary coursed rubble of the surrounding wall face; moreover the whole of this length is marked, about 2 feet above the slits on towers and curtain alike, by a sharply defined horizontal change of build, very plainly distinguishable on the west and south, less easily so on the east, which must be the result of a prolonged pause in building and shows the level, about 8 feet above the water of the moat, to which the greater proportion of the outer line of defence had been carried by the end of the first period of construction, that is to say in or soon after 1298. That this was the earlier and not the later part of the outer curtain to be begun is indicated structurally by junctions west of the north-east corner tower and north of the centre west tower,[1] where the slopes of the different builds show that the work to the north and west is secondary to that to the south and east. Further, the northern and north-western walls and towers are characterised on both their ground and upper storeys by slits having well-cut chamfered ashlar reveals and lintels of a pattern confined on the southern and eastern portions to the upper and later stage only.

The work that had reached an average height of 20 to 28 feet was evidently the great inner curtain, the second figure being equal to nearly 78 per cent of the completed height of 36 feet at which its wall-walks still stand today. The junctions, vertical and horizontal, which in the case of the outer curtain mark a succession of pauses and resumptions of building, are here conspicuously absent, and the unbroken sweep of the inclined scaffold lines climbing from bottom to top of the long east and west walls proclaims the unity of their construction, a unity that likewise extended inwards to meet the side walls of the twin gatehouses; these, with their four towers similarly carried up to a height of 20 feet or more, completed the closure needed to give the degree of defensibility initially required. From gatehouse to gatehouse the curtains maintain a minimum thickness of nearly 16 feet; and whereas at Conway the towers and the curtains are structurally integrated, it can be seen from the plan (Fig. 41) that at Beaumaris the curtains could well have been carried far towards completion, as the 1296 letter allows us to infer they were, independently of any work on the towers at their four corners and against their longer sides.[2]

In calling for a weekly allotment of £250 in 1296 those in charge were only asking for the amount of money that would be needed to maintain building at something approaching the previous season's level, when expenditure had averaged not £250 but £270 a week. But even while St. George and Walter of Winchester

[1] Some slight foundations remain beside this western junction of a cross wall probably built to form a temporary closure to the outer ward when its north-western portion was still unbuilt.
[2] The interpretation of the 'progress' section of the letter of 1296 is discussed in Edwards, 'Castle-building', pp. 26–7. Broadly the same conclusions are reached, but the identification of the 10 outer towers is here put forward for the first time on the evidence of structural and architectural features.

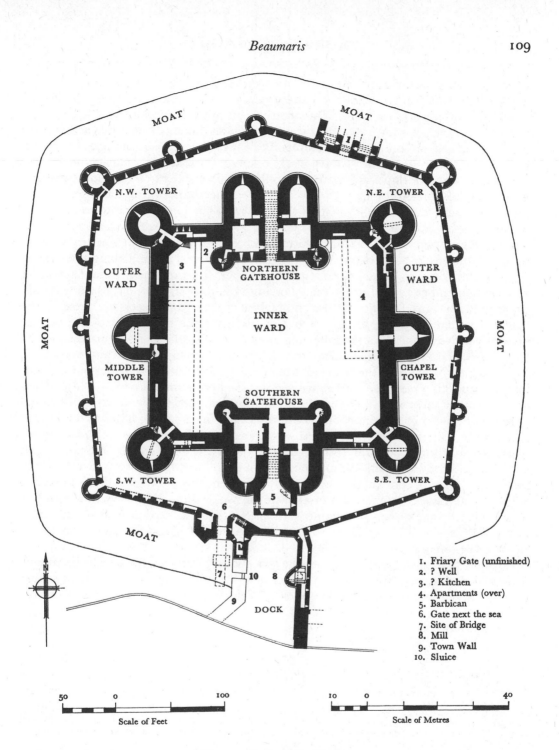

1. Friary Gate (unfinished)
2. ? Well
3. ? Kitchen
4. Apartments (over)
5. Barbican
6. Gate next the sea
7. Site of Bridge
8. Mill
9. Town Wall
10. Sluice

Scale of Feet

Scale of Metres

Fig. 11. Beaumaris Castle.

were submitting their requirements from Conway, the king was making his way northwards from York to Scotland; and already, despite the priority ordered to be accorded to the works in Wales,[1] the Scottish commitment was beginning to retard their progress. On 7 May 1296 there was not enough money at Beaumaris to pay all the workmen,[2] and from then until September expenditure was running not at £270, nor even at £250, but at only £100 a week. Even so, the season's outlay came to some £2323.[3] But with receipts amounting to only £742, the clerk of the works was left with a deficit of no less than £1581 'owed to divers merchants for materials purchased from them, and to divers workmen for their wages'. The kind of quantities for which payments may have been in default can be gauged from such figures as 16,200 freestones quarried at task by four contractors[4] and 32,583 tons of stone transported by sea to the castle, all between Whitsun and Michaelmas 1296. Taking the costs of the two half-years together, some £4185 was spent on the works from September 1295 to September 1296; but for the following year the corresponding sum was only £330, and for 1297–8 £270. At the end of June 1297, £25 a week was fixed as the combined total allotment for works and garrison for the remainder of the season, i.e. until 11 November.[5] In the following twelve months the wages of masons, which had absorbed over £1000 in less than half that time in the summer of 1295, accounted for only £80. Now it was the floors and temporary roofs that were being put in: thus for £33 12s. 8d. 3 perches of planking, 4 great sleeper-beams (*somere*), 54 large joists and 120 other joists were felled in the woods and shipped to Beaumaris to be prepared and placed in position.[6] Finally, as from 30 August 1298, liability for Master James of St. George's daily wage of 3s. was transferred from Walter of Winchester's works account to the account of the keeper of the Wardrobe,[7] a clear indication that with the withdrawal of officials and possibly of building labour also to Scotland the first main phase of construction was nearly at an end. As at Caernarvon, however, activity may have continued on a small scale for two or three years longer: a mandate of 31 October 1300 directs the chamberlain of North Wales to deliver from the issues of his bailiwick to Thomas Danvers, sheriff of Anglesey, £100 for the works of the castle of Beaumaris.[8]

By this time the cost stood at nearly £11,400, all of it—so far as can be judged from the documents—spent on the works of the castle. The town of Llanfaes had been utterly destroyed[9] and the houses of its Welsh burgesses dismantled and carried

[1] Above, p. 89, n. 4.
[2] '. . . quo die soluciones deficiebant in parte'.
[3] £2133 for works, £190 for garrison.
[4] Amongst them John Francis, whom we have previously encountered at Conway (above, p. 53), and John Penne and John of Ellerton whose names are found at Caernarvon.
[5] E 368/68, rot. 34*a*. For details, *see* A. J. Taylor, 'Building at Caernarvon and Beaumaris in 1296', *Bull. Bd. Celtic Stud.* xv, pp. 61–66, where this and other documents illustrating the financing of the works are printed in full.
[6] It is noticeable that at Beaumaris the floors nearly all rested on masonry offsets, allowing the woodwork to be added independently after the masons had finished; at Conway, on the other hand, the joist ends were built right into the walls, requiring carpenters and masons to work hand in hand as building progressed.
[7] *Liber Quotidianus*, p. 102.   [8] E 159/74, rot. 60.
[9] According to an inquisition of 1318 Edward I had entirely demolished the manor and town of Llanfaes after Madoc's rebellion and it still stood unrepaired and uninhabited, the tenants and inhabitants having transferred to Newborough and Beaumaris (C 145/79/12).

off for use in building the new borough nearby.[1] In September 1296 Beaumaris received its charter. Yet though its burgages outnumbered even Conway's,[2] nothing appears to have been spent on equipping it w :h any kind of defences; even the banks and ditches that had sufficed at Flint and Rhuddlan seem here to have been wanting,[3] while the town wall which the inhabitants petitioned Edward II to provide[4] did not materialise till a century later.[5] In considering the apportionment of cost to building achieved, therefore, we do not need to look beyond the castle itself.

After the reference of October 1300 we hear no more of Beaumaris till 1306, when John of Metfield, the newly appointed constable, reported on the castle's condition and made recommendations to the prince's council.[6] It is evident from the chamberlain's account of 1304–5[7] that there had been no resumption of work in that year to parallel Walter of Hereford's renewed activity at Caernarvon, and James of St. George appears to have remained with the king.[8] Metfield enumerated seven 'grievous defaults' in the castle: (i) the gates were much in need of repair and their locks should be changed and new ones sent; (ii) a good, strong barbican should be provided at the gate towards the dock, and the same done at the other gate or else a good barricade put there (*a la porte deuer Le Porth*[9] *covendreyt une bone Barbecane e forte, e al autre porte ensement o bones barres*[10]); (iii) to make the place safe, portcullises were needed; (iv) the castle needed to be closed in, either with a wall of stone and lime or else with a good peel; (v) the ditches should be scoured and made deeper; (vi) the 'little houses' (*petites mesones* ? = gardrobes) in the body of the castle badly needed roofing and repairing, their gutters mending and the 'houses' themselves cleared of dirt and rubbish; (vii) the basements of the towers were foul inside, and the outlets from the gardrobes were full of water and filth so that the bottoms of the shafts were blocked.[11] Plainly these were the shortcomings of a building that had suffered a long period of neglect and where no work to speak of was going on. That at least one of the recommendations was put into effect without delay may be seen not only from a record of wages paid during the first week of May 1306 to a mason and four labourers for work done to obstruct the 'gate towards the field' (*obstruenti portam versus campum*),[12] but also from the actual remains of the stone blocking walls

[1] Ancient Petitions 2803, printed in E. A. Lewis, *Medieval Boroughs of Snowdonia*, p. 295.
[2] With 132¼ and 112 burgages respectively, Beaumaris and Conway were the two largest of the North Wales boroughs.
[3] When the burgesses received a donation of £10 from the prince in 1407 'in aid of making a ditch round the aforesaid town' the wording implies that it was an entirely new work (SC 6/1216/2).
[4] Ancient Petitions 13991, quoted by Lewis, *op. cit.* p. 102.
[5] Thirty burgages were declared 'waste' in 1414 *causa nvve edificacionis nove Muri lapidee* [sic] *circa eandem villam* (SC 6/1152/5).
[6] Printed from E 101/486/20 in *Arch. Camb., Orig. Docts.* (1877), pp. xi–xiii.
[7] SC 6/1211/2, printed in *Bull. Bd. Celt. Stud.* i, pp. 256–75; detailed reference to works at Caernarvon, Conway, Criccieth and Newborough imply *per contra* that Beaumaris was inactive.
[8] He received prests of wages in person at Lincoln on 30 December 1304, Fotheringhay on 11 July 1306 and Newburgh-in-Tynedale on 4 September 1306 (E 101/368/26 and 27); when the Beaumaris rental was compiled in 1305 he was shown as the holder of 6 burgages, but both he and Walter of Winchester were marked as non-resident (Rentals and Surveys, Roll 767, printed in *Arch. Camb., loc. cit.*, pp. xiv–xviii).
[9] Not, as printed in *Arch. Camb., loc. cit.* p. xii, 'dever le *North*'.
[10] The same phrase is used by Villehardouin in describing the defences of the Crusaders' encampment outside Constantinople in July 1203: '...il fermerent tote l'ost de bones lices et de bons merriens et de bones barres' (*La Conquête de Constantinople*, ed. Faral (1961), tome i, p. 168).
[11] Probably the Beaumaris garderobe pits follow the pattern of those at Rhuddlan, which have square drainage channels running under the outer ward to discharge into the moat. [12] E 101/486/2.

which they added against the sides of the northern gatehouse passage in order to diminish its width. That such a measure was necessary at this time provides vivid confirmation that the adjacent sections of the outer curtain had still to be erected, and that the lack of them was felt to endanger the landward defence of the castle.

It seems probable that this summer saw the resumption of continuous building. As from 22 May 1306 the boat that had hitherto been used for ferrying stone from the quarry to the works at Caernarvon was assigned by the prince's auditors to serve the Beaumaris works instead.[1] Moreover, Beaumaris is included amongst the castles on whose works the chamberlain, Thomas of Asthall, accounted for an expenditure of £2040 13s. 8¾d. between Michaelmas 1305 and Michaelmas 1307.[2] Certainly by the latter year Master James of St. George was back in Wales, receiving at Caernarvon on 30 September 1307, as 'master of the works of the castle of Beaumaris', an instalment of wages of £8, pending a decision by the new king or his Council as to whether his services were to be continued.[3] One of the first tasks likely to have been undertaken was the provision of the barbican that Metfield had recommended for the southern gatehouse, for the circular-headed rear-arch over its entrance would suggest that it was built while there were still masons from Savoy on the scene, which probably means in the lifetime of Master James himself or of John Francis. Its building occasioned the moving of a window in the adjacent outer gatehouse to a position commanding a view of the new entry—evidence that the 'gate next the sea' was already standing at least to outer wall-walk height before it was decided to add the barbican behind it.

After Michaelmas 1309 the record of expenditure can be traced continuously until 1326, the annual outlay for these years averaging a little above £175 and giving an overall total of £2995 3s. 3d. If, in addition, we allow estimated sums of £500 for the three years 1307–9 and £400 for the four years 1326–30, we arrive at a total of £3895 3s. 3d., say £3900, for the 24 years during which the second period of construction probably lasted.[4] There can be very little doubt that the principal work of these years was that which gave effect to the most important of Metfield's recommendations, namely the 'closing in' of the castle by the completion of the outer curtain on its north and north-west sides and the heightening of the sections begun in

[1] SC 6/1170/5.   [2] E 372/176, rot. 56d. ii.
[3] He acknowledged receipt . . . *super vadia mea quamquam nondum assignata, octo libr. sterlingorum, quousque dominus Rex vel consilium suum aliud de eisdem duxerint ordinandum in proximo;* if his wages were not confirmed he would have to make repayment to the chamberlain before 1 November (SC 6/1287/1).
[4] Details of £1547 12s. 11¾d. of this amount are set out in Edwards, 'Castle-building', pp. 28–29; but as at Caernarvon there are gaps in the chamberlains' rolls in the SC 6 series, hitherto unaccounted for, which can now be filled in from 'remainders of account' entered on later Pipe Rolls (cf. above, p. 385, note 8); thus Thomas of Chedworth accounted for £489 7s. 6¾d. spent on Beaumaris works between 18 October 1312 and 11 January 1316 (E 372/172, rot. 6d. ii), Edmund of Dinton for £343 1s. 8d. spent between 1 May 1317 and 24 June 1319 (E 372/164, rot. 35, ii); and Robert Power for £274 11s. 1½d. spent between 12 June 1323 and 29 September 1324 (E 372/175, rot. 32d) and £340 9s. 11d. between that date and 29 September 1326 (E 372/174, rot. 23 ii). Nicholas Acton's account of £714 0s. 2½d. spent on the works of the castles between 20 March 1329 and 14 August 1330 (E 372/175, rot. 50d. ii) names Beaumaris with the others, and it is therefore reasonable to allow a nominal £100 per annum for these two years, as also for the years 1327–28 for which John Chiverdon's accounts are wanting. £60 1s. 4½d. is also known to have been spent by Acton's successor Adam of Withiford between 16 September and 16 December 1330 (E 101/487/8, printed in *Arch. Camb.*, *loc. cit.*, pp. lxiiii–lxxii). The possibility, to put it no stronger, that expenditure at the same sort of level may have continued during the 1330's should not be overlooked.

1295. This meant adding about half the finished height of five-eighths of the outer circuit and of the wall flanking the dock as well as building the whole of the other three-eighths. The corbelled parapet of the main curtains, with some of the upper work of the towers of the inner ward, is also likely to belong to this second period. Most of it must have been done under the direction of Nicholas of Durnford, the next master of the works of whom we hear after the death, in or before May 1309, of James of St. George;[1] but unfortunately the surviving accounts, even two series of detailed 'particulars',[2] afford no information as to what parts of the buildings were proceeding at any given time. It appears from a survey of 1321 that in the outer ward three of the four corner towers and six lesser towers, together with the towers over the two outer gates, were all still so far unfinished that no one would like to say how much lead and timber they would require.[3] The corner towers in question must be those at the north-east, south-east and south-west begun in 1295, and the six smaller ones presumably the three on the east, the two more southerly on the west, and the tower containing the water mill in the spur wall. By inference, the gap on the north and north-west had now been closed, the north-west angle tower and three smaller towers finished, and the northern outer gatehouse certainly begun and possibly already carried to the stage at which it stands to-day. A record of the 'perfecting', by David the Dyker of Caernarvon, of $10\frac{1}{2}$ perches of the castle moat between 1312 and 1315 may provide a clue as to when this was done, for the building of new sections of outer curtain might be expected to entail alterations to the corresponding sections of the ditch.[4] At the same time (1321) it was reported that in the inner ward six great towers and a tower over the inner gate (*un tour ultre le Porte deinz*)[5] were only lightly boarded and needed to be properly roofed with framed timber and lead: 35 carrats of lead and 20 lbs. of tin would be required, with at least 220 large joists, 12 'wyvers', 24 wall-posts (*postz pendauntz*), 24 corbels and 24 tie-beams (*lyenz*).

Throughout the 1320's work went slowly on, but at the end of it all Beaumaris, like Caernarvon, was still very much an unfinished castle. Emeldon's survey, made in August 1343,[6] listed 'defects' in its 'walls, towers, houses and other buildings' the remedying of which would cost £684 6s. 8d. The chief items were the great South Gatehouse, the completion of whose two suites of apartments (*camere*) and two rear towers was estimated at £320 (masons' work £200, carpenters' £80,

[1] Durnford may already have been acting as master at Beaumaris before May 1316, when a wage of 1s. a day was granted to him 'during pleasure and good behaviour' (*Cal. Pat. Rolls 1313–17*, p. 457). For his earlier career, see A.J. Taylor, 'A Petition ffrom Master Nicholas de Derneford to Edward II', *Trans. Bristol and Glouc. Arch. Soc.*, xcviii (1981), 171–3.

[2] E 101/485/2 (3 August 1316 to 1 May 1317) and E 101/487/1 (30 September 1319 to 28 September 1320); both are printed in *Arch. Camb.*, *loc. cit.*, pp. xix–lxii, and with the parallel accounts for Caernarvon are analysed from the economic standpoint by Douglas Knoop and G. P. Jones in 'Castle Building at Beaumaris and Caernarvon in the Early Fourteenth Century', *Trans. Quatuor Coronati Lodge*, xlv (1932), pp. 4–47.

[3] 'En la forein bavl sunt iij tours en les angles du Mur, et vj meindres turelles, et ij grauntz tours ultre les deux forein portes du nouel a faires des queux hom ne poet mye bien aymer de certein coe qil couient de plom ne de meryn' (B.L., Add. Roll 7198).

[4] E 372/172, rot. 6*d*. ii; there is also an imperfect record, SC 6/1287/2, no. 10, that Edmund Dinton, chamberlain 1317–19, was allowed 12 marks for making 12 perches of the moat, which had hitherto remained unmade (*iacent' adhuc infacte*) to the damage of the king.

[5] Probably the South Gatehouse, which would be 'inner' in relation to the Barbican and the main entrance beside the dock.

[6] E 163/4/42.

plumbers' and other necessary work £40), the Chapel Tower which it was said could be finished for £128, and the two rear towers of the North Gatehouse for £100. There was no proposal or estimate for completing the other five main towers, although all of them, like the Chapel Tower, had—and still have—little more than the beginnings of their third and final storey; instead their existing roofs were to be repaired as they stood for sums varying from £5 to £10. Nor is there any suggestion for completing the barely started upper-floor suite in the North Gatehouse.

By 1330, if our allowances and calculations are approximately right, Beaumaris's building can have cost little less than £14,400: about the same, that is to say, as the cost of the whole of the· castle and town walls at Conway. One wonders at the ambitious scale on which the work was launched in 1295, and what relation the original estimate bore to the eventual cost of even the uncompleted work. One wonders, too, what purposes and requirements so much accommodation was planned to satisfy. It is evident that there were to be five separate suites of lodgings, one on the east side of the courtyard and two in each of the great gatehouses, each suite having its own hall and chamber with access to further rooms in adjacent towers. Can it be that, by the time Beaumaris was begun, thought was already being given to the day that might come when a royal castle in Wales would need to provide not only for the king's and queen's households but also, and perhaps on occasion simultaneously, for the households of the prince and his consort as well? Such could be the explanation of the double provision of twin-halled gatehouses, with the courtyard apartments here reserved for the constable. Or is it rather that at Beaumaris, where the town would not at first be walled, the castle was intended to contain the lodgings for the justiciar and chamberlain which at Conway were provided in the Mill Gate and other premises nearby? Would one of the suites perhaps have been for the sheriff of Anglesey? To such questions no certain answer can be given, the less so in that so little of what was planned in this way was ever built. What is indisputable is that this last creation of the master of the king's works in Wales achieved a symmetry of design and setting out that makes it the perfect example of the concentric castle; and had it only been destined to achieve the same completeness in its vertical as in its horizontal dimension, it would assuredly have challenged comparison as a piece of military architecture with any one of its predecessors.

Despite its unfinished state, the castle was by no means without military value, and (except during the years 1397–1403, when it was granted first to William le Scrope and then to Henry Percy,[1] and 1422–37, when it was held in dower by Queen Katherine[2]) its maintenance figures regularly in the surviving accounts of the chamberlains of North Wales. No modifications of any importance are, however, recorded, and it stands today substantially as it stood when the works were abandoned early in the reign of Edward III.

By the time construction ceased at Beaumaris and Caernarvon the cost of the works in Wales had mounted since 1277, according to surviving works records, to

[1] *Cal. Pat. Rolls 1396–9*, p. 82; *1399–1401*, p. 155.
[2] *Rot. Parl.* iv, pp. 203–6.

some £93,300.[1] If allowance is made for the probability of further accounts for the period 1330–*c*.1340 being lost, and also for cumulative expenditure on a variety of items properly chargeable to the works but not recorded on direct works accounts,[2] the true cost is more likely to have been somewhere between £95,000 and £100,000, a figure which in modern money values might be approximately equated with an outlay of £10,000,000. Over 80 per cent of the recorded total was spent before 1301, that is to say during the first twenty-four years.

The story of the preceding pages is the story of its spending, insofar as this can be reconstructed from the still formidable though far from complete array of records and accounts kept at the time. Perhaps its most striking feature is the witness it bears to the Plantagenet monarchy's effective command over resources of every kind, often brought to bear over great geographical distances. One recalls first the builders themselves, recruited from every shire from Northumberland to Sussex and Devon to Norfolk, the dykers from the fens, the men skilled and experienced in castle-building brought by the master of the works from the Vaud, the Valais and the Viennois; one thinks of the money to pay them, panniered and pack-horsed from London and Winchester and Nottingham, or brought across the sea from Ireland; of the thirty boatloads of freestone, shipped down the Bristol Channel and round the coast of Dyfed to the works at Aberystwyth, there to be mortared with lime similarly shipped from Tenby; of the limestone, vital to the works at Harlech, brought by sea from Anglesey; or one thinks of the lead for the roofs and pipes and cisterns, mined in Snowdonia[3] and the Isle of Man,[4] carted overland from Mold to Builth, shipped from Bristol to Criccieth and Caernarvon, of the iron and steel from Newcastle-under-Lyme, the 'sea' coal from Flint and the ropes from Boston; one remembers too how the timber-framed halls of the Welsh princes were dismantled and transported from Conway and Aberffraw, Dolbadarn and Ystumgwern, to the castle wards of Harlech and Caernarvon.

What all this could mean in terms of the logistics of a single castle for a single year is shown in Appendix II. What it all resulted in, at least in terms of stone and lime, we are still able to see remarkably completely at Caernarvon and Conway and Beaumaris, and only a little less so at Rhuddlan and Harlech. Of the other royal castles, Flint and Aberystwyth and Hope have suffered rather more severely; Builth lies levelled and buried on its Norman earthworks. The architectural legacy of the

---

[1] Appendix I.

[2] E.g., (i) sheriffs' contributions to labour recruitment and transport costs; during the period 1277–84 *at least* £200 8s. 6½d. was disbursed under this head (inclusion of payments for 'woodcutters' (*coupiatores*) drafted primarily for clearing passes, etc., but no doubt also employed for felling timber used in the works, would make this figure at least half as high again) (Liberate Rolls 53–60); (ii) innumerable works details included in such Wardrobe 'necessaries' rolls as E 101/3/29 and 351/9, and such wages payments as those amounting to £241 made to Perton and James of St. George between 1282 and 1285 and recorded on E 101/4/1 (cf. p. 392, fig. 40); (iii) messengers' services, generally concealed by being inexplicitly recorded on 'nuncii' rolls; and (iv) ancillary charges of the kind listed in the chamberlain's account for £956 14s. 8d. of miscellaneous expenditure incurred between 1286 and 1290, printed in *Cal. Anc. Corr. Wales*, pp. 118–21.

[3] In 1284 Reginald of Ludlow was given lead-mining rights in Snowdonia for three years, reserving to the king one-seventh of all production plus, from the other six-sevenths, 'as much as he shall need for his works in Wales' (*Cal. Welsh Rolls*, pp. 288–9).

[4] In June 1290 safe-conduct was given to certain traders of the county of Chester and the March of Wales 'trading to the Isle of Man for lead for the works of the castles in Wales' (*Cal. Pat. Rolls 1281–92*, p. 358).

works in Wales, to which all but the last-named still contribute, is the more impressive when it is remembered that of Edward I's other great building enterprises Vale Royal has wholly disappeared, the additions to the Tower of London have been disguised within and without by the adaptations and refacings of seven centuries of use, while Westminster preserves only the much restored crypt of the former chapel of St. Stephen. The Welsh castles, on the other hand, stripped though they are of their plaster and timber and glass, of their lead roofs and their iron grilles, have come down to us structurally little altered from the time of their building. It is this, combined with the extent to which it is possible to interpret the phases and techniques of their construction by reference to an abundance of contemporary documentation, that gives them a foremost place among the historical monuments of their age.

APPENDICES

I. *Expenditure on Welsh Castles 1277–c.1330*

1. SUMMARY OF RECORDED TOTALS OF EXPENDITURE*
(a) *1277–1304*

Works	Accounting periods	Reference	Expenditure
			£ s. d.
Builth	3.5.1277–1.11.1282	E 372/124, rot. 24; *ibid.* 126, rot. 6; *ibid.* 127, rot. 2; E 101/485/20, 21; SC 1/55, no. 13	1666 9 5¼
Aberystwyth	1.8.1277–1.8.1289	E 372/125, rot. 2; *ibid.* 134, rot. 2d; SC 6/1218/4	3885 17 11½
Flint and Rhuddlan	16.7.1277–15.11.1277	E 101/485/19	1551 0 10
Flint	23.8.1277–25.12.1286	E 372/122, rot. 28; *ibid.* 124, rot. 29; *ibid.* 131, rot. 26	6068 7 5¾
	30.9.1301–29.9.1304	SC 6/771/1, 2, 4	155 19 9¼
Rhuddlan	30.11.1277–25.12.1285	E 372/122, rot. 28d; *ibid.* 124, rot. 29; *ibid.* 131, rot. 26	9209 8 3¾
	30.9.1301–29.9.1304	SC 6/771/1, 2, 4	83 2 8¾
Hope, Rhuddlan, Conway, Caernarvon, Criccieth, Harlech, West Wales and other places in the Welsh war	22.3.1282–20.11.1284	E 372/136, rot. 33	9414 4 11
Conway	March 1283–19.11.1284	E 372/130, rot. 5d	5819 14 0
	26.11.1284–29.11.1292	E 372/131, rot. 26; *ibid.* 136, rot. 28; *ibid.* 138, rot. 25	7870 1 6¼
	1291	E 372/141	40 11 5
	11.2.1296–26.2.1301	E 101/486/9	31 2 11
Harlech	29.4.1285–29.9.1292	E 372/131, rot. 26d; *ibid.* 136, rot. 28; *ibid.* 138, rot. 25	8184 10 9¼
	1296–1301	E 101/486/9	5 11 7
Criccieth	2.7.1285–29.9.1292	E 372/131, rot. 26d; *ibid.* 136, rot. 28; *ibid.* 138, rot. 25	310 7 9¾
	1296–1301	E 101/486/9	8 9 7
Bere	29.9.1286–29.9.1290	E 372/136, rot. 28	265 5 10¾
Caernarvon	21.8.1284–29.9.1292	E 372/131, rot. 26; *ibid.* 136, rot. 28; *ibid.* rot. 25	6609 17 1
	5.6.1295–10.7.1295	E 372/158, rot. 48; E 101/486/8	170 10 4½
	10.7.1295–19.11.1301	E 372/146, rots. 24, 25	5527 16 4¼
Beaumaris	18.4.1295–29.9.1298	E 372/158, rot. 48	11,289 0 9
	1300	E 159/74, m. 60	100 0 0

Total, 1277–1304 £78,267 11 6

* For a fuller breakdown of the figures for 1277–1301, see Edwards, 'Castle-building', pp. 66–73.

Works	*Accounting periods*	*Reference*	*Expenditure*		
			£	s.	d.
Caernarvon	29.9.1304–29.9.1305	SC 6/1211/2; E 101/486/1	699	8	9
Conway			52	10	3½
Newborough (mill and cross)			86	11	1¼
Miscellaneous			41	9	5
Caernarvon, Beaumaris, Harlech, Criccieth and Conway	29.9.1305–29.9.1307	E 372/176, rot. 56*d*, ii	2040	13	8¾
,, ,,	29.9.1307–29.9.1312	E 372/175, rot. 44*d*	3425	3	7¼†
Caernarvon	18.10.1312–11.1.1316	E 372/172, rot. 6*d*, ii	1321	19	8
Beaumaris	18.10.1312–11.1.1316		489	7	6¾
Conway	20.4.1315–26.10.1315		93	15	3½
Criccieth	29.9.1314–11.1.1316		8	5	4
Caernarvon	11.1.1316–1.5.1317	SC 6/1211/7–9; E 101/485/24; *ibid.* 486/29	650	18	11¼
Beaumaris			409	18	5¼
Conway			88	13	11¾
Harlech			29	18	10½
Criccieth			42	2	7½
Caernarvon	1.5.1317–24.6.1319	E 372/164, rots. 21*d* and 35, ii	663	10	8¼
Beaumaris			343	1	8
Conway			17	9	7
Harlech			40	11	8
Criccieth			52	14	0¼
Caernarvon	Easter 1319–5.6.1323	SC 6/1212/2, 5, 7, 9; E 101/486/30; *ibid.* 487/1, 2, 3	817	19	9
Beaumaris	,, ,,		580	3	11¾
Conway	29.9.1320–29.9.1322		26	13	5
Harlech	29.9.1319–29.9.1322		38	9	4¼
Criccieth	,, ,,		49	16	3¾
Caernarvon	12.6.1323–29.9.1324	E 372/175, rot. 32*d*	365	9	0¼
Beaumaris	,, ,,		274	11	1½
Conway	20.5.1324–16.9.1324		11	10	7½
Harlech	30.9.1323–11.3.1324		67	10	2
Criccieth	18.3.1324–23.9.1324		26	19	2
Caernarvon	29.9.1324–31.10.1327	E 372/174, rot. 23, ii	698	18	5¼
Beaumaris	,, ,,		340	9	11
Conway	29.9.1325–29.9.1326		139	1	8
Harlech	29.9.1324–31.10.1327		50	0	4½
Criccieth	29.9.1325–29.9.1326		21	19	9½
	31.10.1327–20.3.1329	No accounts rendered‡			
Castle works (no separate totals)	20.3.1329–14.8.1330	E 372/175, rot. 50*d*, ii	714	0	2½
Caernarvon	16.9.1330–15.3.1331	E 101/487/8	51	17	5½
Beaumaris	16.9.1330–16.12.1330		60	1	4½
Caernarvon	6.2.1339–25.9.1339	E 101/487/10	144	15	1
		Total II, 1304–39	£15,078	12	5½
		Total I, 1277–1304	£78,267	11	6
		Grand Total, 1277–1339	£93,346	3	11½

† SC 6/1211/3–5 show that £2257 14s. 3d. of this was spent in the three years 1309–12 as follows: Caernarvon, £1423 12s. 10d.; Beaumaris, £557 14s. 0¼d.; Conway, £57 9s. 9d.; Harlech, £175 2s. 8¾d.; Criccieth, £43 14s. 11d.; for the other two years separate figures are not extant.

‡ John Chiverdon, appointed chamberlain on 31.10.1327, died in 1328/9 before rendering his account, and as late as July 1341 his affairs had not been cleared up or fully accounted for (Waters, *Edwardian Settlement*, p. 77, note 2).

2. SUMMARY OF LOCAL TOTALS OF SPECIFIED EXPENDITURE IN ORDER OF MAGNITUDE

(a) *1277–1304*

	£	s.	d.
Conway (1283–1301; mainly 1283–87)	13,761	9	10¼
Caernarvon (1284–1301)	12,308	3	9¾
Beaumaris (1295–1300; mainly 1295–6)	11,389	0	9
Rhuddlan (1277–1304; mainly 1277–80)	9292	11	0½
Harlech (1285–1301; mainly 1286–89)	8190	2	4¼
Flint (1277–1304; mainly 1277–86)	6224	7	3
Aberystwyth (1277–89)	3885	17	11½
Builth (1277–82)	1666	9	5¼
Criccieth (1285–1301; mainly 1285–92)	318	17	4¾
Bere (1286–90)	265	5	10¾
'Unassigned' (1277)*	1551	0	10
'Unassigned' (1282–84)†	9414	4	11
	£78,267	11	6

(b) *1304–c.1330*

	£	s.	d.
Caernarvon (1304–39)	7584	5	3
Beaumaris (1306–30)	3055	8	1
Conway (1304–26)	487	4	7¼
Harlech (1304–27)	401	13	2
Criccieth (1304–26)	245	12	2
Miscellaneous (1304–5)‡	128	0	6¼
'Unassigned' (1305–7)§	1294	19	1¼
'Unassigned' (1307–9)‖	1167	9	4¼
'Unassigned' (1329–30)	714	0	2½
	£15,078	12	5½

(a) and (b) *1277–c.1330*

	£	s.	d.
Caernarvon	19,892	9	0¾
Beaumaris	14,444	8	10
Conway	14,248	14	5½
Rhuddlan	9292	11	0½
Harlech	8591	15	6¼
Flint	6224	7	3
Aberystwyth	3885	17	11½
Builth	1666	9	5¼
Criccieth	564	9	6¾
Bere	265	5	10¾
Miscellaneous	128	0	6¼
'Unassigned'	14,141	14	5
	£93,346	3	11½

* Divided between Flint and Rhuddlan.

† Probably mainly Caernarvon and Harlech (1283–4) and Hope (1282–3); also Conway, Rhuddlan, Criccieth and West Wales.

‡ Newborough mill and cross; minor works (SC 6/1211/2).

§ Balance, after deduction of £745 14s. 7½d. known to be assignable to Caernarvon, of general figure of £2040 13s. 8¾d.

‖ Balance, after deduction of £2257 14s. 3d. assignable to specified works in 1309–12, of general figure of £3425 3s. 7¼d.

II. Harlech Castle

TABLES OF WAGES, CARRIAGE CHARGES, PURCHASES AND PAYMENTS FOR TASKWORK

DECEMBER 1285–SEPTEMBER 1286

A. *Counter-roll of Adam of Wettenhall, comptroller of Master Robert of Belvoir, of the wages of divers workmen working at Harlech from Sunday, 30 December 1285 to Sunday, 15 September 1286 (E 101/485/26)*

1286 3 weeks ending Sunday:	Masons Number	Masons Wages £ s. d.	Quarriers Number	Quarriers Wages £ s. d.	Smiths Number	Smiths Wages £ s. d.	Carpenters Number	Carpenters Wages £ s. d.	Minor Workmen Number	Minor Workmen Wages £ s. d.	Clerks Number	Clerks Wages £ s. d.	Other[p] Items £ s. d.	Total Strength	Total Payments £ s. d.
20 Jan.	2[a]	7 6	16[g]	2 8 0	7[k]	1 15 6	16[l]	4 6 0	20[m]	1 10 0	1[n]	8 0	4 8[q]	62	10 19 8
10 Febr.	1[b]	4 6	23[h]	3 9 0	11	2 13 6	15	4 7 0	40	3 6 8	2[o]	13 3		91	14 9 5
3 March			30[i]	4 10 0	12	2 14 6	17	4 18 6	70	6 7 6	2	13 3		132	19 7 9
24 March			40[j]	6 0 0	15	3 9 9	24	6 15 6	116	13 9 6	2	13 3		197	26 10 9
21 April[c]	29[d]	9 13 4	48	12 5 3	18	5 4 8	23	8 19 0	123	18 15 6	3	1 4 8		244	56 2 5
12 May	131	39 1 6	73	15 19 6	18	4 7 6	33	9 8 6	468	51 17 1½	4	1 4 3		727	121 18 4½
2 June	155	46 12 0	98	20 1 0	18	4 7 6	27	7 12 6	582	69 12 0	4	1 4 3	4 2 6[r]	884	153 11 9
23 June	199	57 10 0	93	19 13 6	18	4 7 0	22	6 14 6	572	61 1 0	4	1 4 3	12 3 0[s]	908	162 13 6
14 July	227[e]	64 14 0	115	22 19 6	30	7 1 0	22	6 11 0	546	55 5 9	4	1 4 3		944	157 14 0
4 Aug.	163	47 18 9	89	18 17 6	32	7 7 6	35	10 2 0	579	60 18 9	4	1 4 3		902	146 8 6
25 Aug.	145	43 18 9	80	16 18 0	31	7 4 6	33	9 15 6	572	64 19 7½	5	1 6 3	5 5 0[t]	866	149 7 1¾
15 Sept.[f]	181	57 4 9	82	14 11 0	18	7 16 6	27	7 16 6	463	51 3 8	6	2 7 3	5 4 0[u]	777	137 15 8
37 weeks		£367 4 1		£157 12 3		£55 0 8		£87 6 0		£454 10 7		£13 7 2	£21 19 2		£1156 19 11

B. *Counter-roll of Adam of Wettenhall of the costs of carriage at Harlech in the 14th year (E 101/485/27)[v]*

	Paid to	Cost of	Commodity carried	From	To	Amount £ s. d.
10 Febr.	Adam Boynard[w] and Robert Scot.	Hire of 6 horses	Iron	Caernarvon	Harlech	2 0
3 March	Adam Boynard, Robert Scot, Madoc Crath, Stephen Janitor, Robert of Walden and Gilbert clericus.	Hire of 27 horses	Stone for the kiln in the castle; iron, steel, nails	The free quarry / Caernarvon	„ / „	6 9
24 March	Collard clericus, Robert of Walden, John le Hore, Adam Boynard and John le Colier; Robert Scot.	Hire of 11 horses	Iron		„	3 8
		Hire of 4 horses	Sand	The sea	The castle	12 0

						£	s.	d.
21 April[c]	Robert of Walden, Gilbert clericus, Collard, Gilet, Perottus clericus and others; Adam Boynard.	Hire of 57 horses	Lime; iron;	Conway	"Harlech	4	4	0
		Hire of 1 horse	William the Plumer's tools	Harlech	Criccieth			3
12 May	William le Verior, Robert of Chepstow and 11 men;	Shipping	Stone	The quarry	The castle	3	18	0
	Robert of Walden, Robert Scot, Madoc Crath, Stephen Janitor, Perottus clericus and Collard clericus.	Hire of 38 horses	Lime and sand	,,	,,	5	18	9
2 June	Robert of Walden, Robert Scot, William of Lampader, Adam Boynard, Gilbert clericus, Gylet and Collardus; Richard of Derby.	Hire of 46 horses	Lime	Caernarvon	,,	9	0	0
		Hire of 1 horse	Crossbows	Harlech	Harlech			4

(*a*) Master Peter Morel and Albert de Menz, making the chimney of the *camera* of Sir John de Bevillard and other necessaries in the castle.

(*b*) John de Nez, trimming (*sculpant*) stones for the kiln in the castle.

(*c*) This period included Easter (April 14) and is of 4 weeks.

(*d*) Philip Run and Thomas del Mened are the named masons in this and the next 3 periods; they each receive 2s. a week in the first and the next 3 periods; they each receive 2s. a week in the first and the three following periods.

(*e*) For the rest of the account the named masons are Philip Run and John de Osk, one receiving 3s. and the other 2s. 6d. a week until 4 Aug., after which both are paid 3s.; other masons are paid at graduated rates from 2s. 6d. down to 1s. 2d. a week. Ralf de Ocle (who also built the kiln at Conway) worked on the limekiln in June–July.

(*f*) The close of the account does not mark a break in the work, the next accounting period running straight on from this day (E372/136, rot. 28). In 1286 the Harlech, Caernarvon and Conway accts. end on Sundays 15, 22 and 29 Sept. respectively; in 1287 the Caernarvon, Harlech and Conway accts. end on Sundays 7 Sept., 12 Oct. and 9 Nov. respectively; and in 1288 the Conway, Caernarvon and Harlech accts. on Sunday 3 Oct. and Tuesday and Sunday 21 and 26 Dec. respectively. In 1286 at least this points to a timed progress of auditors from castle to castle.

(*g*) John Stauald and William Routh are named; quarriers all receive 1s. a week.

(*h*) For the remainder of the acct. those named are Hugh de Salop' and William Routh.

(*i*) *operant' in quarr' de Hardelagh et quarr' de Egrin.*

(*k*) John Birch and Nicholas de Flint, at 2s. 8d. and 2s. 6d. respectively, are named throughout the account.

(*l*) Named carpenters at the castle are Thomas de Nova Aula and Maykin (3s. and 2s. 6d. a week respectively); Stephen de Norton and Cabot are employed in the woods.

(*m*) Nicholas le Harpor, William del Pek and Eynon of Oswestry are named; the category includes pick-men (*pickarii*), barrow-men (*bayard'*) and free hodmen (*libri hottarii*); most receive 1½d. a day.

(*n*) Nicholas 'clericus', who throughout pays the wages of the 'minuti operarii'.

(*o*) Nicholas, and John of Merston, the latter being responsible for the quarriers.

(*p*) All but the last of these are payments for carriage and belong more properly to section B.

(*q*) 2s. 8d. to Adam Boynard and Robert Scot for 8 horses hired from them to carry iron from Caernarvon to Harlech; 2s. to Madoc Crath, John Colier and Stephen Janitor for hire of 12 horses to take lime to the castle.

(*r*) Wages of boatmen, viz. (a) Robert of Chepstow and 5 men, (b) Roger of Oswestry and 2 men carrying the workmen's tools to the forge (probably quarriers' tools from Egryn— see next note), and (c) William le Verior and 6 men.

(*s*) Wages of boatmen, viz. (a) William le Verior, Robert of Chepstow and 11 men, (b) Jordan of Lynn (Len) and 5 sailors carrying lime from Caernarvon to Harlech in the king's barge for 9 weeks from 21 April, and (c) John Broun and Alan of Kirkeby and 4 sailors carrying stone from the free quarry of Egrin to the castle in 2 of the king's barges. 'Egrin' is probably Egryn in Llanaber, about 7 miles SSE of Harlech.

(*t*) Wages of boatmen, viz. Henry de Lanpader (Aberystwyth) and Michael of Chepstow, and 4 sailors carrying lime and stone from Caernarvon to Harlech in the king's barge for 9 weeks from 23 June.

(*u*) Expenses of Madoc Seys, going to London with letters to John de Kirkby (Treasurer of the Exchequer) on the king's affairs.

(*v*) E 101/485/26 and 27 originally formed a single continuous roll of particulars of wage, carriage, purchase and task-work payments, all four categories being included in the total at the end of 485/27.

(*w*) For Adam Boynard and others here named, see Appendix C. III, 9 (p. 1038).

Date	Paid to	Cost of	Commodity carried	From	To	Amount £ s. d.
23 June	William of Lampader, Roger del Wode, Michael of Chepstow and Robert of Chepstow;	Shipping	148½ tons of stone	Caernarvon	Harlech	14 17 0
	Robert de Hoxle, Robert of Walden and 18 others.	Hire of 67 horses	Lime, stone and sand			11 3 3
14 July	Robert of Walden, Gilbertus clericus, Gylet, Perrottus clericus, Collardus, Madoc Crath and 15 others;	Hire of 117 horses	Lime, sand and stone	The quarry	The castle	19 18 9
	Adam of Dundalk, Adam Lovegod, John Beleyter, Robert Secumbe, Nicholas Deneys, Adam of Singleton and 21 others;	Shipping	384 tons of stone	Quarry in Anglesey	Harlech	38 8 0
	Thomas of Lampader and William le Verior;	Shipping	112 tons of stone	The free quarry of Egrin		2 16 0
	Thomas Cokayn;	Shipping	70 tons of stone	,,		1 15 0
	Jordan de Mundeniz.	Shipping	59½ tons of stone	,,		1 9 9
4 Aug.	Gilbertus clericus, Robert of Walden, Thomas de Nova Aula and 15 others;	19 carts	Stone	,,	Harlech	8 5 0
	William of Montgomery, Robert Scot, John le Hore;	7 carts	Stone	,,		2 12 6
	John Colier, Gylet, Collard clericus, Perrottus clericus and 22 others;	Hire of 77 horses	Wood for the plumbers; sand and lime			12 0 7½
	Robert of Chepstow and Michael of Chepstow;	Shipping	202 tons of stone	The free quarry	The castle	3 7 4
	John de Oxon', Richard de Salop', William Seysel and three others;	Shipping	238 tons of stone and lime	Caernarvon	Harlech	23 16 0
	Walter de Corleye;	Carrying	120 measures of iron	Depot (celar) of Jordan de Bradeford	Ship in R. Dee at Chester	10 0 0
	Walter Billy;	Shipping	Same iron	Chester	Harlech	4 0 0
	Walter Billy.	Shipping	Two barrels of steel; nails, ropes	Chester	Harlech	4 4 0
25 Aug.	Robert of Walden, Gilbertus clericus, Perrottus clericus, Collard, Gillet, John of Paris and 26 others;	41 carts	Stone; wood for the kiln	The free quarry	The castle	15 15 0
	William de Hoxle, William Pollesden, Adam Boynard, Madoc Crath, Richard de Bradele and 36 others;	Hire of 65 horses	Lime and sand	The sea	The castle	10 3 1½
	Roger del Wod, Michael Fiere, William Long and Walter of Stratton.	Shipping	243 tons of stone and lime	Caernarvon	Harlech	24 6 0

Date	Paid to	Quantity / Commodity	Purpose		Bought at	Cost £ s. d.
15 Sept	William de la Sale, Maurice de la Haye, Henry of Acton, Nicholas of Eccleshall and Thomas of Greenham; Robert of Walden, Gilbertus clericus, Gilet, Collard, Perrottus, Peter de Tours, Robert de Hoxle, Adam Boynard, Madoc Crath and others; Roger del Wode, William le Verior, William Long, Wildebor and 26 others.	30 carts	Wood for the kiln; stone	The free quarry	The castle	11 9 4
		Hire of 84 horses	Lime, sand, earth lime	The sea		14 0 0
		Shipping	405 tons of stone and lime	Caernarvon	Harlech	40 10 0
				Total for carriage:		£285 2 5

C. *Counter-roll of Adam of Wettenhall of divers purchases made at Harlech in the 14th year* (E 101/485/27)

Date	Paid to	Quantity	Commodity	Purpose	Bought at	Cost £ s. d.
20 Jan.	John Colier and Robert his partner (*socius*);	30 qrs.	Charcoal	The king's forge		5 0
	Madoc the Welshman;	4 qrs.	Lime	Making chimney in *camera* of Sir John de Bevillard	Abermau	8
	Nicholas clericus.	1 lb.	Tallow	Greasing crossbows		
		1 lb.	Yarn	Making crossbow strings		1 11
		1	Ox-hide	For use of Simon the Artiller		
10 Febr.	John Colier.	50 qrs.	Charcoal	The king's forge		8 4
3 March	John Colier;	50 qrs.	Charcoal	The king's forge		8 4
	John le Gayte.	17	Bands (*cingli*)	For barrows		1 5
		6	Pieces of small cord	Measuring the ditch (*fouea*)		4
24 March	John Colier;	80 qrs.	Charcoal	The king's forge		13 4
	Robert Colier;	10 qrs.	Charcoal	Forge at free quarry		1 10¾
	John of Drayton.		Sticks and straw	Roofing the houses in the castle		8 9
21 April[a]	John Colier;	100 qrs.	Charcoal	The king's forge		16 8
	Robert Colier;	17 qrs.	Charcoal	Forge at free quarry		3 2¼
	Madoc the Welshman;	88½ qrs.	Lime			1 9 6
	Robert of Bedford;	120	Clayes	For the scaffold		7 6
		200	Hods			8 0
		20	Large hods			0 6
	John le Gayte;	1	Door	For smithy at the free quarry		3¾
	Perrottus clericus.	2 doz.	Bands	For barrows		1 6
		2	Empty tuns	Measuring lime in		2 2

	Paid to	Quantity	Commodity	Purpose	Bought at	Cost £ s. d.
12 May	John Colier;	106 qrs.	Charcoal	The king's forge		1 2 8¾
		27 qrs.	Charcoal	Forge at free quarry		
	Adam of Newcastle-under-Lyme.	20	Sheaves of steel			1 5
2 June	John Colier;	141 qrs.	Charcoal	The king's forge		1 5 8
	Jordan of Bradford;	70	Sheaves of steel			4 1 6
	Adam of Newcastle;	9000	Nails	For boards		13 6
	Robert of Bedford;	100	Clayes	For the King's Works		17 6
		100	Hods	,, ,, ,,		
		100	Barrows	,, ,, ,,		
	Madoc the Welshman;	7,640 qrs.	Lime	*pro feodo cyment'*		14 3 8½
	Robert Scot.	1	Battering tool (*aries*)			13 4
23 June	John Colier;	144 qrs.	Charcoal	The king's forge		1 4 0
	Madoc the Welshman;	122 qrs.	Lime		Newcastle-under-Lyme	1 0 4
	Ralf of Newcastle;	120	Measures of iron			48 0 0ᵇ
	John FitzThomas;	2	Barrels of steel		,,	7 0 0ᵇ
	Ralf and John aforesaid;	20,000	Nails	For barrows (@ 6s. per 1000)	,,	12 1 8
		30,000	Nails	For boards (@ 18d. per 1000)	,,	
		40,000	Nails	For mortarboards (@ 16d. per 1000)		
		40,000	Nails	For laths (@ 7d. per 1000)		2 4 4
	Ralf of Newcastle.	2	Great cables	Great cables	St. Botolph's	15 0
		4	Small ropes		,,	13 4
		5	Other ropes			3 2 5
			Small cords	Measuring the works		
14 July	John Colier;	182 qrs.	Charcoal	The king's forge		1 10 4
	Madoc the Welshman;	588 qrs.	Lime			6 2 10½
	Philip le Mercer;	30 ells	Canvas	Sail of one of the king's barges		5 0 0
	Robert of Bedford.	100	Scaffold poles	For the works		10 0 0
4 Aug.	John Colier;	170 qrs.	Charcoal	The king's forge		1 8 4
	Madoc the Welshman;	183 qrs.	Lime			1 10 6
	John le Gayte;	4 doz.	Corners (*angli*)	For barrows		3 0 6
	John of Northampton;	3 ells	Black cloth	Covering the exchequer of Harlech		3 6
	John le Gayte;		String and pitch	For the masons		4 4½
25 Aug.	John Colier;	176 qrs.	Charcoal	The king's forge		1 9 4
	Madoc the Welshman and his partners;	303 qrs.	Lime			4 14 3
	David ab Eynon of Lanuays;	4	Ropes			10 0 0
		3	Small ropes			5 0 0
	William Marshall.	1	Great cable			1 10 0

	Paid to		Quantity		£	s.	d.
15 Sept.	John Colier; Jordan of Bradford; Madoc the Welshman; Robert of Bedford.	Charcoal	114 qrs.	The king's forge	19	0	0
		Image	1	For the chapel of Harlech	10	8	8
		Lime	37 qrs.			2	0
		Little hods	60			8	4
		Scaffold poles	120	For the king's works			
				Total for purchases:	£125	17	5¾

(a) This period included Easter (April 14) and is of 4 weeks.
(b) Includes cost of carriage from Newcastle-under-Lyme to Chester.

D. *Task-works in* 1286 (E 101/485/27)

	Paid to	Task	Rate	£	s.	d.
10 Febr.	Richard of Longslow (Wlonkeslowe)	Making a smithy at the free quarry			12	2½
	Robert of Bedford	Making a scaffold			17	6
	Richard de Roden and Albert de Menz	Quarrying and dressing 1040 stones, each 2 ft. by 1½ ft. by 1 ft.	25s. per 100	25	10	0
	,,	Quarrying and dressing 56 steps for the stairs of the towers	18d. per step	4	4	0
	,,	Quarrying and dressing 200 ft. of string-course (*tabellamentum*)	2d. per foot	1	13	4
	,,	Quarrying and dressing 40 ft. of voussoirs	2½d. per foot		8	4
	,,	Quarrying and dressing 80 ft. of reveals of arrow-slits for the towers (*de Archer' turrium*)	5d. per foot	1	13	4
			Total for task-work:	£34	18	8½

Sum total of expenditure on wages, carriage, purchases and task-work for the works of Harlech, 37 weeks, 30 Dec. 1285 to 15 Sept. 1286: £1602 18 6¼

III. Notes on Savoyard and other foreign craftsmen employed by Edward I in Wales[1]

1. *Philip the Carpenter*. Philip 'Sente', principal carpenter for the construction of the roof of the Great Tower at Flint in 1286, is presumably identical with the Philip 'of Ewyas' named as a principal carpenter at Caernarvon Castle in June–July 1295;[2] with the 'Philip of Ewyas' named at Vale Royal Abbey in 1278–80;[3] and with 'Philip the carpenter' who (i) appears as a burgess of Caernarvon in 1298,[4] (ii) was paid for executing the timber work of the 'Beleestre' tower in Caernarvon Castle in 1305[5] and (iii) was the leader of ten carpenters felling and preparing timber in Nantconway for the hall over the King's Gate at Caernarvon in July 1320.[6] That he is to be identified with the 'Philip the carpenter of St. George' who received *ex gratia* payments ('dona') of 40s. from Count Philip of Savoy at his castle of St. Georges-d'Espéranche in December 1274 and July 1275[7] is also highly probable. He would not have been the only English carpenter working for the counts of Savoy at about that time: Berteletus, one of the principal carpenters employed on Peter of Savoy's works at Chillon in 1265–6,[8] is named in the following year at the castle of Yverdon, where he shared the 'task' of building two superimposed halls (*pro duabus aulis una super aliam*), as Bartlet the Englishman (*Berteleto anglico*).[9] It also appears likely that the Master Theobald de Waus, 'king's carpenter', who in 1277 was appointed to carry timber from Hampshire to the Tower of London and who in that connection rebuilt the key bridge over the Kennet at Burghfield near Reading,[10] is to be identified with the Master Theobald the carpenter who was working with Bartlet and others at Chillon in 1266[11] and with Philip at St. Georges-d'Espéranche in 1274–5 (when he also received 'dona' of 40s. and made and put up three shutters ('fenestre') in the count's wardrobe there), and who appears in Savoy again at intervals from 1281 to 1290 when, as 'Master Theobald of St. George, carpenter', he was sent for to assign 'tasks' (*pro taschiis dandis*) at the count's castle of Le Bourget.[12] If these identifications are correct, we have the extremely interesting picture of two carpenters working together, probably in association with Master James of St. George, at St. Georges-d'Espéranche in 1274–5; moving to England, the one to the works of the Tower of London, the other to those of Vale Royal, two years or so later; the one, Theobald, returning to Savoy when the Tower works were finished and remaining there probably for the rest of his career; the other, Philip, staying on in the king's service in Wales to what by 1320 must have been no inconsiderable age. It is noteworthy that, of the two, Theobald is generally, Philip never, referred to as 'magister'.

2. *Master Bertram*. A military engineer of long experience, probably of Gascon origin. Appears as Master Bertrand de Saltu (Sault de Navailles, Basses-Pyrénées), *ingeniator*, in 1248;[13] served at the siege of Bénauges (Gironde) in 1253;[14] in charge of construction of the

---

[1] For the career of the principal master of Edward's Welsh castle works, see A.J. Taylor, 'Master James of St. George', in *Eng. Hist. Rev.* LXV (1950), pp. 433–457, and *The History of the King's Works*, I, ed. H.M. Colvin (London 1963), pp. 203–5.   [2] E 101/486/8.
[3] *Ledger-Book*, pp. 201–12.   [4] P.R.O., Rentals and Surveys, 17/86.   [5] Above, p. 91.
[6] E 101/487/2.   [7] Turin, Archivio di Stato, Inv. Sav. 38, Fo. 46, mazzo 1, no. 4.
[8] A. Naef, *Chillon: La Camera Domini* (Geneva, 1908), p. 46 and n. 22.
[9] Turin, Inv. Sav. 70, Fo. 205, mazzo 1, no. 1.
[10] *Cal. Pat. Rolls 1272–81*, pp. 214, 408; *Cal. Inq. Misc.* i, p. 350; Liberate Roll no. 58.
[11] Turin, Inv. Sav. 69, Fo. 5, mazzo 1, no. 3(c).
[12] Chambéry, Archives de la Savoie, Inv. Sav. 50, Fo. 154, mazzo 1, no. 1(ii).
[13] *Close Rolls 1247–51*, p. 82.   [14] *Close Rolls 1253–4*, pp. 194, 302.

king's engines at the Tower of London from April 1276;[1] present at siege of Dolforwyn (Montgomery) in March–April 1277, and considered as possible supervisor of subsequent repairs to that castle;[2] engaged on Rhuddlan works in 1277–8; named in London context in 1280;[3] received wages for service with king in war in Wales 1 November 1282 to 29 February 1284,[4] about which time he died and was buried at Caernarvon, the cost of his funeral being allowed to the constable of the castle.[5] Was at Castell-y-Bere 3 May to 6 June 1283, apparently directing repair of castle following its surrender by the Welsh.[6] Granted custody of Dee mills at Chester, October 1277[7] and succeeded therein by Master Richard the Engineer in or before summer of 1282.[8] Though specialising in *ingenia* and siege operations,[9] his employment in connection with building works is established by the evidence for Dolforwyn, Rhuddlan and Bere, as also by his presence at Caernarvon in 1283–4.

3. *Stephen the Painter.* Stephen was no doubt the same artist as had been engaged by Master James of St. George in 1274–5 for the painted chambers of the count and countess of Savoy in Count Philip's new castle of St. Laurent-du-Pont in the Viennois.[10] A year earlier (May–July 1273—exactly the time when Edward I was Count Philip's guest at St. Georges-d'Espéranche), Stephen had carried out the redecoration of Westminster Hall in preparation for Edward's coronation, then possibly to take place that year.[11] If, as is very probable, Stephen was also responsible for the only slightly earlier and still surviving decoration in the *camera clericorum* at Chillon,[12] we have some idea of a style of wall-painting likely to have been used originally in some of the more important chambers in the North Wales castles. Its characteristic motif, an alternating red and white chevron pattern, survives in contemporary work in this country only on the splay and soffit of the reredos arch in St. Faith's Chapel in Westminster Abbey, where the correspondence of the original colours, now scarcely distinguishable, with those employed at Chillon is vouched for by Schnebbelie's watercolour of 1790.[13] Neither at Westminster nor at Rhuddlan nor at St. Laurent-du-Pont is Stephen named as *magister*, though his commissions were evidently not unimportant.

4. *Master Manasser de Vaucouleurs.* From Vaucouleurs in Champagne. It is of note that payment for the 'task' assigned him by Master James on the well at Hope was calculated at 6d. the *toise* (*pro teysa*); he was paid for 7 *toises*, i.e. about 60 feet. The *toise* was the normal unit of measurement for masonry surfaces in the castle works of the counts of Savoy.[14] Thus by an instrument dated at St. Georges-d'Espéranche on 24 April 1280 Tassin of St. George, mason, contracted with the count to build two *toises* of walling in the castle of Falavier, one *teysa muri* to be 3 feet and the other 2 feet in thickness;[15] similarly

[1] C 47/35/7, nos. 24, 25; *Cal. Close Rolls 1272–9*, pp. 278, 315; E 101/467/7(7) contains his accounts of payments and purchases *circa ingenia domini Regis* for 1278–9.
[2] *Cal. Anc. Corr. Wales*, p. 31.   [3] *Cal. Pat. Rolls 1272–81*, p. 362.   [4] E 101/4/1, m. 19.
[5] *Cal. Welsh Rolls*, p. 294.   [6] C 47/2/4.   [7] *Cal. Close Rolls 1272–9*, p. 406.
[8] *Cal. Close Rolls 1279–88*, p. 202.   [9] Cf. J. Harvey, *Mediaeval Architects*, p. 31.
[10] . . . *Pro camera domini pingenda ad precium factum per Stephanum pictorem per manum Magistri Jacobi, lx.s. Pro camera domine pinguenda per dictum Stephanum per manum predicti Magistri Jacobi, lx.s. Pro capella et garderoba domini pinguenda . . . factum per dictum Stephanum per manum ipsius Magistri Jacobi, l.s.*, Chambéry, Archives de la Savoie, Inv. Sav. 32, Fo. 14, mazzo 1, no. 66 (2).
[11] *Pro Stephano pictore Regis. Liberate de thesauro nostro Stephano pictori nostro xl.s. in partem solucionis vadiorum suorum circa dealbacionem et decoracionem magne aule nostre Westmonasterii'*, Liberate Roll no. 49, m. 4, 25 May 1273; and mm. 2, 3.
[12] Naef, *op. cit.* Pl. IX(b); also *ibid.* p. 37, fig. 32.
[13] Soc. Ant. Lond., Westminster MSS.; figured in monochrome in Pamela Tudor-Craig, 'The Painted Chamber at Westminster', *Arch. Journ.*, cxiv, Pl. XXIIA.
[14] L. Blondel, *L'Architecture Militaire au temps de Pierre II de Savoie: les Donjons Circulaires*, in *Genava* xiii (1935), p. 300.   [15] Chambéry, Archives de la Savoie, Inv. Sav. 135, Fo. 17, pqt. 14, pièce 7.

the contract of Tassin and his brother Master Giles of St. George, mason, for building the tower which still stands at Saxon, in the Valais, in 1279, was *pro turre Sassonis in tascha facienda de altitudine decem teys*.[1] In 1283–4 Master Manasser was employed as master and director of the diggers at Caernarvon,[2] where he became a burgess and where before his death (1293 or earlier) he held office as one of the town bailiffs.[3]

5. *John Francis*. There is reason to believe John Francis came to Wales from Savoy and that he is to be identified with the 'Johannes Franciscus' who is named with other masons and carpenters (including Bartlet the Englishman—*Berteletus Anglicus*—,*Jaquetus de sancto Jorio* and Master John the father of Master James) in the Chillon accounts of 1266.[4] This Johannes Franciscus is in turn likely to be the 'Franciscus cementarius' who executed task-work for the new *turris* at Peter of Savoy's castle of Conthey (canton Valais) in 1258,[5] built the *turris* at Saillon (canton Valais) in 1261[6] and was joint-builder of two chambers at Chillon in 1260–61.[7] He was probably also the builder of the castle of Brignon (canton Valais) in 1261–2.[8] His tower at Saillon still stands to nearly its full height, together with much of the curtain wall and flanking towers and the contemporary town wall and its gateways. In their siting in relation to the terrain, in the texture and *appareil* of their masonry, and in constructional technique (use of inclined scaffolds), they show marked affinities with Conway.

6. *William Seysel*. Probably from Seyssel (depts. Ain and Haute-Savoie), a castle of the counts of Savoy on the Rhône, south-west of Geneva. A *Perronetus de Saysello* is named among builders working at the count's castle of Le Bourget (dept. Haute-Savoie) in 1291–2 on taskworks assigned by Theobald of St. George.[9]

7. *Gillot de Chalons*. Possibly, in the light of what we now know of the provenance of Master James of St. George, from Chalons (dept. Isère), 10 miles south-west of St. Georges-d'Espéranche. Before coming to Conway, where he settled and acquired 3¼ burgages,[10] he is likely to have worked at Rhuddlan, one of the towers of Rhuddlan Castle being named Gillot's tower (*turris vocata Gillot'*) in an account of 1304.[11]

8. *Albert de Menz*. In 1286 Albert de Menz was one of those paid for making a chimney for the chamber of Sir John de Bonvillars in Harlech Castle and for the quarrying and dressing of a variety of freestone details.[12] In 1289 he was paid for further similar work, including the making of window mullions (*columpne*) for the castle hall.[13] Is likely to have come from Savoy, perhaps from Le Mintset (old forms 'Menze', 'Mintze') in Martigny-Combe (canton Valais).[14]

9. *Master Giles of St. George and Adam Boynard*. In the Harlech accounts for 1286[15] 'Gilet', Adam Boynard, John of Paris and Peter of Tours appear with others, named and unnamed, merely as suppliers of horses and carts used to bring heavy materials to the

[1] Turin, Archivio di Stato, Inv. Sav. 69, Fo. 69, mazzo 1, no. 1. For Master Giles, see also 9, below.
[2] Above, p. 80 and note.   [3] *Cal. Welsh Rolls*, p. 352.
[4] Turin, Archivio di Stato, Inv. Sav. 69, Fo. 5, mazzo 1, nos. 3(c), 4.
[5] M. Chiaudano, *La Finanza Sabauda nel. sec. XIII* (Turin, 1933–38), i, pp. 25–6.   [6] *Ibid.* pp. 58, 68.
[7] *Ibid.* p. 62.   [8] L. Blondel, 'Le Château de Brignon', *Vallesia* (Sion, 1949), iv, pp. 29–34.
[9] Chambéry, Archives de la Savoie, Inv. Sav. 50, Fo. 154, mazzo 1, no. 1. For Theobald, see 1. above.
[10] SC 12/17/87.
[11] E 101/486/15; cf. the reference (1267) to 'Coton's Tower' (*turris Cothonis*) and 'William de Passu's Tower' (*turris Wellelmi de Passu*) at Yverdon (canton Vaud), so called from the names of the masons who had built them *ad tascham* a few years previously (Chiaudano, *op. cit.* i, pp. 59–60, 117); cf. also the tower called 'Beleestre' at Caernarvon Castle (above, p.91, note 4) and the 'Penne' tower on Caernarvon Town Wall (above, p. 93, note 2).
[12] E 101/485/26, 27.   [13] E 101/501/25, no. 63.
[14] H. Jaccard, 'Origine des noms de lieux . . . de la Suisse romande', *Mems. et Docts., Soc. d'histoire de la Suisse romande*, 2nd series (Lausanne, 1906), vii, p. 271.   [15] E 101/485/27.

site.[1] Three of the group, Collardus, Gilbertus and Perrottus (the last an especially common name-form in Savoy records), are sometimes qualified as *clericus*, seemingly in the context an unlikely pointer to their real status. The presence amongst them of Robert de Walden[2] suggests that on the contrary they were probably masons. This accords with the further suggestion that 'Gilet' is to be identified with the *Giletus de sancto Georgio* who built Philip of Savoy's still surviving *donjon* at Saxon (canton Valais) in 1279–80[3] and who appears as Master Giles of St. George at Aberystwyth in 1282;[4] with him at Saxon there worked another leading figure who in Savoy records appears variously as 'Beynard King' (*Beynardus rex ribaldorum*) and 'Adam King' (*rex qui dicitur Adam*) and who thus seems likely to be none other than his Harlech associate Adam Boynard; he became a burgess of Harlech and acted as bailiff in 1291–2.[5] While nothing is certainly known of Peter of Tours or John of Paris, it at least seems probable if this identification is correct that Giles of St. George and Adam Boynard may have held key positions under Master James in the earlier stages of the Harlech works. It is perhaps significant that one of the distinctive architectural features of contemporary castle-building in Savoy, the full-centred semi-circular arch, is found only in the eastern towers at Harlech and there only on the two lower floors.

---

[1] Appendix II above.
[2] Cf. J. H. Harvey, *Mediaeval Architects*, 2nd edn., revised (Gloucester, 1984), p. 311.
[3] Turin, Archivio di Stato, Inv. Sav. 69, Fo. 5, mazzo 1, no. 7; Fo. 69, mazzo 1, no. 1.
[4] Above, p. 13, n. 4.   [5] E 372/138, rot. 25*d*.